3000 800045 69529
St. Louis Community College

D0087542

Florissant Valley Libra
St. Louis Community College
3400 Pershall Road
Ferguson, MO 63135-1499
314-595-4514

Making Connections

The long-distance bus industry in the USA

Margaret Walsh

Ashgate

Aldershot • Burlington USA • Singapore • Sydney

© Margaret Walsh, 2000

All rights reserved. No part of this publication may be reproduced, stored in a retrieval system, or transmitted in any form or by any means, electronic, mechanical, photo-copying, recording, or otherwise without the prior permission of the publisher.

The author has asserted her right under the Copyright, Designs and Patents Act, 1988, to be identified as the author of this work.

Published by
Ashgate Publishing Limited
Gower House
Croft Road
Aldershot
Hants GU11 3HR
England

Ashgate Publishing Company
131 Main Street
Burlington
Vermont 05401-5600
USA

Ashgate website: http://www.ashgate.com

British Library Cataloguing-in-Publication data

Walsh, Margaret.
    Making connections: the long-distance bus industry in the USA
    1. Bus lines – United States – History
    I. Title
    388.3'22'0973

Library of Congress Cataloging-in-Publication data

Walsh, Margaret.
    Making connections: the long-distance bus industry in the USA / Margaret Walsh
        p.   cm.
    Includes bibliographical references.
    1. Bus lines – United States – History.   2. Transportation, Automotive – United States – History.
    I. Title
    HE5623.W35 2000
    388.3'22'0973–dc21   00-029982

ISBN 0 7546 0207 9

Typeset in Times by N²productions and printed on acid-free paper by Athenaeum Press, Ltd., Gateshead, Tyne & Wear.

Contents

List of Tables

List of Figures

Acknowledgements

During the past fifteen years I have been carrying out research and writing articles on aspects of the history of the long-distance bus industry in the USA. These articles have appeared in a variety of books and journals on both sides of the Atlantic. As the pieces have not always been easily accessible it seemed useful to pull the majority together in a single volume and to write two new articles, an introduction and a bibliography, thereby offering concerted insights into what has been a badly-neglected part of American transport and economic history.

I wish to thank the following editors and publishers for permission to reprint: as chapter 2, 'The Early Growth of Long Distance Bus Transport in the United States' in T.C. Barker (ed.) (1987), *The Economic and Social Effects of the Spread of Motor Vehicles*, Macmillan Press Ltd., London, pp. 81–96; as chapter 4, 'Tracing the Hound. The Minnesotan Roots of The Greyhound Bus Corporation', *Minnesota History*, **49/8**, Winter (1985), pp. 310–21) and as chapter 5, 'Minnesota's Mr Bus: Edgar F. Zelle and the Jefferson Highway Transportation Company', *Minnesota History*, **52/8**, Winter (1991), pp. 307–22 the Minnesota Historical Society; as chapter 6, 'Iowa's Bus Queen: Helen M. Schultz and the Red Ball Transportation Company', *Annals of Iowa*, **54**(3) (1994), the State Historical Society of Iowa, pp. 329–55; as chapter 7, 'The Motor Carrier Act of 1935. The Origins and Establishment of Federal Regulation of the Interstate Bus Industry in the United States', *Journal of Transport History*, 3rd Series, **8**(1), (1987), pp. 66–80 and as chapter 9, 'Not Rosie the Riveter: Women's Diverse Roles in the Making of the American Long-Distance Bus Industry', *Journal of Transport History*, **17**(1) (1996), pp. 43–56, Manchester University Press. These articles are reproduced from the original text except for editing for style, rewriting the notes into a consistent form throughout this book, and except for the additional references to materials available since the original publication of the articles. Some of the original photographs have been reproduced; others have been omitted because of space considerations. Tables have been altered.

Chapter 10 has used material from 'Serve/See America Now. Advertising Bus Travel in the United States During The Second World War', *Journal of Advertising History*, **11**(1), published in association with the *European Journal of Marketing*, **22**(4), (1988), pp. 41–60 (MCB University Press), to expand the original 'See This Amazing America. The Long-Distance Bus Industry's Use of Advertising in its First Quarter Century', *Journal of Transport History*, 3rd Series, **11**(1) (1990), pp. 61–88 (Manchester University Press) in order to create one article on bus advertising. Small sections of chapter 3 are derived from 'The Intercity Bus and Its Competitors in the United States in the Mid Twentieth Century' in Chris Wrigley and John Shepherd (eds) (1991), *On the Move: Essays in Labour and Transport History Presented to Philip Bagwell*, London, pp. 231–51 (Hambledon Press).

Other bus articles and bus-related articles which are not reprinted in this volume, but which are related to this collection are 'Coordination, Cooperation or Competition: The Great Northern Railway and Bus Transportation in the 1920s', in R. Cameron and L.F. Schnore (eds) (1991), *Cities and Markets. Studies in the Organization of Human Space*, Lanham, MD, pp. 163–89; 'In Whose Interest? Public Policy and Transport during Depression and War', in R.A. Garson and S.S. Kidd (eds) (1999), *The Roosevelt Years: New Essays on the United States, 1933–1945*, Edinburgh, pp. 11–29; 'Railroad Responses to the Development of the Long-Distance Bus Industry in the United States Prior to Federal Regulation in 1935' in G. Boyes (ed.) (forthcoming), *Cooperation and Competition. The History of the Railways' Relationship with Other Transport Modes*, York and 'Passenger Connections: Views of the Intercity Bus Terminal in the United States', in W. Bond and C. Divall (eds) (forthcoming), *Suburbanising the Masses: Public Transport and Urban Development in Historical Perspective*, Aldershot.

Very little of this research could have been undertaken without generous financial assistance. In particular, I am indebted to the Nuffield Foundation which enabled me not only to have a year's research fellowship in 1990–91, but also funded research trips to the USA. I am also grateful for financial support from the Wolfson Foundation, the British Academy, the American Philosophical Society, the United States–United Kingdom Educational Commission, the School of Social Sciences at the University of Birmingham, the University of Nottingham, the Center for Humanistic Studies at University of Kansas, the American Heritage Center at University of Wyoming and the Minnesota Historical Society.

In the long search for sources I have encountered considerable and generous assistance from librarians, archivists, historians and people connected with the bus industry who have given me access to their personal collections, have patiently answered my questions or have either talked to me or allowed me to interview them when they would otherwise have been engaged in their own business affairs. Though it may seem slighting to single out specific institutions and individuals, I do wish to thank in particular the librarians at the American Heritage Center, University of Wyoming and the archivists and librarians at the Minnesota Historical Society, where I undertook the bulk of my primary research; the interlibrary loan librarians at the University of Kansas, whose patience in processing several sets of journals was remarkable; the interlibrary loan librarians at the Universities of Birmingham, Nottingham and Queen's University, Belfast; Bill Carner, curator at the photo archives, Ekstrom Library, University of Louisville and Donald M. Coffin, former secretary-treasurer of the Motor Bus Society, consultant to the Greyhound Corporation and third vice-president of the Museum of Bus Transportation. William A. Luke, former editor of *Bus Ride* (1965–1996) and Chris Wrigley deserve thanks for their long-serving and continuing support and enthusiasm.

Persons in the bus industry or bus-related industry who have generously given me their time include Robert Bowen, son of Ivan Bowen, general counsel for the Greyhound Corporation; Russell A. Byrd, former bus driver and author; Frederic D. Fravel, senior associate at Ecosometrics Inc.; the late James E. Fuller, bus driver, St Paul; the late John P. Hoschek, vice-president, librarian and archives manager, Motor Bus Society, and author; Thomas D. Jones, library director, Motor Bus Society; Mary Martin, daughter of Helen Schultz, bus entrepreneur; Eugene Nicolelli, director of the Greyhound Bus Origin Museum; Susan Perry, senior vice-president, Government Relations, American Bus Association; Mary Jean Picknelly, senior vice-president, Peter Pan Bus Lines Inc.; George A. Rossman, son of Laurence A. Rossman, newspaper owner and consultant to the Greyhound Corporation; the late Robert Slater, bus driver, St Paul; George M. Smerk, professor of transportation and director of the Institute for Urban Transportation, Indiana University; the late Robert A. Tracy, bus driver, Mason City, Iowa; the late Charles A. Webb, former president of the National Association of Motor Bus Owners; Charles Zelle, president and chief executive officer, Jefferson Lines, and Louis N. Zelle, former president and chief executive officer, Jefferson Lines. The late Esther Bubley, photographer, also generously talked to me about her bus photography.

I have worked in many other libraries and archives in the USA during my lengthy search for varied bus materials. I wish to take this opportunity to thank the numerous librarians, archivists and employees who have helped me to locate information or find materials in the American Bus Association records, Washington, DC; the Atchison, Topeka and Santa Fe Records, Topeka, Kansas; the Department of Communications Library, the University of Illinois, Urbana; the Hagley Museum and Library, Wilmington, Delaware; the Hibbing Public Library, Hibbing, Minnesota; the then Interstate Commerce Commission Library and Archives, Washington, DC; the Iowa Department of Transportation Library, Ames, Iowa; the Iron Range Research Center, Chisholm, Minnesota; the James J. Hill Reference Library, St Paul, Minnesota; the Kansas State Historical Society, Topeka; the Library of Congress, Washington, DC; the Mason City Public Library, Mason City, Iowa; the Midwest Regional Resources Center, Chicago; the Minneapolis Public Library; the Minnesota

State Library, St Paul; the National Archives at both Suitland Maryland and in Washington, DC; the National Museum of American History at the Smithsonian Institution, Washington, DC; the National Tramway Museum, Crich, Derbyshire; the Nebraska State Historical Society, Lincoln, Nebraska; the Northeast Minnesota Historical Center, University of Minnesota, Duluth; the State Historical Society of Iowa, Des Moines; the J. Walter Thompson Archival Records, then in New York City; the Transportation Research Board, Washington, DC; the Union Pacific System Records, Omaha, Nebraska; the University of Minnesota Library, Minneapolis and the US Department of Transportation Library, Washington, DC.

I have also had assistance from librarians and archivists whose institutions I have not visited: namely the California Historical Society, San Francisco; the Iowa State Historical Society, Iowa City; the Missouri Pacific Railroad Company, St Louis; the Oregon Historical Society, Portland and the Southern Pacific Transportation Company, San Francisco.

In this volume I have tried to examine the American long-distance bus industry with the insights of both the historian and the social scientist. At times my outside position as an academic and as a 'foreigner', albeit one with experience of several years' residence in the USA, has put me at a disadvantage, especially in respect to access to research materials and to contact with persons in the industry. But distance does have its advantages, not least in gaining perspective and in living where passenger travel by public carrier has wider acceptability. I am grateful to all the institutions and individuals acknowledged above. I alone remain responsible for the contents of the essays.

Note: Americanisms and Spelling

The research materials used in this volume were written and spoken in US English. I usually write in UK English. To help prevent any confusion among UK English users I here explain some Americanisms which have been retained in the text. For the benefit of Americans I am also noting some UK English terms and spellings which have been used.

For readers of UK English I have used automobility (domination of society by the car), fall (=autumn), gas man (=garage mechanic), line (=queue), lot (=subdivision of a block in a city or town), movie (=film), movie theatre (=cinema), railroad (=railway), store (=shop), truck (=lorry), vacation (=holiday), washroom or restroom (=toilet or w.c.). Some words like uptown, midtown, downtown or upstate have both general and specific meanings. Generally uptown means towards the upper part of a city or town, and is usually the part away from the main business district. Depending on the size of the city or town the uptown can often be residential. Downtown is towards the lower part of a city or town. Midtown is the centre of the town or city, which is often the business district. Upstate means the northern part of the state. Downstate means that part of the state which is further south. Downstate Minnesota is southern Minnesota, whereas midtown New York City is the central section of Manhattan and downtown New York City is Canal Street and south.

For readers in North America, I have used three words, automobile, auto and car interchangeably throughout the text. I have used engine rather than motor (i.e. diesel engine rather than diesel motor) and have used UK English spelling throughout. So, for example, center has become centre, theater has become theatre, learnt has became learned, and transportation has become transport. There is little, however, that is not easily understood.

List of Abbreviations

Archives, associations and journals.

AA	*Advertising Age*
ABA	American Bus Association
AR	*Annual Report*
AMTRAK	National Railroad Passenger Corporation
BF	*Bus Facts*
BR	*Bus Ride*
BT	*Bus Transportation*
Cont., *AR*	Continental Trailways, *Annual Report*
D	*Destinations*
EFZR	Edgar F. Zelle Records
FSA	Farm Security Admininstration
FO	*Fleet Owner*
GC, *AR*	Greyhound Corporation, *Annual Report*
GCR	Greyhound Corporate Records
GL	*The Greyhound Limited*
GNR	Great Northern Railway Company Records
HT	*Highway Traveler*
IBRC, *AR*	Iowa Board of Railroad Commissioners, *Annual Report*
ICC	Interstate Commerce Commission
ICC, *AR*	Interstate Commerce Commission, *Annual Report*
JTC	Jefferson Transportation Company
JHTC	Jefferson Highway Transportation Company
JWT	J. Walter Thompson
LARR	Laurence A. Rossman Records
MCA	*Motor Coach Age*
MR&WC, ATCD, *BR*	Minnesota Railroad and Warehouse Commission, Auto Transportation Company Division, *Biennial Report*
NARG	National Archives Record Group
NAMBO	National Association of Motor Bus Owners (formerly Operators)

NAMBO, Mins	National Association of Motor Bus Owners, Minutes of the Board of Directors
NAMBO, *Procs*	National Association of Motor Bus Owners, *Proceedings*
NGLBTT	*Northland Greyhound Bus Timetable*
OWI	Office of War Information
RA	*Railway Age*
RVM	*Rear View Mirror*
SEP	*Saturday Evening Post*
SONJ	Standard Oil (New Jersey)
T&BO	*Truck and Bus Owner*
TbB	*Travel by Bus*
Tr	*Trailways*
WALR	William A. Luke Records

1   Introduction

For young Europeans of the 1960s and 1970s 'Going Greyhound' across the USA had great appeal. It was not only that 'taking the daaawg' was for many their equivalent of the film *Easy Rider*; it was also that Greyhound was and still is a part of American history, having a brand name to rank with Coke, Levis and McDonalds. The sleek Greyhound logo and the blue, red and white lines of the Americruiser were and still are a symbol of travelling vast distances, viewing ever-changing and often dramatic scenery, at a reasonable price and in remarkable company. For many the coach also became the motel and provided overnight accommodation, with interesting interludes at Greyhound terminals and refreshment stops at Post House inns or other food chains. American bus travel was both a means of travel and a cultural experience, not to be missed.[1]

Yet while young Europeans, whether as students or tourists, were pleased to 'Go Greyhound', relatively few Americans followed suit either with Greyhound, National Trailways or one of the nation's regional motor carriers. The bulk of the intercity bus industry's domestic clientele were students, pensioners, the unemployed and minority groups, often travelling alone and all sharing the common ingredient of low income, though pensioners might also be non-drivers because of age or ill health. These regular customers were joined occasionally by members of the armed services, business travellers, truck drivers returning from a one-way trip by surface to save money and wives with children when the family's second automobile was out of action. Few would choose to travel by bus. Like the majority of their compatriots they would prefer to fly if speed was a priority, or to drive themselves to their destinations at a time and at a speed of their own choosing, without sharing the ride and without having to get picked up at the other end or make their own way to and from the bus terminal. Many Americans in the 1960s and 1970s thought intercity bus travel was distasteful and was to be avoided.

This consensus had not always been held. In the first half of the twentieth century Americans enjoyed bus travel. In the 1920s they were pleased to gain unexpected mobility and new horizons, and all without the expense and risk of private motoring. Buses were exciting and liberating, albeit uncomfortable and somewhat unpredictable. In the depressed 1930s bus travel expanded because it was more flexible than train travel and remained cheaper than using private automobiles. Americans might be suffering from the worst economic downturn

1

in their experience, but many remained geographically mobile. War then dramatically increased the numbers of bus passengers because private motoring became very difficult, if not impossible. As a result, people used motor coaches to enable them to travel rather than for the pleasure of travelling.

Neither the bus industry nor its clients fully recovered from the legacies of the Second World War. Problems of overcrowding, poor rolling stock, erratic timetabling and changing bus personnel left a negative image of being 'on the buses'. Though major improvements were made to the vehicles, the terminals and the auxiliary facilities, passengers left as soon as they could. In part they abandoned the buses in protest against enforced coach travel under difficult circumstances; in part they took to their automobiles thanks to better conditions which included more and superior automobiles, the move to the suburbs and the improvements in roads. As the bus industry struggled to keep pace with changing conditions both internally in business management, and externally in facing competition from air travel and a recharged train service in the shape of Amtrak, its status waned. The passengers who remained tended to be those who had few, if any, alternatives and there seemed little hope of attracting more clients other than the tourists, the chartered passengers and incurably romantic riders.

Making Connections explores the varied fortunes of the long-distance or intercity bus industry from its beginnings in the second decade of the twentieth century to deregulation in 1982. Originally, I had hoped to examine the industry by writing a business history of its leading company, the Greyhound Corporation. Such an approach would have considered both the internal dynamics of business administration and the external patterns of marketing and public relations in the changing economic and social conditions of the twentieth century. Not only did the forms and financing of business operations change markedly, but companies had to adjust to severe fluctuations in the economy. The expansion of the service sector and the growth in personal mobility also required that much more attention be paid to consumer demands. A coherent body of corporate records, together with public records from the government and from the industry generally, would have provided the means of undertaking such a business history.

Unfortunately, the accessible corporate records were inadequate to provide the spine for the projected analysis. Though two substantial bodies of Greyhound materials were available in St Paul, Minnesota and in Laramie, Wyoming and a third archival resource, then in Grand Rapids, Minnesota, offered more direct company information, there was no cooperation from the Greyhound Corporation in Phoenix, Arizona.[2] Certainly, much information had been lost in the moves of corporate headquarters and in the changes in the regional divisions of the corporation. But written archival materials, bus artefacts and access to personnel through interviews were available to the officially-sponsored corporate biographer. Without cooperation or some substantive appraisal of the nature and value of historical materials still held by the corporation, an academic evaluation of the history of the bus industry through its major participant was impossible.

I thus shifted my sights to investigate alternative ways of analysing long-distance bus transport. The accessible Greyhound materials could be used as a base for discussing the early growth of the intercity bus industry and the public records as a base for the growth in the years after the Second World War. Case studies of regional companies and aspects of business management could then illuminate some of the diversity within bus operations and some of the ways of dealing with specific problems in a consumer-driven industry which was subject to both local and federal regulation. Clearly, more case-studies could be undertaken of bus companies at the local level, but detailed investigations, using public records and whatever archival materials can be traced, require substantial amounts of time and energy. Such efforts might well be undertaken in the form of dissertations at either the Masters or Doctoral level.

Making Connections became a series of articles because of access to or lack of access to primary sources; it became this specific collection of articles because of materials which were made available to me personally or to which historians working in other fields drew my attention. 'Digging' for resources is always central to historical research; perseverance is a characteristic which is also necessary when trying to gain access to private resources. Much relevant material on individuals and small enterprises still remains in family hands; tracing relatives often depends on the good will, cooperation and initiatives of librarians and archivists who 'know their area', whether city, county or state. Had it not been for generous assistance at this level, in passing on or finding out information about specific people, then much of the local detail about Minnesota and Iowa which appears in this volume would have been lost.

Colleagues in women's history and in American studies directly and indirectly also pointed me to routes which I would not have taken had I remained simply an economic and business historian. Ten years of teaching women's history has convinced me that much is missing from both the framework and the content of what might be called traditional or mainstream history. To change this framework and content requires not only new sources and new historians, but also different ways of analysing existing sources. Women have always been significant in bus travel, initially as consumers, but then also as producers and retailers. Their presence has been hidden in records generated by men and primarily for male readers, government officials or accountants. Women were and are, however, part of the business world of the twentieth century and an understanding of their contributions significantly alters historical perspectives.

These perspectives emerge in part through visual as well as written evidence, and *Making Connections* is enhanced both by an excursion into bus photography and by the use of photographs as illustrative examples. Some photographs have been retrieved from the dust of historical archives: others have emerged from private collections. A rich vein remains to be mined in perceiving and visioning the changing ways in which buses were operated and used by passengers. Yet more pictorial evidence in the form of advertising artwork published in popular magazines and newspapers directed my attention to the style and substance of promotion and public relations in a consumer industry. Interdisciplinary approaches to visual materials can add new and rich dimensions to the study of history.

The 'spine' of *Making Connections* or its 'main routes' examines the growth, decline and struggle for stability in the national bus industry. In the years before American entry into the Second World War the industry moved from birth and youth to come of age as a viable form of surface transport (see chapter 2). The origins of commercial passenger motor transport lie in the experiments made by numerous individuals throughout the nation to expand a taxi service into a 'jitney' by stretching out automobiles and picking up passengers either on the streets or at fixed points such as hotels or stores. The success of these improvised ventures encouraged pioneers to seek out manufacturers of longer vehicles which might be called buses. Competition between local companies brought bankruptcy for some and enlarged regional status for others as the better-organized entrepreneurs seized the opportunity to merge with or buy up weaker operations. There was more adventure than stability in this youthful bus industry.

The major depression of the 1930s shortened the bus industry's adolescence. Then all bus companies faced the prospects of declining business. Many small carriers collapsed as passengers and revenue fell, but some of the larger regional firms, and the Greyhound Corporation in particular, were able to consolidate their markets. They modernized their financial structures and they reorganized their administrative structures to ensure system-wide economies. The larger operators were then well placed to promote and to capture the increase in passengers in the second half of the decade. By this time federal legislation, the Motor Carrier Act of 1935, designed to ensure business stability and to promote the public interest, was influencing bus business. It favoured protecting existing operators provided that they could meet sound economic practices and standards. The larger companies dominated the long-distance trade while the sound, small companies which weathered both the major economic crisis and the new regulatory regime ran intrastate routes and specialized services.

America's involvement with and then entrance into the Second World War altered the shape and the perception of the intercity bus industry (see chapter 3). War and the general upturn in the American economy brought full business and increased revenues to most operators. The necessity of moving both the armed forces and civilian workers, combined with a shortage of both fuel and automotive spare parts, forced Americans to use public transport. Buses and their rivals, the railroads, flourished in what has been described as their 'halcyon days'. But the impressive growth of business was achieved under duress. Shortages of vehicles, difficulties in running existing buses which were ageing and in poor condition, and lack of modern new vehicles/rolling stock, together with overcrowding both on the buses and in the terminals, instilled a negative image of coach travel among both adult and young passengers. This memory was difficult, if not impossible, to eradicate in the post-war years.

Bus executives and managers were well aware of the need to take some bold decisions if they were to promote their business when the war ended. They had to invest in new and much improved vehicles and in new terminals, garages and administrative offices and they had to reshape their tarnished image by a public relations campaign in the media. Yet progress in both areas was agonizingly slow. Sharp inflation in the immediate post-war years increased the costs of both labour and commodities and the revenues that the industry had accumulated during the war were inadequate to fund necessary replacements, let alone expansion. Then the lengthy federal government inquiry into bus fares which lasted from summer 1946 until late 1949 impeded both planning and actual developments. Companies simply did not know what fares they might expect to set and whether they would be judged to have acted fairly and honestly during the war. The hesitation, if not hiatus, in moving confidently forward cost the motor carriers dearly. They did not banish their poor wartime reputation and they were ill-prepared to meet rising competition.

The buses could compete with the trains for a proportion of the intercity travel market and they were not yet significantly threatened by commercial air flights. They failed, however, to deal with competition from private cars. The 25.8 million automobiles registered in 1945 had increased by a further 14.6 million in 1950 as Americans eagerly acquired new vehicles. Perhaps coaches would never have matched the freedom which cars gave to individuals, but operators could have made a better case for using buses more often if they had been able to put their plans into operation more quickly and more assertively.

They were not idle. Many innovations were introduced in vehicles, types of service and facilities, and new levels and styles of advertising were adopted. But progress was impeded by external barriers and internal inertia. Intercity buses were not only subject to federal government regulations, but also to diverse rules imposed by individual states. These included vehicle registration, fuel taxes, and size and weight limitations. If managers wished to significantly improve the quality of their coach service by adopting larger and heavier buses, then they needed uniform standards throughout the nation. They also wanted reciprocal agreements between states to apportion taxes according to usage.

Long delays in achieving consistency between the states slowed down the introduction of new equipment.

Perhaps more damaging, in the long term, was the slow engagement with changes in the consumer market and the failure to establish a fashionable image and good public relations. Passengers increasingly had more options about their mode of travel and they had more money in their pockets. They thus needed to be wooed onto the buses. It was no longer a question of informing people about travel opportunities, but of persuading them that the bus was the best choice. This message was not communicated; nor was the message that bus operators were actually friendly people, anxious to please and satisfy customers. Buses were developing a poor profile in more ways than one.

By the 1960s the bus industry had become reconciled to obtaining a small share of the national passenger transport business. Faced with the increasing popularity of automobiles, improvements in road engineering which made personal driving easier, and the advent of the jet plane which stimulated air travel, bus managers accepted the growing segmentation of the travel market. Coaches, like trains, could and did attract customers, but more as a niche than a mass market. Bus operators could make a difference at the margins by keeping up to date with technological innovations and by taking retailing initiatives. Their progress would depend on their ability to seize new connections.

The large companies at the heart of the bus industry, namely Greyhound and Trailways, but in particular Greyhound, set the pace. Managers increasingly were trained in the theory as well as the practice of the modern business world and mechanics were required to gain diplomas as well as practical experience. Bus industry personnel were to be thoroughly educated. New approaches to publicity were also adopted. These included paying more attention to radio and television and to targeting specific audiences. Accepting that most passengers using scheduled services had low incomes and that they travelled by bus because they could not afford the alternatives, operators ensured that these groups were well informed and knew about any special offers. They also sought to increase the core business of the regular routes by building a light freight trade, especially to centres which had no alternative public carrier. But a more lucrative market lay in middle-income Americans. If these would not take the bus regularly, they might be persuaded by better marketing strategies to take the bus for special occasions. Increasingly, bus managers made plans to attract middle-income groups by building up special passenger services. Through a range of holiday packages, charter trips to events and connecting links to airports, they offered a type of social self-selection whereby the otherwise car-driving Americans could be reasonably confident that they would be travelling with their own sort of people. Regular bus services would be supplemented by and occasionally overtaken by special services.

Such strategies which enabled bus operators to expand their passenger business in the 1960s did not, however, stand them in good stead in the ensuing years when stagflation and energy crises weakened the economy and when regulatory policies altered the terms of competition. The industry suffered from escalating expenses and erosion of profits during the troubled economic years of the 1970s. As in the immediate post-war years, higher bus production costs consequent on inflation were not matched by receipts. Attempts to reduce expenditures, improve efficiency and boost passenger numbers by advertising and developing more special services met with little success. The competitive position of the industry was further weakened when the federal government created and sustained the National Rail Passenger Corporation, better known as Amtrak, to run rail passenger service. Subsidized rail fares threatened the income generated by motor coaches in urban corridors. Further federal government policy, in the shape of the deregulation of the airlines in 1978, brought more problems. Sharply declining air fares consequent on competition between air companies attracted some long-distance bus passengers who increasingly found that it was as cheap, if not cheaper, to fly to their destinations. The question then arose, could or should the federal government now assist the bus industry? Subsidy was considered as a way forward, but in the growing conservative ethos of the late 1970s and early 1980s free enterprise won the day. Future developments, whether limited or expansive, would take place in an era of deregulation.

The general analysis of the growth of the long-distance bus industry in the USA masks diverse patterns of company development. Having emerged from its pioneering years of a plenitude of small firms, the industry became an amalgam of two large companies at the centre, several notable regional operations and many small ventures. Though the numbers of small bus operators declined markedly in the Great Depression, they spiralled again when economic conditions picked up in the post-war years. However, the surge was temporary. Economies of scale and greater private automobility put severe pressure on local firms. By 1975 there were an estimated 950 firms in the industry in contrast to the 3,610 firms in 1925 (see table 1.1). Something of the variety of bus enterprises and their significance at a grass roots level is reflected in three regional case studies in the Midwest.

The regional origins of the Greyhound Corporation have generally been traced to northern Minnesota in the second decade of the twentieth century (see chapter 4). Though other claims have been made for Californian roots, the corporation itself has endorsed Hibbing as its mainspring, a sanction which has recently been enhanced by the opening of the Greyhound Bus Origin Museum there. The account of Greyhound's beginnings, however, might be replicated throughout the nation because early bus ventures were little more than communal taxi services in stretched-out automobiles. Entrepreneurs needed to establish regular routes and timetables, to use vehicles which were specifically designed and built as motor coaches, and to introduce systematic management and accounting techniques before they could put their bus business on a sound footing. That the Hibbing operators were more successful than their counterparts in expansion, whether through growth or acquisition of rival companies, was due in part to finance and in part to managerial vision.

The Great Northern Railway, whose lines dominated northern Minnesota, was not as antithetical to the emerging bus industry as were many of its rail counterparts. Though recognizing the potential loss of passenger business to the more flexible and cheaper carrier, Great Northern officials were willing to cooperate and even coordinate, rather than compete and so try to throttle the bus trade.[3] Financial assistance from the Great Northern enabled the Northland Transportation Company to expand its routes and services, while managerial advice from railmen with long experience of working in transportation improved business administration. Yet bus entrepreneurs like Eric Wickman and Orville Caesar were not content to be subsidiary to the railroads. They recognized that to make the best use of the highways, they needed to be independent. To this end they sought alliances with other bus companies showing regional potential. By the late 1920s these stronger concerns had

Table 1.1   The intercity bus industry in the USA: selected statistics 1925–1985

Year	Number of companies	Number of vehicles	Route miles	Bus miles (millions)	Passenger miles (billions)
1925	3,610	21,430	218,601	n.a.	n.a.
1930	3,520	14,090	318,715	1230	7.1
1935	2,120	11,160	330,216	960	7.6
1940	1,830	12,200	313,136	820	10.1
1945	2,320	23,210	360,856	1400	27.0
1950	2,480	24,420	412,284	1350	21.2
1955	2,600	27,200	410,000	1375	21.9
1960	1,150	20,974	265,000	1092	19.3
1965	1,100	19,800	263,000	1156	23.8
1970	1,000	22,000	267,000	1209	25.3
1975	950	20,500	274,000	1126	25.4
1980	1,330	21,400	279,000	1162	27.4
1985	n.a.	20,100	263,000	997	23.8

Sources: B.B. Crandall (1954), *The Growth of the Intercity Bus Industry*, Syracuse, NY, appendix A, table A-2, pp. 280–82; National Association of Motor Bus Owners (1976), *1926–1976: One-Half Century of Service to America*, Washington, DC, p. 23; *The Fleet Owner* (1957), **52**, p. 138; F.A. Smith (1986), *Transportation in America. Historical Compendium, 1939–1985*, Westport, CN, p. 12; American Bus Association, *Bus Facts for 1982*, p. 2; American Bus Association, mss statistics, c. 1988.

proved their viability and were recognized as good investment risks on the stock market. The merger which created the Greyhound Corporation in 1929 was financed partly by existing railroad money and partly by new investments.

Pioneer bus ventures in Iowa resembled those in Minnesota. Entrepreneurs ran a taxi-like service in their autos. If they succeeded, they acquired another larger vehicle and then a specially-designed bus. They expanded further if they could secure financial loans and if they gained managerial expertise. The early history of Iowa bus firms provides different perspectives in that one of its leading entrepreneurs was female (see chapter 5). Gender presented complications in an industry which was male-dominated and which was associated with such male characteristics as assertiveness, confidence in the world of work and suitable training or education. Helen Schultz succeeded in establishing and expanding her bus company as a young and (initially) single woman. She built up her enterprise into a regional operation partly by her forceful personality and partly because she was able to attract enough capital and acquire enough business acumen to consolidate her early start. She stayed in business for eight years and then sold her company as a going concern to a larger and more systematically organized bus rival. It was probably a wise decision because she was already running into financial and administrative difficulties. How many of these difficulties were specifically related to her gender rather than her entrepreneurial skills is not now possible to assess, but she clearly demonstrated a role which would not become acceptable for another half century.

Helen Schultz sold the Red Ball Transportation Company to Edgar Zelle of the Jefferson Highway Transportation Company in 1929. Edgar Zelle was another Minnesota pioneer bus operator, but he had built up his enterprise in the southern part of the state (see chapter 6). Having negotiated with the Northland Transportation Company about bus routes in northern Minnesota in 1925, he turned his attention southwards to consolidate routes in southern Minnesota and to expand through Iowa to the important gateway of Kansas City, Missouri, where he could connect with other major companies for nationwide destinations. Part of this expansion included buying the rights to bus routes, including those of Helen Schultz. The flourishing regional bus concern needed injections of capital, which were supplied by local bankers and businessmen, and a keen awareness of business management, which was supplied by Zelle himself. An educated man who kept up to date with motor-coach activities locally and nationally, he successfully negotiated the economic depression of the 1930s as an independent carrier by careful planning, economy drives and lobbying state officials. During the war he worked for the government as an auxiliary transport aide at both the local and national level. He also continued to manage the Jefferson company which emerged from the war as a viable and profitable concern. Like all operators he faced difficult times in the post-war years when passengers were anxious to leave the buses for their autos. He succeeded, however, in reshaping the operation before he gradually took a back seat as his former right-hand man, Lester Wakefield, and then his son managed the independent regional company.

Case studies of individual intercity bus firms demonstrate the range of concerns entrepreneurs faced in running a public venture. Central to all such operations was a good working relationship with the government, at both state and federal level. Any transport enterprise affected society's well-being by virtue of its status as a common carrier or as a private carrier using the shared highways or skyways. Other than in the hectic pioneering days, buses were subject to local ordinances. Then as ventures grew, states licensed vehicles and required driver insurance and competency. As traffic grew, state governments turned their attention to economic issues like competition and fares (see chapter 7). Arguing that the public had to be protected, they determined whether carriers were financially secure enough to run their businesses and whether any new proposed transport service was necessary and useful to the community at large.

Individual state governments wrestled with the competition between trains and buses and between trains and trucks in the 1920s and early 1930s. Most state railroad commissions sanctioned motor-carrier operations despite the opposition of railroad corporations and their protests about unfair terms of trade. Soon similar issues were being debated at federal level as bus companies expanded beyond state boundaries and became potentially subject to federal scrutiny. The federal government acted indecisively for several years and only with the passage of the Motor Carrier Act of 1935 did it permanently subject buses and trucks to regulation. This act ensured that buses carrying passengers between states complied with strict rules governing safety, insurance, finance, accounting and record-keeping. Existing companies who conformed to these standards were protected, but they and any newcomers had to establish, publish and adhere to rates which were reasonable and non-discriminatory. The bus industry had now entered a new regulatory era. Like the railroads and shortly to be joined by the airlines and internal waterways, it was accountable for its behaviour to public officials and had to plead its case in a regulatory environment which was neither uniform in its agencies and enforcement nor fixed in its ideological construction.[4]

If the bus companies had to observe regulations established by an external authority, they were free to chose how to promote their own activities. Even before buses became a viable means of transport, advertising had become an integral part of business practice, either to inform an impersonal market of the nature and availability of a product or a service or to promote sales in a competitive market. The large bus companies soon realized how essential advertising was in a newly developing service industry (see chapter 8). They divided their potential clients into two groups. They advised regular customers by messages in local newspapers, supplemented by timetables picked up at the local terminal. They hoped to attract the middle classes by placing pictorial advertisements in popular magazines aimed at the leisure market of holidays, tourism and entertainment. For both groups of clients buses were envisaged as comfortable, safe and convenient modes of travel and all at a reasonable price. Whether the recreational messages in magazines had a major impact during the years of the Depression remains uncertain, but the number of such advertisements was increased. During the war the bus industry as a whole tried to persuade the increasing numbers of passengers that the poor conditions of overcrowding, old equipment and inadequate timekeeping were purely a temporary result of emergency conditions. Clearly, this wartime propaganda was not very successful. Despite the new and striking post-war advertisements in glossy magazines and newspapers, and despite ventures in documentary films and new approaches on the radio and television, promotional campaigns did not bring back clients. They may only have helped halt a further drift downward.

The little customer survey information that is available about bus travel in the twentieth century does not reveal the impact of company publicity. What it does suggest, as do several observations in company and trade association files, is that the majority of bus passengers have been female. Yet the bulk of historical records about buses and bus transport are solidly masculine. Certainly these records are producer-oriented and concentrate on the operations and administration of companies, on industry statistics, types of buses, government regulations, intra- and inter-industry competition and personnel. The public relations materials and the advertising copy demonstrate a visual perception of women as employees and as customers, but little written attention was given to female work skills or to female concerns as distinct from passenger issues. Occasional references to women working in the travel bureaux or answering telephone inquiries and staffing the information desk were sufficient.

Yet the bus industry has enjoyed more female connections than it has acknowledged. The most obvious association, and that frequently made by male historians – namely as a reserve labour force during the Second World War – is both true and at the same time dismissive of a regular involvement (see chapter 9). Certainly, until equal opportunities legislation in the 1960s and its more effective enforcement in the 1970s, there were few women owners and managers. Even now women at the top of the business pyramid are scarce. Yet they have existed and do perform well, offering examples of female managerial competence. More numerous, and frequently hidden, have been women working in white-collar positions, such as accountants, depot managers, tour organizers, directors in a family concern and public relations officers. Now, in a post-industrial economy dominated by the service sector, such female staff have been renamed 'middle management', but they have always made an active contribution to the running of bus operations. So, too, have their pink-collar counterparts who worked as typists, clerks or telephonists in the business offices and their blue-collar sisters who cleaned the buildings and the vehicles and who worked in the restaurants. Women produced as well as consumed, and both functions need much more attention.

More evidence about women has emerged through visual representations of the bus industry at work. Pictures of the daily routines of maintaining and repairing vehicles, selling tickets, offering information, waiting for buses, making bus journeys and using auxiliary services like cafeterias or concessions available in terminals demonstrate a division of the sexes which approaches the norm. Such photographs also show an industry which is sometimes vibrant, sometimes struggling to survive. 'Living' pictures of buses and bus people at work and passengers in transit are rarely found in historical archives. Many bus manufacturers, bus companies and bus enthusiasts have preferred to take and keep images of vehicles in pristine condition, often set against a distinctive background and without passengers or workers; or, at best, adorned by one or a small number of people who might add to the distinction of the industry. Sometimes these pictures were taken solely to record the make and style of the vehicle and to ensure that the engine number was visible. At other times the pictures were designed to present a wholesome and upwardly-mobile image of the business and might be used for promotional purposes. Documentary photography undertaken by observers outside the industry reveals an alternative and participatory side of the bus business.

During the New Deal and the Second World War the federal government established two agencies to assemble an extensive record of American life through documentary photographs. The images stemming from these projects provide remarkable evidence of a past which rarely emerges through written documents. As part of her assignments for the Office of War Information, Esther Bubley took her camera on a cross-country bus trip in 1943. Four years later in 1947 she again photographed Greyhound buses, this time working for Standard Oil (New Jersey) (see chapter 10). Both collections of photographs offer an outsider's view of an industry and its workers as they were adjusting to abnormal conditions. The pictures thus provide irreplaceable evidence of a set of transport circumstances which the photographer cannot and has not created. The investigative photographer was able to select the timing, the location and the angle of the bus-based scenes and so could impose a personal perspective, but this does not thereby become a fixed viewpoint. It can be interpreted and reinterpreted many times, bringing new light to interpretative analysis. The Esther Bubley photographs from 1947 are here explored to dissect a bus system and a bus culture which operated in the USA in the years immediately after the Second World War.

Intercity buses have been visible throughout the USA since the 1920s. Their role in the economic and social development of the nation has rarely been analysed and is here only partially discussed. More can be accomplished both from existing public resources and from collections which are still privately owned, provided that historians have sufficient interest, perseverance and energy. The long-distance bus industry in the USA has offered a useful and necessary service and it deserves to be given its place in the nation's history.

Notes

1. These remarks draw on personal reminiscences of European students who became academics and L. Elliott, 'Rocky ride for an American dream', *The Guardian*, 11 June 1994, p. 40.
2. For more detailed information on available archival materials see the bibliographical essay, pp. 219–37.
3. For more information on the role of the Great Northern Railway in the early growth of the bus industry see M. Walsh, 'Coordination, Cooperation Or Competition: The Great Northern Railway and Bus Transportation in the 1920s', in R. Cameron and L.F. Schnore (eds) (1997), *Cities and Markets. Studies in the Organization of Human Space*, Lanham, Md, pp. 163–89.
4. For more information on the public policy and transport see M. Walsh, 'In Whose Interest? Public Policy and Transport during Depression and War', in R.A. Garson and S.S. Kidd (eds) (1999), *The Roosevelt Years: New Essays on the United States, 1933–1945*, Edinburgh, pp. 11–29.

Part One

Main Routes

2 From Jitney to Giant: The Early Growth of Long-Distance Bus Transport in the USA

Bus transport in the USA started in the second decade of the twentieth century when numerous entrepreneurs in all parts of the country operated local services between nearby communities using automobile sedans. Encouraged by their early success, ambitious pioneers built up longer networks by connecting their routes to those of like-minded venturers and by acquiring more reliable and comfortable vehicles. For those who could meet the requirements of state government regulations and withstand the competition from both railroads and other bus operators, prospects looked good. By the late 1920s the possibility of national lines suggested increased business; but the onset of the Great Depression forced reorganization in the burgeoning and highly competitive industry. Many small carriers went out of business when passengers and revenue declined, while the larger companies had to restructure their operations to reduce costs at the same time as improving services. Federal regulation of motor carriers in the mid-1930s strengthened the position of surviving and larger companies who were able to retain their trade. By the end of the decade long-distance bus travel was established as a permanent and important part of the nation's economy.

Origins. Local services link up

At the turn of the twentieth century Americans who wished to travel between cities either for work or for pleasure had limited options. The steam railroad offered the best, the most reliable and the fastest means of transport. Electric railways provided reasonable intraurban and short-distance intercity travel. They also offered some longer lines, but only in certain parts of the country. The horse-drawn coach was neither a competitive nor a comfortable alternative given the deplorable state of the nation's highways; and though bicycles were popular in both town and country, they, too, were hampered by poor road surfaces. It took the mass production and ownership of cars, together with

17

increased attention to road construction, to bring the major breakthrough in travel in the 1920s. And alongside the rapid spread of the popular and individualistic auto came the slower, but no less significant, growth of bus transport. Not only did buses replace trams and trolleys in urban mass transit; they also opened up new avenues of intercity travel both to those Americans who could not afford cars and to those car owners who preferred to leave distance driving to others.[1]

No particular date marks the beginning of the American intercity bus industry because so many individuals were attracted to it at about the same time by the large profits available to those who could carry fare-paying passengers over public highways. These ubiquitous bus pioneers came from all walks of life. Few knew much about transport or about business, but they were willing to chance their hand in a new venture which had low entry costs. Frequently driving used vehicles, these 'carriers' concentrated on local services operated on a consumer-demand basis with the driver taking cash fares. There were no formal schedules or routes, though some bus owners who carried men to work, began and finished their journeys either at hotels or stores. Others, however, loaded anywhere on the street where likely passengers stood waiting. Word of mouth or newspaper advertisements announced the existence of the new service, but a regular commitment was not guaranteed. Bus men frequently did not start until they had got a payload; and those who travelled on the early buses were satisfied with reaching their destination rather than enjoying a fast or comfortable journey.[2] The early 'jitney' or taxicab-style days were exciting and promising, but were not particularly stable.[3]

The experiences of pioneers in the two states which led the way in long-distance bus travel, California and Minnesota, suggest the flavour, problems and possibilities of this new form of transport. In northern California Wesley E. Travis, who had previously worked in subcontracting the postal service in the Mountain and Far West regions and then in the taxicab business in Chicago, in 1907 set up another taxi service in San Francisco. Following his early success, he incorporated this enterprise as the California Taxicab Company in 1909 and gradually acquired forty taxicabs. But these vehicles were unsatisfactory both in terms of size and reliability, so he decided to improve their design and construction. Soon other carriers, such as the auto-stage operators of Stockton, wanted to buy his new elongated vehicles and this interest prompted him to investigate the possibilities of interurban as well as intraurban road transport.[4]

In 1912, ex-miner A.L. Hayes started an auto-stage line in southern California to take sightseers from San Diego to Oceanside. This proved to be so popular that he began another service to El Centro and then gradually built up longer routes and more regular schedules, later extending his Pickwick Stages to Los Angeles, a distance of 132 miles, where he joined up with another bus pioneer, Charles Wren. Wren had started off in suburban 'jitney' transport in

1913 with service between Los Angeles and Venice, some 14 miles away. Persuading other city taxi and longer-line operators to use his depot as a terminal, he moved into intercity transport with a route to San Fernando, 20 miles to the north. Shortly after this, he extended this line to Santa Barbara, 99 miles away. By 1918 he had organized a number of rental-car drivers into a small auto-stage association operating between Los Angeles and San Francisco. Following consolidation with Hayes's San Diego line, Pickwick Stages became a state network of sorts using the coastal route.[5]

In the Iron Range district of northern Minnesota, early bus operators started up business by carrying men between mining locations. In Hibbing, in 1914, Eric Wickman, a former diamond driller, entered the bus trade when he could not sell the first car shipped to his Hupmobile agency. Acquiring two partners, Andrew G. Anderson and Arvid Heed, they built up a regular service to the nearby community of Alice. The entrepreneurs then bought another auto and started a new route to the mines at Mahoning. As trade was brisk and their carrying capacity inadequate, they hired a local blacksmith to build elongated bodies welded onto truck frames. By 1915 they needed more capital and more drivers. So they acquired new partners and formed the Mesaba Transportation Company. Soon the firm was operating a fleet of eighteen buses with routes extending as far as Grand Rapids, 40 miles away.[6]

These California and Minnesota experiences were replicated throughout the USA in the years between 1910 and 1920. Men from all walks of life who had touring cars carried passengers short distances for reasonable fares. If they worked hard and set up fairly regular services, either undercutting or amalgamating with nearby competitors, then they made enough money to expand and acquire more vehicles to develop these local routes. In most areas the possibility of operating over longer distances was prevented by the slow speed of travelling on dirt-top roads, in the rural areas in particular, and the frequent breakdowns. It was more difficult for drivers to make repairs on the road if they were far from their base. Any attempts to establish longer-distance services took the form of uncoordinated links with the local services of other entrepreneurs. Passengers were left with the discomfort of long waits.

State legislation, technical development and better organization hasten change

But change was on the horizon. It came in two main ways: externally in the shape of state government regulations and internally through improvements in mechanical engineering and business organization. Prompted by the need to finance better roads and to ensure public safety, and increasingly lobbied by railroad interests anxious to curb the new freight and passenger competition at an early stage, state governments moved to regulate motor carriers. By 1920, eleven states had imposed some control on bus operators. In the next five years, twenty-six more states followed suit, making three-quarters of the total, including those most heavily populated. Regulations varied widely, but most states insisted that buses, as public utilities, should be subject to laws protecting passengers from unnecessary and inefficient lines, high charges, unsafe vehicles and inexperienced drivers. Many of the new requirements, such as those ensuring that drivers had licences and insurance coverage, that buses had brakes and lights, and that companies kept to advertised schedules, were difficult to enforce, particularly in rural areas. But a start had been made to ensure that bus lines observed basic standards.[7]

Within the bus industry advances in mechanical engineering and competition, both between small independent carriers and between buses and trains, stimulated improvements in motor-coach equipment and in operating practices. In terms of design and technology, the new buses of the early 1920s were much superior to the improvised elongated auto sedans of earlier years which had been constructed on truck chassis and seated only up to seventeen persons. In 1921 the Fageol brothers of Oakland, California, produced the Safety Coach, a low-slung twenty-two-seater with sedan doors all along the side and equipped with a four-cylinder 60-horsepower airplane-type engine. The following year the White Company of Cleveland, Ohio moved from a commercial chassis to one specially designed for bus use. Other auto and truck manufacturers like Pierce-Arrow of Buffalo, New York, General Motors of Pontiac, Michigan, and Mack Motor Truck Company of New York City also started to specialize in bus production, while several bus operators constructed motor coaches to meet their particular needs.

When larger and more comfortable vehicles with more powerful engines were called for, Fageol adopted a six-cylinder 100-horsepower engine, and stretched the wheelbase and widened the body of his safety coach to accommodate twenty-nine rather than twenty-two passengers. Other leading bus manufacturers made similar design changes and worked to improve safety and comfort through introducing air brakes, sturdier frames, heating and ventilating systems, interior baggage racks, and even toilet facilities. By the mid-1920s some ambitious firms were experimenting with two-level (or duplex) vehicles, with seating capacity for fifty-three passengers, and were designing night coaches which would provide sleeping and seating accommodation for twenty-six people. This general quest for improved vehicles in its turn brought systematic maintenance checks and more repair facilities in well-designed garages and terminals.[8]

Changes internal to the bus industry were equally important in contributing to the growing popularity of passenger travel in the 1920s. Modern business practices similar to those adopted by the railroads were essential to ensure smooth operation, profitability and customer satisfaction. Ambitious bus entrepreneurs in companies like California Transit and Pickwick Stages in California, or Mesaba Transportation and Jefferson Highway in Minnesota, thus began analysing traffic flows, planning routes and connections more carefully, and developing rational fare structures. They installed new accounting procedures and created divisional lines of control. They then published schedules regularly and advertised services widely, taking care to draw attention to the comfort of the buses, the safety-consciousness of the drivers, the amenities at the terminals and the ease of purchasing tickets.[9]

Bus entrepreneurs were anxious to systematize their procedures not only to increase profits but also to compete more effectively against steam and electric railways. In this they were so successful that many rail companies decided to use buses themselves or to work in collaboration with bus concerns rather than to try and limit their operations through restrictive legislation and heavy taxation. Accepting the economic facts that buses offered advantages of greater flexibility and cheaper running costs, especially for short and immediate-length journeys and for routes in sparsely populated areas, the number of railroads operating buses rose remarkably in the mid-1920s. There were only three steam railroads running buses in January 1925, but by the end of that year thirty-one companies were using 375 vehicles. Encouraged by the successful example of major pioneers like the Great Northern, the Pennsylvania, and the New York, New Haven & Hartford Railroads, other rail companies quickly adopted buses on a system-wide basis. By 1929, sixty-two steam railroad companies ran 1,256 buses over 16,793 miles of route.[10]

Railroads might attempt to retain their passengers by setting up bus auxiliaries in the late 1920s, but the larger bus companies, now with a decade of operating experience, looked further afield and threatened long-distance rail services. They announced their intention of providing nationwide routes using improved buses and interline connections. By 1927 the major Californian companies, Pickwick Stages and California Transit, had routes which stretched north to Portland, Oregon, south to San Diego, California, and east into the Plains and south-western states of Arizona and New Mexico. In the centre of the continent the Minnesota-based Motor Transit Company, having bought numerous small lines, started to acquire operating subsidiaries beyond the Middle West. The California Transit Company, reorganized as the American Motor Transportation Company, headed by Wesley Travis, had the distinction of putting together the first coast-to-coast bus service in 1928. For a one-way fare of $72 the adventurous traveller who could endure a journey of five days and fourteen hours, incorporating 132 stops, could travel by road from Los Angeles to New York on the longest bus line in the world. Motor Transit shortly thereafter, in 1928, offered a transcontinental service through cooperative arrangements with Pickwick Stages.[11]

But Motor Transit needed to make more systematic arrangements, and stringent controls were necessary to build up regular transcontinental passenger services. A national bus company had to be forged. In 1929, having put together a marketable portfolio of motor transport stocks, Midwestern investment bankers consolidated a sprawling bus empire consisting of four fully-owned operating, three fully-owned ancilliary and six partially-owned operating companies with routes in forty-one out of the forty-eight states. This expansion carried the company from a total of 5 million coach miles in 1927 to 20 million in 1930. Early the following year, Motor Transit officially adopted the name already used by most of the recently acquired companies and became the Greyhound Corporation. There were high hopes for the future. In the space of a few years entrepreneurs had successfully introduced a new component into the transport sector and were offering economic, speedy and safe travel on a nationwide basis (see table 1.1 on page 8).[12]

Problems of the 1930s

The adolescence of the intercity bus industry would, however, be more painful than its birth pangs and infancy. Coming of age in the major depression of the 1930s, all bus companies faced the prospects of declining traffic (see table 1.1 on page 8). Many small carriers collapsed when passengers and revenue fell, while the newly-merged large corporations, experiencing both a capital and cash flow shortage, had to reorganize both their financial and administrative structures and had to ensure system-wide economies in order to survive. Having weathered their first national crisis in the early 1930s, motor-coach entrepreneurs then had to comply with federal regulations. Still more economies and major improvements in vehicles and operating practices, along with widespread advertising campaigns, were necessary to come through the recession of the late 1930s. But by the end of that decade bus travel in the USA was well established.

The impact of the Great Depression was felt throughout the intercity bus industry in the early 1930s as passenger traffic failed to continue its upward momentum. Though the decline in business was not as severe as that experienced in many branches of manufacturing, bus companies had to face shrinking demand. Certainly, large operators had analysed traffic flows when establishing new routes or when buying existing lines, but they had generally assumed that they could persuade the public of either the necessity or the enjoyment of bus travel. Workers could get to their existing jobs more easily or could find better jobs in new locations. Women had more opportunities to go shopping and families were able to visit each other regularly. Furthermore, buses were admirably suited to serve the growing interest in tourism and to provide for holiday traffic. But with unemployment rising and incomes falling, fewer people rode distances to work. Fewer still rode the buses for social and recreational reasons. Bus operators would have to reassess market potential.

The number of intercity bus companies fell notably between 1929 and 1932 from 3,910 to 2,760. Many small and weak firms collapsed because their unsound accounting methods and inadequate maintenance facilities could not withstand the strain of competition for decreasing passenger traffic. Their larger and more ambitious counterparts, now in consolidations underwritten by investment financiers, were also in difficulties. Unable to repay the short-term loans used to float the mergers which created them, some companies declared bankruptcy, while others had to refinance and then to apply themselves systematically to both reducing costs and increasing business.[13] The manoeuvres undertaken by the newly formed Greyhound Corporation illustrate the problems of surviving the early years of the Depression.

The Greyhound Corporation

Following the stock market crash of October 1929 Greyhound was dangerously overcapitalized. Much of the corporation's rapid expansion in 1928 and 1929 had been financed by short-term loans which could not be repaid as earnings fell. Two recapitalization schemes were essential to meet current obligations in 1930 and in 1933. On the first occasion, before the Depression reached its nadir, Greyhound's major investment broker, Glenn Traer, managed to persuade bankers to take a $4 million issue of three-year notes. But the corporation's financial position did not turn around in the next three years. Low profits in 1930 and 1931, and a net loss in 1932, meant that there was no money to repay the notes as they fell due in spring 1933 or to service the current debt of $1,640,000. More ingenuity and salesmanship were needed if Greyhound was to stay in business.

Turning first to the floating debt, Traer and top Greyhound officials, Eric Wickman and Orville Caesar, persuaded General Motors, who had been manufacturing buses for Greyhound since 1930, to take over a substantial portion. They were then able to get extensions on the remainder. Next they arranged a new issue of five-year notes in exchange for the maturing three-year notes. These measures, however, were insufficient to resolve the company's financial problems. The capital stock situation remained very unhealthy. Greyhound lagged badly in paying its cumulative preferred dividends and the common stock had never yielded any dividends. Recapitalization created a new common stock in exchange for shares of the second preferred stock and the old common stock, while retaining the first preferred at par. Some stockholders took a loss under the rearrangements, but that alternative was deemed preferable to the company's demise.[14]

The nation's largest bus concern was still not out of its quagmire. The company had to make more money if it was to progress. Divisional restructuring promised savings when the two uneconomic companies in the system, Western Greyhound and Southland Greyhound, were reorganized into a sounder unit, Southwestern Greyhound.[15] Careful attention to maintenance facilities and to improving equipment also reduced operating costs. On the more positive side, company managers sought out and won new business by, for example, providing transport to and organizing tours at the Chicago World's Fair in 1933 and 1934. They also conducted a huge mass-media campaign which included scenes on a Greyhound bus in the 1934 film *It Happened One Night*, starring Clark Gable and Claudette Colbert. Bus passengers travelling on Greyhound increased in 1934 and 1935 and prospects started to look better.[16] The experiences of Greyhound during the troubled years of the 1930s may not be typical, but they do suggest that considerable attention would have to be paid to better business methods, sounder financing and innovative marketing if the bus industry was to grow.[17]

Legislation favours existing operators, especially the larger ones

While bus companies were still struggling to combat the economic impact of the Depression, they were faced with further changes imposed by law. By the mid-1920s most states had regulated intrastate motor-carrier operations, not only on the grounds of public safety and financing road construction, but also with a view to controlling economic issues like the degree of competition and the level of fares. When, however, Supreme Court decisions rendered state regulation of interstate motor traffic ineffective in 1925, calls for federal legislation became frequent and loud. But the process of enacting this legislation was slow and painful. Congressional hearings in 1926, 1928, 1930, 1932 and 1934, and investigations by the Interstate Commerce Commission (ICC) starting in 1926 and 1930, convinced or persuaded enough politicians that the new motor-carrier industry, particularly the trucking section, should not yet be regulated and no fewer than forty bills failed to pass both Houses of Congress between 1925 and 1935. Most bus operators, the railroads and taxpayers represented by state associations, favoured some regulations in the interests of reducing cut-throat competition, but little headway could be made while diverse interest groups fought over specific issues and methods of administration.[18]

Indeed initial federal guidelines emerged from the flurry of legislation which was passed in the First Hundred Days of Franklin D. Roosevelt's administration in 1933. Under the National Industrial Recovery Act, the motor bus operators met government mediators and representatives of labour and consumers and drew up a code of self-regulation. Companies signing the code agreed to respect existing state regulations, to eliminate destructive competitive practices, to observe maximum hours and minimum rates of pay for workers and to promote the fullest use of the industry. This Motor Bus Industry Code, however, had little impact on the shape of long-distance bus transport in 1933 and 1934. By this time depressed business conditions had eliminated sub-standard operators and most of the active firms had already adopted many of the suggested administrative practices and were following safety provisions. Though the trade association, the National Association of Motor Bus Operators (NAMBO), favoured the principle of self-regulation rather than regulation by a government agency, the code had little chance to be effective, for in 1935 the National Industrial Recovery Act was declared unconstitutional.[19] Later that year, however, the long-awaited specific federal regulation came into effect with the Motor Carrier Act, alternatively known as Part II of the Interstate Commerce Act.

The objectives of the Motor Carrier Act were to prevent wasteful and destructive competition within the bus and truck industries in particular, and in the transport sector in general, and to promote and protect the public interest. The ICC, as regulatory agency, would achieve these aims by exercising three main controls. In the first place entry into the bus industry would require a certificate of public convenience and necessity which could be suspended, changed or revoked. Mergers and issues of securities also had to be approved. Second, bus operators had to conform to regulations governing safety, insurance, finance, accounting and records. For example, drivers had to be qualified, certain safety devices were made compulsory, insurance protection was required and companies had to comply with specified accounting procedures. Third, carriers had to publish and to adhere to rates and fares and they had to give thirty days' notice of any changes. The ICC could suspend these changes and could prescribe maximum, minimum and actual rates to be charged. Long-distance bus transport had now entered a new regulatory era.[20]

The terms of the Motor Carrier Act worked in favour of large companies and those with existing routes. Certification protected most companies already in business while the establishment of operating standards did not significantly affect those with adequate capital. Although the newly established Motor Carrier Bureau[21] did not follow a consistent policy in interpreting the 1935 Act, officials seemed to lean towards a course of regulated monopoly by limiting competition between long-distance bus operators. Existing companies contested applications for competitive routes, and on establishing that the service was adequate, new applications were often turned down. Mergers of existing carriers were allowed when it was clear that the volume of traffic for two carriers was inadequate. Bus subsidiaries of railroads could not acquire

competing motor carriers if the sole purpose was to eliminate competition; but
if traffic flow was light only one company would be certified. Small operators
did continue to offer service, but the large firms dominated. National Trailways,
an association of independent bus firms with each component retaining
individual membership, offered transcontinental services; but Greyhound had
no serious rival. And Greyhound proceeded to clarify its position under the
Motor Carrier Act, grouping its twenty-nine companies into seven operating
divisions. These mergers, known as 'The Greyhound Mergers of 1936',
simplified the corporate structure at the same time as consolidating and
strengthening Greyhound's position.[22]

Greyhound's continuing prominence in bus transport, and its ability to grow
during depressed economic conditions in the late 1930s, stemmed as much
from the continued improvements in operating practices as from mergers and
the changing legal environment. Bus officials hoped that increased passenger
traffic would follow from improved internal management and better public
services. They also realized, however, that they would have to stimulate bus
travel through a systematic advertising campaign in major journals and
newspapers, supported by travel brochures and window displays. Business
needed to be encouraged.

Greyhound managers pursued various avenues of improvement simul-
taneously. A proportion of the bus fleet was annually updated. The introduction
of the aluminium and steel cruiser in 1936 and the diesel engine in 1938
constituted the two outstanding technical innovations, but many small changes
were made to engine parts, particularly transmissions and brakes. In the
maintenance division, the regular servicing carried out at terminals was now
supported by periodic overhauls undertaken at large garages specifically built
at key points for that purpose. Many modern terminals were constructed not
only to provide central offices, but also to offer those amenities such as waiting-
rooms, cafeterias, baggage-checking, improved washrooms and travel bureaux,
now demanded by passengers. Steps were also taken to improve one of the
negative facets of bus travel, namely those intermediate rest stops run by
concessionaires. Indeed, in 1937 Greyhound started buying and building its
own Post Houses, to be run by trained managers. As for the travelling itself,
better interdivisional coordination brought superior timetabling arrangements,
while more travel agencies in key cities provided full information on both the
new schedules as well as the planned and expense-paid tours.[23]

Where Greyhound led, other long-distance bus operators tended to follow.
As rates and fares were now subject to the authority of the ICC, competitors
could no longer win passengers by cutting fares. Nor could they offer new
routes without government permission. Instead, they had to provide better
services, and for the most part this meant improving the safety, comfort and
speed of travelling. Given this greater care and attention, bus operators

Table 2.1 Intercity travel in the USA by Mode (billions of passenger miles, 1929–1989)

Year	Total intercity travel Amount	%	Private carrier Total[1] Amount	%	Automobile Amount	%	Air Amount	%	Public carrier Total[1,2] Amount	%	Bus Amount	%	Rail Amount	%	Air Amount	%
1929	216.0	100	175.0	81.0	175.0	81.0	-	-	40.9	18.9	7.1	3.3	32.5	15.0	-	-
1934	219.0	100	191.0	87.2	191.0	87.2	-	-	27.5	12.6	7.4	3.4	18.8	8.6	0.2	0.1
1939	309.5	100	275.5	89.0	275.4	89.0	0.1	-	34.0	11.0	9.5	3.1	23.7	7.7	0.8	0.3
1944	309.3	100	181.4	58.6	181.4	58.6	-	-	127.9	41.4	27.3	8.8	97.7	31.6	2.9	0.9
1949	478.0	100	410.2	85.8	409.4	85.6	0.8	0.2	67.8	14.2	24.0	5.0	36.0	7.5	7.8	1.6
1954	668.2	100	598.5	89.6	597.1	89.4	1.4	0.2	69.7	10.4	22.0	3.3	29.5	4.4	18.2	2.7
1959	762.8	100	689.5	90.4	687.4	90.1	2.1	0.3	73.3	9.6	20.4	2.7	22.4	2.9	30.5	4.0
1964	892.7	100	805.5	90.2	801.8	89.8	3.7	0.4	87.2	9.8	23.3	2.6	18.4	2.1	45.5	5.1
1969	1,134.1	100	985.8	86.9	977.0	86.1	8.8	0.8	148.3	13.1	24.9	2.2	12.3	1.1	111.1	9.8
1974	1,306.7	100	1133.1	86.7	1121.9	85.9	11.2	0.9	173.6	13.3	27.7	2.1	10.5	0.8	135.4	10.4
1979	1,589.9	100	1337.9	84.2	1322.4	83.2	15.5	1.0	252.0	15.8	27.7	1.7	11.0	0.7	212.7	13.4
1984	1,687.2	100	1401.1	83.0	1388.1	82.2	13.0	0.8	286.1	17.0	24.6	1.5	10.8	0.6	250.7	14.9
1989	1,936.0	100	1563.9	80.8	1550.8	80.1	13.1	0.7	372.3	19.2	24.0	1.2	13.1	0.7	335.2	17.3

Source: National Association of Motor Bus Operators, *Bus Facts*, (1966), pp. 6, 8; F.A. Smith (1986), *Transportation in America. Historical Compendium 1939-1985*, Westport, CN, p. 12; F.A. Smith (1990), *Transportation in America. A Statistical Analysis of Transportation in the United States*, Washington, DC, p. 7; R.A. Wilson (1997), *Transportation in America. Historical Compendium, 1939-1995*, Lansdown, VA, p. 21.

Notes:
1 Percentages do not always total 100 because of rounding up.
2 Early figures take count of waterways as well as railroads, buses and airlines.

Table 2.2   Intercity travel in the USA by public carrier 1929–1989
(passenger miles – percentage distribution)

Year	Total	Bus	Rail	Air
1929	100	17.4	79.5	-
1934	100	26.9	68.4	0.7
1939	100	27.9	69.7	2.4
1944	100	21.3	76.4	2.3
1949	100	35.4	53.1	11.5
1954	100	31.6	42.3	26.1
1959	100	27.8	30.6	41.6
1964	100	26.7	21.1	52.2
1969	100	16.8	8.3	74.9
1974	100	16.0	6.0	78.0
1979	100	11.0	4.6	84.4
1984	100	8.6	3.8	87.6
1989	100	6.4	3.5	90.1

Source: Calculated from table 2.1.

maintained a small proportion of the nation's intercity travel in the 1930s while increasing their passenger mileage from 7.1 billion to 9.5 billion in the same period (see tables 2.1 and 2.2). Though private automobiles accounted for the bulk of long-distance travel in the Depression years, buses were making inroads into the public carrier sector. Within the space of a quarter of a century a new public transport facility had grown to maturity and was able to offer passenger service comparable to, and in many cases superior to, those offered by the long-established railroad.

Notes

1. For general discussions of the condition of roads and the prospect of highway travel in the late nineteenth and early twentieth centuries see J.B. Rae (1971), *The Road and the Car in American Life*, Cambridge, MA, pp. 22–39; American Association of State Highway Officials (AASHO)(1964), *A Story of the Beginning, Purposes, Growth, Activities and Achievements of the American Association of State Highway Officials*, Washington, DC, pp. 31–40; C.L. Dearing (1941), *American Highway Policy*, Washington, DC, pp. 29–59, 224–40. For an overview of steam and electric railways see J.F. Stover (1961), *American Railroads*, Chicago, and G.W. Hilton and J.F. Due (1960), *The Electric Interurban Railways in America*, Stanford, CA.

2. For general information on early bus activity see A.E. Meier and J.P. Hoschek (1975), *Over the Road. A History of Intercity Bus Transportation in the United States*, Upper Montclair, NJ, pp. 1–9; B.B. Crandall (1954), *The Growth of the Intercity Bus Industry*, Syracuse, NY, pp. 6–13; F.K. Edwards (1933), *Principles*

of Motor Transportation, New York, pp. 5–9. Detailed information is available in local newspapers, for example, the *Hibbing Daily Tribune*, 1915–27.

3. In California car owners pulled up at trolley stops and offered rides for a 'jitney' or nickel. The name 'jitney' was frequently used before the manufacture and use of longer vehicles which might be called 'buses' or 'motor coaches'. In 1915 the newly incorporated Mesaba Transportation Company was described as a 'jitney company', *Hibbing Daily Tribune*, 18 December 1915.

4. C.H. Gohres, 'History of Pacific Greyhound Lines', pp. 2–8, box 3, Greyhound Corporation Records, University of Wyoming, Laramie (hereafter cited as GCR); W.E. Travis, 'Statement', Folder 'Greyhound History: Pacific Greyhound Lines', box 1, GCR.

5. Gohres, 'History of Pacific Greyhound Lines', pp. 18–20; J.P. Hoschek (1960), 'Greyhound's Western History', *Motor Coach Age*, **12**(2), p. 5; Edwards, *Principles of Motor Transportation*, pp. 5–6.

6. F.H. Schultz (c. 1954), 'Greyhound The Greatest Name on the Highway', thesis, n.p., pp. 5–7, box 4, GCR; C.G. Schultz, 'Notes on Son's Thesis', folder 3, box 3, GCR; 'Jitney into Giant', *Fortune*, **10**(2) (1934), pp. 42–3, 110; *Hibbing Daily Tribune*, 25 June 1946; H.V. Anderson (1954), 'A History of the Beginnings of the Bus Industry with Grass-Roots in St Louis Country', unpublished manuscript, pp. 5–13.

7. General discussions of the state regulation of motor carriers can be found in S. Szto (1934), *Federal and State Regulation of Motor Carrier Rates and Services*, Philadelphia, pp. 9–189; Crandall, *The Growth of the Intercity Bus Industry*, pp. 38–97; J.J. George (1929), *Motor Carrier Regulation in the United States*, Spartanburg, SC, pp. 1–213; E.R. Johnson (1938), *Government Regulation of Transportation*, New York, pp. 510–27. More detailed information is available either in trade journals like *Bus Transportation* (hereafter cited as *BT*), **1–4** (1922–1925), and *Railway Age* (hereafter cited as *RA*), **70–79** (1921–1925), or in state publications and local newspaper reports of state commission hearings, as, for example, Minnesota Railroad and Warehouse Commission, Auto Transportation Company Division, *Biennial Reports* (1926), (1928), (1930) and *Minneapolis Journal* (1925).

8. Meier and Hoschek, *Over the Road*, pp. 17–20, 22–5, 43–6; Gohres, 'History of Pacific Greyhound Lines', pp. 4–5, 7, 12–13, 25–7; Eli Bail (1984), *From Railway to Freeway; Pacific Electric and the Motor Coach*, Glendale, CA, pp. 51–2, 55; Anderson, 'Beginnings of the Bus Industry', pp. 12–15; 'The Fageol Safety Coach Story', *Bus Review*, **1**(3) (1968), p. 4; *Minneapolis Journal*, 3 February 1924, 1 February 1925, 6 February 1927, 25 September 1928. *BT*, **1–3** (1922–1924), contains sections advertising buses manufactured by different companies.

9. For general information on business practices see Bus Transportation (1932), *Making Bus Operations Pay*, New York. For more specific insights see the trade journals, *BT*, **1–8** (1922–1929); *The Truck and Bus Owner* (hereafter cited as *T&BO*), **1–2** (1922–1924); and *Travel by Bus* (hereafter cited as *TbB*), **1–3** (1924–1926).

10. Extensive information on railroad involvement with buses can be found in *RA*, **76–87** (1924–1929). Statistics on railway-operated buses are available in National Association of Motor Bus Operators (NAMBO), *Bus Facts for 1927–1930* (hereafter cited as *BF*), Washington, DC. By 1929 electric railroads operated over 10,000 buses, *BF* (1930). For an analysis of railroad involvement with buses in California and in the upper Midwest see G.L. Thompson (1993),

The Passenger Train in the Motor Age. California's Rail and Bus Industries 1910–1941, Columbus, OH, especially pp. 63–90 and M. Walsh, 'Coordination, Cooperation or Competition: the Great Northern Railway and Bus Competition in the 1920s' in R. Cameron and L.F. Schnore (eds) (1997), *Cities and Markets. Studies in the Organization of Human Space*, Lanham, MD, pp. 163–89.

11. Gohres, 'History of Pacific Greyhound Lines', pp. 8–17, 20–23; Bail, *From Railway To Freeway*, p. 59; M. Walsh, 'Tracing the Hound: The Minnesotan Roots of the Greyhound Bus Corporation' (chapter 4); *Highway Traveler*, **1**(2) (1929), pp. 10–11, 28–9; **2**(1) (1930), pp. 16–17, 29 (hereafter cited as *HT*). *RA*, **82**(4) (1927), pp. 329–31; **85**(25) (1928), pp. 1261–5.

12. 'The Greyhound Corporation', pp. 1–10, Greyhound history folder 1, box 3, GCR; F.H. Schultz, 'Greyhound, The Greatest Name on the Highway', pp. 11–15; Walsh, 'Tracing the Hound', chapter 4, pp. 82–4; 'Jitney into Giant', p. 42.

13. For a general discussion of the problems faced by the larger bus operators in the early 1930s, see *BT*, **9–13** (1930–1934).

14. F.H. Schultz, 'Greyhound, The Greatest Name on the Highway', pp. 17–22; 'Jitney into Giant', pp. 34–43, 110, 113–14, 117; Greyhound Corporation, *Annual Reports* (1929–1932), (hereafter cited as GC, *AR*); 'A Brief History of the Greyhound Lines', *Mass Transportation*, **September** (1956), p. 56; O. Schisgall (1985), *The Greyhound Story. From Hibbing To Everywhere*, Chicago, pp. 29–33. The loans from the General Motor Corporation have been the subject of considerable controversy and discussion, much of which has been focused on whether General Motors supported the bus industry in order to undermine electric rail mass transit in North America. See US Congress, Senate, 93 Cong. 2 Sess. (1974), Hearings, *The Industrial Reorganization Act*, pt 4A, 'American Ground Transport' and 'The Truth About "American Ground Transport" – A Reply by General Motors'; T.P. O'Hanlon (1984), 'General Motors, Nazis and the Demise of Urban Ground Transit', *Government Publications Review*, **11**, pp. 211–32; V. Wilkins (1995), 'The Conspiracy Revisited', *The New Electric Railway Journal*, **7**(4), Summer, pp. 19–22; B. Snell (1995), 'The Conspiracy Explained', *The New Electric Railway Journal*, **8**(1), Autumn, pp. 26–9.

15. Both Western Greyhound and Southland Greyhound had too many routes and low passenger traffic and both faced competition from the railroads who were cutting rates. F.H. Schultz, 'Greyhound, The Greatest Name on the Highway', p. 22.

16. GC, *AR*, (1934 and 1935); *HT*, **4**(4) (1932), p. 41; **6**(2) (1934), p. 34. C. Jackson (1984), *Hounds of the Road. A History of the Greyhound Bus Company*, Bowling Green, OH, pp. 45–8; Schisgall, *The Greyhound Story*, pp. 39, 41.

17. The structure of the bus industry in the early 1930s consisted of a majority of operators who owned a handful of buses and a very small number of larger firms, of whom Greyhound was the leading concern. Many operators would not have faced major problems of corporate financing, but they would have needed loans from local banks or other sources.

18. M. Walsh, 'The Motor Carrier Act of 1935', (chapter 7), pp. 138–44.

19. United States National Recovery Administration (1934), *Codes of Fair Competition*, nos 58–110, **II**, 'Code of Fair Competition for the Motor Bus Industry', Washington, DC, pp. 110–17; *BT*, (1933–1935), **12–14**, contains discussions of the bus industry's attitude to the code; Crandall, *The Growth of the Intercity Bus Industry*, pp. 123–6; Szto, *Federal and State Regulation*, pp. 267–77.

20. US Congress, 74 Cong. (1935–1936), *Statutes at Large*, 49, (being Public Laws of the USA), 'Motor Carrier Act, 1935', pp. 543–69; W.H. Wagner (1935), *A*

Legislative History of the Motor Carrier Act, 1935, Denton, MD; J.C. Nelson (1936), 'The Motor Carrier Act of 1935', *Journal of Political Economy*, **44**, pp. 471–97; I.L. Sharfman (1937), *The Interstate Commerce Commission: a Study in Administrative Law and Procedure*, part 4, New York, pp. 102–22; P. McCollester and F.J. Clark (1935), *Federal Motor Carrier Regulation*, New York, pp. 88ff; W.J. Hudson and J.A. Constantin (1958), *Motor Transportation. Principles and Practices*, New York, pp. 476–82.

21. The Motor Carrier Act was to be administered by the ICC. The Federal Coordinator of Transportation had recommended, in his third report, *Report of the Federal Coordinator of Transportation, 1934*, US Congress House, 74 Cong. I Session, 1935, Document 89, that the ICC should be reorganized to deal with regulation of motor and water carriers, but Congress failed to act on this suggestion. Nevertheless, it was clearly understood that special divisions for handling each kind of transportation were essential if regulation was to be effective. See Wagner, *A Legislative History*, pp. 13–14 quoting Senator Wheeler, 79 Cong. Rec. 5650, 5656, 5657. On 1 October 1935 the ICC did reorganize, reducing the number of its divisions from seven to five and establishing Division 5 as the Bureau of Motor Carriers.

22. F.H. Schultz, 'Greyhound, The Greatest Name on the Highway', pp. 31–5; *RA*, **100**(17) (1936), pp. 692–6; **100**(21) (1936), pp. 837–8, 844–5. *Mass Transportation*, **September**, (1956) p. 57. Crandall, *The Growth of the Intercity Bus Industry*, pp. 166–220, provides the best summary of those early motor carrier cases which affected buses. ICC, *Annual Reports*, from 1937, lists the most important decisions made by the Bureau of Motor Carriers, but frequently these decisions are concerned with trucks.

23. For details of improvements made by Greyhound see *HT*, **7–12** (1935–1940). For a summary of some of these improvements see, 'Greyhound Still Growing', *Fortune*, **30**(3) (1944), pp. 121–5, 236–9, 242. For a discussion of terminals in the 1930s see M. Walsh, 'Passenger Connections: Views of the Intercity Bus Terminal in the United States' in W. Bond and C. Divall (eds) (forthcoming), *Suburbanising the Masses: Public Transport and Urban Development in Historical Perspective*, Aldershot.

3   Missing Connections:
The Long-Distance Bus Industry in
the USA from the Second World War
to Deregulation

In the first quarter-century of its existence the long-distance bus industry in the USA developed from a struggling, disconnected set of lines, a pioneering experiment, into a reasonably well-organized network of routes which had become an integral part of the nation's transportation system. In the emergency years of the Second World War it increased its share of intercity passenger travel and could anticipate buoyant business prospects in peacetime. But many problems needed to be resolved if the industry was to retain its Depression, let alone its wartime, share of the transport market.

In the thirty years following the war, bus operators ran a useful service which annually carried millions of Americans. They did not, however, make significant headway in intermodal competition. Private carriers, primarily the automobile, retained over 80 per cent of passenger miles for most of the post-war years (see table 2.1 on page 27). The public carriers faded proportionately during the 1950s and early 1960s and only increased their share subsequently because of the growing popularity of air travel. Buses certainly fared better than their traditional rivals, the railroads, in their efforts to find a niche in the late twentieth-century transport pattern, but their role prior to deregulation in 1982, though valuable, was limited.

Was the bus industry fated to be a minor part of the nation's transport network in the second half of the twentieth century? Why did the potential, which was visible in the 1920s and 1930s, not develop? Did management fail to resolve the internal operating problems of the industry, and if so, does much of the blame then lie with the major corporations, Greyhound and Trailways, which dominated the industry in these years? Or were the general conditions of running bus lines so constrained by externalities that bus operators could never make more than a limited impact? Were their managerial efforts negated by government regulations and the existence of alternative modes of transport which were more attractive to individualistic and highly mobile Americans?

The evidence suggests both internal weaknesses and external problems beyond the control of bus-industry management.

The legacy of the Second World War

Any examination of the modern bus industry must start with the impact of the Second World War. During these years the public carriers played an important part in keeping the nation moving. By 1944 they were responsible for 41.4 per cent of passenger miles in contrast to 11.0 per cent in 1939. Within the public sector buses served the nation well, contributing 8.8 per cent of total passenger miles in 1944 (see table 2.1 on p. 27). The numbers of passengers carried showed a more remarkable contribution because bus journeys, which averaged 32 miles in 1942, tended to be shorter than train and air journeys. In 1942, intercity carriers hauled 134.2 per cent more passengers than in 1941. In the four-year wartime period 1942–1945, buses carried 3,745,980,000 passengers, while in the last full year of the war, 1944, it was estimated that buses had quadrupled the business handled in 1939. As early as 1942 Greyhound, the largest bus operator, reported a load factor, or ratio of seats to occupancy, of 69 per cent in contrast to the 56 per cent of the previous year, while the much smaller Midwestern company, Jefferson, reported a 75 per cent load factor in 1943. Buses were an essential part of the nation's wartime transport pattern.[1]

Yet this growth in activity was achieved under duress and despite numerous shortages in vehicles, spare parts, fuel and labour. Stopgap solutions to overcome these shortages would create a deferred maintenance and replacement predicament which would take the industry years to resolve, while travelling conditions on buses instilled a negative image which proved very difficult to dispel. How did this happen? The lack of new equipment and spare parts entailed the use of vehicles beyond their 'sell-by date'. The problem was manageable in 1942 because orders placed before the outbreak of war were filled and buses in service rose by 30 per cent. In 1943, however, practically no new intercity buses were produced. Greyhound managed to convert tractor-trailers into utilitarian 'victory buses', which with their seats for forty-five passengers and standing room for fifty people, served to move larger numbers of war workers. Some new 'adult school' buses were made available. The following year, 1944, the War Production Board approved the manufacture of only a limited number – 1,927 – of intercity buses, leaving the carriers hungry for new equipment. Even when virtually all of the bus production of 1945 went into civilian service, intercity operators continued to be badly stretched for viable vehicles.[2]

The industry thus 'made do' by curtailing non-essential services, by patching up older vehicles and by encouraging higher maintenance and driving standards. By July 1943 the industry had already complied with the Office of Defense Transportation's requirements for limiting express services, services with less than a load factor of 40 per cent, and services to amusement places. Efforts were also being made to pool competitive bus services covering the same or closely parallel routes and to stagger bus resources. Given the dire shortage of metal and rubber, new welding techniques were used on such essential parts as crankshafts, cylinder heads and axles while fabricated worn parts were given a new lease of life by a metallizing process, which, though expensive, kept vehicles on the road. By the end of 1943 over 4,000 of the industry's 21,480 buses had been in service for the more than the life expectancy of a normal vehicle of eight years. It was thus essential that closer inspection of vehicles at servicing ensured that wheel alignments and other vehicle adjustments affecting tyre life were properly maintained. Drivers were cautioned to be very careful in applying brakes and in reducing speed when rounding bends. Such measures to reduce wear and tear, however, assumed competent and well-trained mechanics and drivers. Increasingly, the industry faced shortages of such personnel as men moved to higher-paying war industries, joined the armed services or were drafted. Though women were employed in many capacities from 1942, skills were in short supply.[3]

Not only were older buses kept in service during the war, but they were driven more slowly. To conserve fuel and rubber the federal government imposed a 35 miles per hour speed limit in October 1942. Opposed by the industry because it had no evidence of savings from lower maximum speeds, the measure was also resented because it restricted already weakened fleets, increased man hours for drivers and lengthened schedules. Passengers, as well as operators, faced difficult conditions. They encountered packed, often uncomfortable older buses which were more liable to break down, and they undertook long journeys in these tiresome conditions. Furthermore, as bus travel increased, terminals became more crowded and it was impossible to make any improvements for the millions who faced tedious waits. Lack of materials prevented any construction or alterations to terminals and garages other than completing the projects started before Pearl Harbor. Denied the use of their cars, passengers could now only be exhorted to be patriotic citizens and be patient. The unfavourable impressions of inconvenience and discomfort, however, remained with many wartime travellers.[4]

At their first meeting in four years, in 1946, the executives of the National Association of Motor Bus Operators (NAMBO) congratulated their members on their significant wartime achievements. They also, however, warned operators of the need to resolve diverse and complex problems before settling down to normal conditions. New modern terminals, garages and offices were required to update facilities which were inadequate and even obsolete. Old buses needed to be replaced by larger, more comfortable and mechanically superior vehicles. More careful attention was required in scrutinizing operating costs and practices, which had been neglected during the hectic emergency years of the war. Managers would have to improve travelling conditions significantly if they were to maintain a high proportion of the traffic carried on scheduled routes during the war. Then, as travel restrictions were lifted, entrepreneurs needed to expand the leisure market by encouraging people to regard buses as a friendly, relaxing and convenient mode of recreational travel. Both regular and special services could grow, provided that costs, especially labour costs, were kept under control. The agenda was there, but could the bus industry respond? Many Americans had been obliged to use public transport by wartime shortages and they were anxious to gain or regain their mobility through car use. New vehicles and parts production, however, could not satisfy demand in the late 1940s. There were thus still captive as well as willing passengers on the buses and both needed to be persuaded about the merits of these vehicles if the industry was to flourish.[5]

Post-war financial adjustments

The immediate post-war framework within which bus managers worked was influenced by government regulations at both the federal and state levels, by rising costs, by strong intermodal competition and by delays in refurbishing the industry. Finance, in the shape of fares and adequate earnings, emerged as the top priority in the quest for economic viability and a sound competitive position. This issue was raised, not by the motor-bus operators, but officially by the Interstate Commerce Commission (ICC), which in July 1946 instituted a nationwide investigation of bus fares. Mandated to administer a national transport policy which served the public interest and in which the different modes of transport could coexist, the regulatory body responded to concerns which were expressed about the honest, efficient and economical management of the intercity bus industry, its profit margins during and after the war and the lack of uniform bus fares. The federal government agency thus decided to undertake the first comprehensive study of intercity buses fares and charges in order to establish a fair rate structure.[6]

The ensuing lengthy hearings, from July 1946 to December 1949, recognized that the wartime revenue of the bus industry had increased as bus traffic expanded. Price controls during the war had prevented similar rises in wages and in the cost of materials used by bus carriers. Net operating income thus notably increased. The government appropriated a considerable proportion of this money in income and excess profit taxes and the industry subsequently invested much of the remainder in expansion and renovation. As for fares and charges, in the post-war years the commissioners found that these were just and reasonable. Inflationary trends, revealed most notably in wage rises and in increased capital requirements, accounted for most of the higher rates. The lack of uniformity in rates within the country was not due to discrimination and inefficiency but stemmed from the response of local and regional carriers to variations in operating, traffic and service conditions. Differential rates should thus remain.[7]

But what were appropriate profit margins in this era of regulated transport policy? The standard operating ratio, taken as the ratio of operating expenses to operating revenues, was to become the accepted method of determining industry income, with an operating ratio of eighty-five, before federal income tax, officially deemed to yield a fair return.[8] The first monitoring of motor-coach rate levels by the federal regulatory agency gave intercity carriers what government officials considered to be a reasonable chance of success in a period of changing intermodal competition. Could the industry seize the initiative?

In the late 1940s and early 1950s buses faced three rival carriers for intercity travel: airlines, cars and trains. As yet, commercial aviation was in its infancy and did not pose a significant threat. Though increasing numbers of middle- and upper-income Americans were taking scheduled domestic flights for long-distance travel in the 1950s, popular use of air transport awaited the widespread adoption of jet planes in the 1960s. Cars, however, were becoming more plentiful. Registrations increased from 25.8 million in 1945 to 40.4 million in 1950, the year in which motor-vehicle output exceeded 8 million for the first time in automotive history. Despite the poor quality of national highways, rivalry from the private automobile was a threat to bus transport, particularly for short journeys. Some longer car journeys were also looking competitive. Though high post-war construction costs caused delays in developing national networks, the federal government had already authorized a limited expenditure on roads in the Interstate and Defense Highway Act of 1944. Meanwhile, state governments looked to self-financing toll roads to provide a better local network for motorists.[9]

Bus operators acknowledged that many car owners at mid-century would increasingly drive themselves rather than go by bus. Yet they still remained more concerned about the competitiveness of their traditional public-sector, intermodal rival, the railroad. Clearly the train, though inflexible in terms of its route, offered the advantages of higher speeds and a more luxurious service in the shape of dining cars, lounge cars and freedom of movement while in motion. Worried about this challenge, bus carriers, especially in the Northeast, urged that bus fares, as in the 1920s and 1930s, should generally remain lower than corresponding rail fares. But if the trains continued to impose an effective ceiling on bus fares in the late 1940s, buses, like the railroads of the earlier years, would run into debt. Increasing operating expenses threatened the ability of bus companies to run a profitable service while offering their customers the advantages of cheap fares.[10] Why were bus companies so concerned about rising costs?

State government regulations provided part of the answer. As these regulations were not uniform on economic and safety aspects of interstate bus operation they impeded the financial development of the bus industry. Following the expansion of long-distance and thus interstate travel, bus companies increasingly found that they had to pay a larger number of state registration and motor-fuel taxes as well as federal excise taxes. They and their trade association, NAMBO, were concerned to secure reciprocal agreements about such items as licences, taxes and regulatory laws. With respect to licences, for example, they lobbied for arrangements for the payment of a composite licence whose cost was apportioned according to the use of vehicles in each state. Bus managers did not want to register vehicles in each state through which individual buses travelled. In the mid 1940s only twenty-three states granted reciprocity for common carrier buses which operated exclusively on an interstate basis and only fifteen states for those which operated on both interstate and intrastate routes. Differential gasoline and tonnage (ton mile) taxes also caused bus companies extra expense and considerable work.[11]

In addition to financial regulations, individual state governments also imposed size and weight limitations on vehicles and these influenced the selection and improvement of buses. Now freed from wartime restrictions, bus entrepreneurs were very concerned to streamline their service and provide faster speeds. An increase in vehicle size, power and weight was essential. Bus design advances, such as moving the engine to the back of the coach, had already increased passenger and luggage capacity by as much as 30 per cent. However, other alterations such as the use of new metals for bus construction, wider seats and aisles, more leg room, better lighting, and the addition of toilets and air conditioning depended substantially on the changes which could be made in state size and weight limitations. In 1948 only two states allowed a maximum width of 102 inches and only thirteen allowed a maximum length of 40 feet or over, dimensions which were considered basic for the new post-war bus. NAMBO tried to persuade the mediating agency, the American Association of State Highway Officials (AASHO), to press for liberalized laws relative to bus operation. AASHO, however, was cautious in its response, partly because any new regulations would apply to trucks as well as buses. If the maximum dimensions and load weighting of trucks were increased, road construction and maintenance would require significantly more investment. Bus operators thus faced indecision and delays in developing modern passenger fleets. They thus lost savings in cost per seat mile and had to be more adaptable about their use of buses at a time when competition was high.[12]

Uncertainties in state regulation notwithstanding, bus entrepreneurs did invest in new vehicles. Buses were ordered as soon as wartime restrictions were lifted and significant numbers were delivered in the late 1940s, practically all being of the integral body and chassis type and many with diesel engines. But delays due to shortages of materials and strikes in production plants meant that veteran coaches were still in use. Hundreds of older models were rebuilt and restyled to meet passenger demand, which remained relatively high in the late 1940s and early 1950s. The costs involved in buying new vehicles at the same time as maintaining and remodelling older vehicles which would normally have been retired, were significant. Depreciation charges were also of major concern. Greyhound, for example, faced peak charges on both its new and restyled vehicles in 1949 and so further acquisition of more modern cruiser-type buses was deferred until 1952, when the company estimated that annual depreciation charges would level off and normal replacement of equipment could be resumed.[13]

A programme of new and improved terminals, garages, depots, agencies, offices and restaurants also involved high capital investment. Clearly, facilities which had been constructed, converted or leased in the early years of the bus industry or during the Depression required refurbishment or replacement, while larger, purpose-built terminals were needed to retain and attract passengers. Customers expected improved loading and baggage-handling arrangements, more comfortable waiting-rooms, satisfactory restrooms and eating facilities where good, reasonably-priced food was available. The industry needed to demonstrate to the travelling public that it was progressive, consumer-oriented and capable of modernizing.[14]

The industry was willing and capable, but finance was not readily available. Funds accumulated during the war had been earmarked for investment in a variety of buildings, but these funds proved to be inadequate as inflation sharply increased the costs of construction and materials. For example, Greyhound, the leading company, planned to spend $20 million on terminals and garages in 1946, but postponed much of its construction programme. In 1947 and 1948 the corporation's plans progressed slowly because of continuing difficulties with building costs, and only the most necessary facilities received attention. Not until operating expenses started to level off in 1949 and 1950 did the company place more emphasis on refurbishing buildings. Smaller companies, like Jefferson Transportation of Minneapolis, also found their plans to streamline their plant were delayed and downsized.[15] Why were accumulated wartime revenue and current revenue, the main source of bus-industry finance, not readily available for fixed-capital investment?

Bus operators suggested that part of the answer lay in high taxes, part in relatively low fares and part in labour costs. During the war the industry had been subject to both normal income tax and excess profits tax. In the ten-year period 1938–1947, Class I carriers paid some 60 per cent of their net income in taxes, a percentage which fell to 40 in 1948. Yet even after the reduction of tax rates in the late 1940s, motor operators claimed that these generally were higher than before the war and thus they had less money to invest in plant and equipment. Not only were taxes high, but fares had not risen sufficiently to match the increased expenses involved in providing an improved service. Indeed, they had been reduced. The ICC 'Investigation of Bus Fares' reported that the 1939 fares averaged 64 per cent of those of 1934 and even the impact of wartime and post-war expenses had only raised bus charges by five percentage points to 69 per cent in 1947. An increase in fares would help, but would not resolve the financial problems of the bus industry.[16]

Managers and trade association officials considered that increased labour costs were in large part responsible for their post-war difficulties. Wages and salaries had risen from 35.2 per cent of total expenses in 1939 to 42.7 per cent in 1949. Operators thus felt that there had been a disproportionate rise in bus company payrolls. Unions, however, claimed that increases in the cost of living merited wage rises. As in other industries, they used the strike weapon and collective bargaining to press for pay increases, improved working conditions and fringe benefits such as overtime premiums after fewer hours, meal concessions, increased holiday entitlements, uniform allowance and sick pay. An estimated 16.5 per cent of bus workers in 1945 and 11.7 per cent in 1946 were involved in strike action. Managers were uneasy about post-war labour relations and looked forward to a more stable period of industrial relations following the passage of the Taft-Hartley Act in 1947 and the negotiation of longer work contracts. Certainly, subsequent strike action in the 1940s was more localized, but management also became more attuned to collective bargaining and looked to ways of improving labour productivity to reduce expenses.[17]

They also sought improvements in public relations as well as in industrial relations. Before the Second World War advertising had played an important part in selling bus services. During the war, however, the industry cooperated with the government and advertised the vital role of bus transport. Patriotism was more important than profit. But with intra- and intermodal competition now developing, and the legacy of poor wartime travel conditions still remaining, it was important to create a positive bus image quickly. In 1946 NAMBO and the National Bus Traffic Association (NBTA) set up promotional programmes to persuade Americans to use buses for recreational purposes. Recognizing that demand for leisure activities was high and that money was available, managers predicted an expansion of vacation business and the growth of charter business. If these services were friendly, efficient, comfortable and convenient, more passengers would want to ride the buses more often. Operators thus restored travel bureaux, trained travel agents and publicized escorted tours. The two major companies, Greyhound and Trailways, set the pace in this burgeoning market by increasing their advertising campaigns and by emphasizing the need for courtesy and consideration by their personnel. While there was a flurry of business in 1946 and 1947 because of postponed spending and car shortages, the lag in investment on plant and equipment did not enhance the bus reputation in either vacation or regular travel.[18]

Misplaced optimism: moving into the 1950s

Though bus operating expenses continued to rise in the early 1950s, major contributory factors such as wages, maintenance costs, depreciation and fuel costs showed signs of levelling off. Modest increases in both intrastate and interstate fares provided some funds for investment. An expansion in chartered military traffic also helped boost the bus industry temporarily. Deeming that the industry was now on a stable post-war basis, bus managers made more progress in refurbishing their buildings and equipment and paid considerable attention to improving public relations. Nevertheless, the industry's share of intercity

Table 3.1   Intercity travel in the USA by public carrier 1939–1989 (passengers carried in millions)

Year	Total	Bus		Rail[2]		Air	
		Passengers	% total	Passengers	% total	Passengers	% total
1939	585.5	132.6	22.7	451.0	77.0	1.9	0.3
1944	1393.2	475.6	34.1	913.2	65.6	4.3	0.3
1949	955.7	348.9	40.3	554.5	58.0	16.3	1.7
1954	730.3	256.6	35.1	438.6	60.0	35.1	4.8
1959	598.8	191.2	31.9	352.3	58.8	55.3	9.2
1960[1]	748.5	366.0	48.9	325.7	43.5	56.8	7.6
1964	752.8	360.0	47.8	313.0	41.6	79.8	10.6
1969	851.8	396.0	46.5	295.9	34.7	159.9	18.8
1974	851.9	386.0	45.3	274.2	32.2	191.7	22.5
1979	958.2	368.0	38.4	295.0	30.8	295.2	30.8
1984	964.1	352.0	36.5	286.9	29.8	325.2	33.7
1989	1109.7	337.0	30.3	351.4	31.7	421.3	38.0

Source: F.A. Smith (1986), *Transportation in America. Historical Compendium, 1939–1985*, Westport, CN, pp. 14–15 and R.A. Wilson (1997), *Transportation in America, Historical Compendium, 1939–1995*, Lansdown, VA, p. 22.
Notes:
[1] New series after 1959 that covers all classes of intercity bus carriers.
[2] Rail figures include commuting passengers.

travel, as measured by passenger miles, gradually declined both in absolute and relative terms (see table 2.1 on page 27) and the number of passengers carried also fell (see table 3.1). In the 1950s buses were only a minor part of the transport sector. Though they fared better than the railroads, they failed to persuade Americans to turn away from their cars.[19]

Despite the delays in obtaining nationwide agreements about the size and weight of intercity buses, operators, especially the major companies, Greyhound and Trailways, experimented with new types of motor coaches and improved existing models. Larger buses with diesel power, air suspension and air conditioning offered more comfortable and enjoyable rides and, given the better condition of roads, also a faster journey. By 1951 two-thirds of Greyhound's bus fleet had diesel engines. In 1953 the second-largest bus company, Continental Trailways, was ordering vehicles with air suspension and large picture windows. Two years later, in 1955, their new Vista Liners rivalled Greyhound's Scenicruiser – a bus advertised as having not only air suspension, but extra room for passengers, spacious seats, washroom facilities, and an observation deck for greater enjoyment of the scenery. Motor coaches had to offer amenities comparable to those of trains and these buses needed to be in top running condition. New and centrally-located garages ensured the quicker and smoother journeys increasingly required from passengers with higher post-war standards.[20]

The programme of terminal and depot construction and remodelling offered improved facilities in both major cities and small towns. New terminals ranged in size from the large union Port Authority Bus Terminal in Manhattan in midtown New York and the five-storey Greyhound terminal in downtown Chicago to more modest stations in smaller cities like Stevens Point and Green Bay in Wisconsin, Coos Bay in Oregon, and Corsicana, Texas. Such bus stations with their well-planned facilities were designed to be inviting places where people could come for information and tickets, to wait for buses, to meet friends and to enjoy beverages or food. Companies further urged employees to maintain clean and courteous services, especially in the restrooms and cafeterias. Washrooms were recognized as a source of lost business because of their inadequacy and lack of hygiene. Restaurants like the high-class Continental Restaurants, and station cafeterias were made sufficiently welcome to attract local residents as well as passengers. On the road, rest stops were significantly improved. Greyhound, for example, expanded its subsidiary Greyhound Post Houses to 154 by 1954, to ensure that good food was available at modest prices. Other carriers preferred, whenever possible, to use chain operations. By the mid-1950s bus operators were providing good amenities and ones which could rival those available to private automobile drivers and possibly to airline passengers.[21]

These bus operators also publicized their facilities to convince consumers that travelling by bus had become a much better experience than in the war and immediate post-war years. They both promoted the advantages of bus accessibility and flexibility to reach all points in the nation, and they built a reputation for courtesy and for reliable, safe and restful journeys. Basic knowledge about the location of bus terminals and the availability of bus timetables was communicated in local newspapers. Once at the bus station, would-be passengers found scheduling and cost information at travel bureaux and tour offices as well as at the ticket counter and in convenient racks. Telephone advice was also available. New improved standards on scheduled routes and recreational opportunities, however, had to be communicated not only at terminals by company employees, but nationally in popular magazines, on the radio, in films and even on the new visual media, television. A faster, through service with limited stops, and a luxury service with hostesses and snacks, both at a slightly higher price, tempted businessmen travelling between large cities, while regular coach service continued to offer economical and dependable service. Americans were also encouraged to be more adventurous and 'take the bus' on holiday, either on a variety of escorted tours or through chartering vehicles for day trips. Bus advertising was now capitalizing on a nation having more paid vacation time and bus operators were searching for other markets such as the carriage of small freight and the US mail.[22]

Despite these considerable efforts to modernize equipment and buildings and to advance business through improved public relations and widespread advertising, by the mid 1950s managers realized that their business was declining. Intercity transport remained highly competitive. Even though significant improvements in highway construction would not take place until the 1960s, the private automobile was winning the contest for short-distance travel under 400 miles. Americans liked personalized transport. Registration of cars increased by 64.7 per cent between 1946 and 1953 and in 1960 there were 61.7 million cars in the USA, or one for every 2.9 persons. Despite many and varied plans, bus companies were finding it very difficult to persuade car owners to turn to buses although the cost of using their car was higher than travelling by bus. Moreover, these owners enjoyed greater convenience from driving themselves, whether for business or pleasure. Americans were becoming wedded to their cars in a growing automobile culture.[23]

Bus carriers thus knew that they must improve both long-distance regular route trade and special operations. In this they were certainly ahead of the railroads whose passenger trains were not only losing money, but were being discontinued. Between 1951 and 1956 state commissions approved 981 applications to terminate services involving 33.3 million train miles. But as one public sector competitor faded another loomed large. Commercial airlines offered speed and prestige and were successfully selling an attractive and more frequent service to business executives and those passengers who were abandoning the Pullman and sleeper trains. On some routes they also offered a low-price air-coach service to help promote their mode of travel, which could be costly and was often inconvenient in terms of schedules, access and inadequate terminals. Recognizing the growing appeal of air travel, bus entrepreneurs attempted to make links with airlines through connecting air-bus services, but they failed to make significant headway.[24] The bus industry needed to be more aggressive and inventive about promoting itself in a period of growing competition.

To achieve a higher profile and a better performance, some executives improved their internal management. Arthur S. Genet, who became president of the Greyhound Corporation in 1956, considered that bus managers lacked the discipline and initiative essential to introduce new ideas and new ways of operating. There was too much lethargy among the older bus pioneers and their appointees, and there were too many operating divisions within the company. Under Genet, Greyhound downsized its corporate groupings from thirteen to seven, thereby aiming to raise efficiency in the use of equipment, procedures and personnel. Training programmes were introduced for all staff. Executives were not only required to attend business school to learn the theory of modern management techniques but they also had to acquire practical on-the-job experience before specializing in their fields. Appointments would no longer be made for personal reasons of friendship and family. On the shop floor mechanics were given more and better training which often included courses in colleges as well a two- to four-year apprenticeship. To deliver first class maintenance it was necessary to be competent in the most recent engineering technology. The Greyhound Corporation took on a more professional look.[25]

This new personnel 'shake-up' was extended to public relations. A different agency, Grey Advertising, with headquarters in New York, was brought in to take a fresh approach to advertising. This focused on radio and television as well as the printed media, and targeted customers by niche marketing and by developing a favourable public image. Two distinct types of scheduled travel were promoted – the ordinary, perhaps 'second-class', used by lower-income passengers, and a luxury 'first class' which cost and offered more. In terms of special services, the vacation and sightseeing businesses were advanced more aggressively at both the local and national levels. Travellers were reminded of the benefits of well-planned, escorted tours and the flexibility of charters. Other fields of transport-related business, such as freight, carrying mail, van lines and rent-a-car were also marketed in a more assertive manner. Greyhound's first broad public-relations programme recognized the growing affluence and consumer-consciousness of Americans as well as the already proven advantages of economy. Rather than using a silhouette of a greyhound as its trademark, the corporation decided to use a real greyhound as a living symbol. By the early 1960s 'Lady Greyhound' was appearing nationally at bus terminal openings, travel and civic events, fashion shows and public service functions for the benefit of the sick, the needy and children. Considerable positive publicity followed not only for Greyhound, but for the industry at large.[26]

Searching for a place in the transport sector

But neither the streamlining of the leading company nor the steady improvements in plant, equipment and services undertaken by Greyhound and other operators improved the relative standing of the industry as an intercity carrier. Despite an increase in passengers from 366 million to 396 million and an increase in total bus miles of 5.6 billion in the 1960s, the industry's share of the nation's intercity total fell from 2.5 per cent to 2.2 per cent. Car travel remained the dominant mode of transport, especially for journeys under 500 miles. The popularity of the automobile continued unabated, with 89.3 million registered in 1970, representing one vehicle per 2.3 persons. The rise in families with multiple car ownership from 15 per cent in 1960 to 35 per cent a decade later merely consolidated the greater use of cars in preference to public transport. And the modernization of the road system facilitated easier and faster individual journeys for both work and pleasure. By 1969, 65 per cent of the 41,000 miles (eventually expanded to 42,500 miles) of federally supported Interstate Highway network was open, encouraging longer-distance driving. Major improvements in state-financed highways and primary roads fostered more intensive local and regional mobility. The age of mass automobility had arrived.[27]

Within the public sector the train continued to decline as a mode of intercity passenger travel and as a competitor in the 1960s. The Transportation Act of 1958 shifted control over route termination from individual states to the ICC. That federal body reduced annual passenger train mileage from 275 million in 1957 to just over 180 million in 1964. By 1965, there was no passenger service on over half of the nation's rail network, and on routes where trains still ran their frequency had declined, even in the densely populated Northeastern urban corridor. Train travel was falling into disuse. Buses did not, however, have a clear pathway to long-distance travel because planes were becoming more popular. The rapid expansion in commercial air travel from 30.5 billion passenger miles in 1959 to 111.1 billion passenger miles in 1969 (see table 2.1 on page 27) clearly demonstrated the growing preference of more Americans for speed over cost. The long-term decline in real air fares had encouraged middle-ranking people to consider using airlines. Companies had responded to consumer demand by improving speed, safety and comfort with jet planes, and by expanding capacity with larger aircraft and regional and commuter flights. The changing technology which allowed cheaper and more flexible air transport, such that it became an accepted part of American mobility, pushed bus companies towards a smaller share of an expanding travel market in the 1960s.[28]

Different interpretations, however, were placed on these intermodal figures. Reacting positively, bus operators proudly reported their ability to keep and even increase their passengers. Unlike the trains, buses remained attractive. Their appeal, however, was becoming limited to specific groups of people. On the scheduled routes where faster, more comfortable and economical service was available because of improved roads and modern vehicles, customers now tended to be those who, for financial or age reasons, did not drive a car. Indeed, Greyhound's famous 1960s slogan 'Go Greyhound and Leave the Driving to Us' seemed to emphasize the lack of a car. Their equally famous marketing ploy of the $99 fare for up to ninety-nine days, initially for overseas travellers and for Americans in the off-seasons, was extended and copied by other companies, thereby encouraging lower-income groups to travel long distances. College students, senior citizens and minorities rode the buses as did rural Americans for whom the motor coach was often the only means of 'for-hire' transport. These Americans, however, took the bus by default rather than by choice. They were a captive niche market and would remain so. Bus operators failed to make scheduled service attractive to the higher-income passengers or to a significant proportion of the 34.9 million passengers who left the trains in the 1960s. Despite notable improvements in terminals and buses, and despite providing through services between major cities and luxury services with amenities such as radios, pillows and hostesses, middle-income Americans preferred either to drive their cars or to fly. In their own cars or in an airport terminal or on a plane they were less likely to encounter people whom they perceived to be 'undesirable'.[29]

Yet these 'better-off' groups could be persuaded to travel by bus for specific purposes. The holiday package and charter trips offered a type of self-selection, and middle-income Americans could be reasonably confident of travelling with 'their sort of people'. Special passenger services were becoming the source of higher proportions of bus company revenue in the 1960s. Continental Trailways, for example, reported that their income from escorted tours more than quadrupled between 1961 and 1965 and they looked to the European as well as the American market with their 'Visit USA Program'. Special events also became a focus for increased bus business. The New York World's Fair in 1964 and 1965 aroused noteworthy interest. Greyhound was the official carrier, and the company obtained considerable patronage from operating the ground transport at the fair. Both Greyhound and other bus companies found that other similar events like the Seattle World's Fair of 1962, the Montreal Exposition of 1967 and the Hemispheric Fair in San Antonio in 1968 yielded tourist dollars. Special group services provided yet more income. The military, athletic teams, bands, clubs and school parties, to mention a few, hired vehicles for days, weekends, holidays or other occasions. For such groups, chartering a bus was often the easiest, most effective and cheapest way to organize events and trips. This growing importance of charters was reflected in their changing share of bus operating revenue. In the 1960s charter and special service income rose from 7.8 per cent to 11.1 per cent of total operating revenue, and by 1970 intercity buses carried some 19 million charter passengers who comprised 10.9 per cent of their total traffic.[30]

Bus managers also developed other sources of revenue in the 1960s. Freight carriage, in particular, proved to be profitable. Buses had always carried small packages as part of their service, but in the 1960s more systematic efforts were made to develop an express package service. The decline in rail services meant that many small towns did not have an effective regular delivery for small shipments of freight, for mail and for newspapers. Though other small-shipment carriers were very competitive, the bus industry worked hard to capture a share of this market. Highway improvements enabled not only regular, but also fast deliveries to the 5,000 cities and towns having Greyhound terminal facilities capable of handling packages. Furthermore, Greyhound buses could pick up or drop off parcels at any point along the company's 100,000 miles of route in North America. It was thus not surprising that buses were increasingly used for conveying a variety of small freight, ranging from car repair and replacement parts, through electrical parts, film and photographic equipment, to sporting goods, clothing and drugs. By 1968 Greyhound Package Express contributed $52.2 million or 12.4 per cent of the company's total revenue. Greyhound was not exceptional. Package express was a flourishing part of other companies' business strategy. By 1970 Class I companies had more than doubled the proportion of their income obtained from this auxiliary service, to 14.2 per cent of the total. Together, charters, tours and package express accounted for a quarter of their operating revenue. The bus industry was successfully finding money-making complements to its regular route income. Companies were becoming multi-product firms.[31]

The dominant carriers, Greyhound and Trailways, who relied more heavily than other bus carriers on regular route revenue, looked to yet other ways of maintaining their position. They participated in the conglomerate movement, a notable feature of American business in the 1960s. Greyhound, with over 50 per cent of the intercity bus traffic in the late 1960s, had started to diversify early in the decade. Reorganization as a holding company in 1964 facilitated this process. While buses and auxiliary transport services, now including Greyhound Van Lines, a nationwide household-goods moving company, and Motor Coach Industries (MCI), the largest builder of intercity buses in North America, remained at the centre of the operation, the Greyhound Corporation Inc. broadened its base. It moved into financial, food, consumer, pharmaceutical, equipment leasing and general activities, with groups of related companies headed by corporate vice-presidents. In 1969 the largest and most important merger took place, with the diversified meat-packing and pharmaceutical corporation Armour-Dial. By then, Greyhound's slogan 'Greyhound's got more going for you than buses' was being beamed into millions of houses in a new television advertising campaign. Three years later the Greyhound conglomerate, with its new corporate headquarters 'Greyhound Tower' in Phoenix, Arizona, was ranked by Fortune Magazine as the twenty-ninth largest industrial concern in the USA. Trailways, the second leading intercity bus carrier, also diversified, acquiring real estate, accident insurance, restaurants, car parking and ocean cargo shipping operations. Changing its name to TCO Industries Inc. in 1967, bus operations were placed in a wholly-owned subsidiary called Continental Trailways while the corporation's other interests, mainly transport-related, were run by various subsidiaries. The two leading intercity carriers thus hoped that diversification would realize substantial benefits and would improve the business prospects for motor coach carriers in the 1970s.[32]

Smaller intercity bus companies could not follow the lead of Greyhound and Trailways. They tended to remain primarily in transportation services. Regional carriers operated scheduled routes, often on an interstate basis, with charter and special services providing important financial returns. Companies like the Jefferson Lines Inc., which became the eighth largest firm after its acquisition of Crown Coach Company in 1966, operated in Minnesota, Iowa, Missouri and Arkansas. Peter Pan Bus Lines Inc. also worked on this basis in Massachusetts, Connecticut and New York. Both found that charter work was necessary to economic well-being. Local operators, like Badger Coaches in Madison and Milwaukee, Wisconsin, or Wolf's Bus Line of York Spring, Pennsylvania, relied to a considerable extent on charter and special work, often within a 200-mile radius. When they ran regular scheduled lines, these plied intrastate routes.[33] There was considerable variety among regional and local bus companies nationwide, not only in terms of their size, but also in terms of their working arrangements and revenues. A uniform bus industry did not exist; individual carriers frequently responded to particular markets. Looking to the future, it seemed that flexibility provided some avenues for survival, if not success, in an intercity passenger market where buses had a limited role.[34]

Crises, challenges and opportunities in the 1970s

Flexibility, however, proved to be inadequate in the changing transport market of the 1970s. In a period of stagflation and energy crises, all modes of transport faced difficulties, but the economic losses of the railroads and the buses brought major inquiries and these in turn suggested changes in federal government policy.[35] Clearly, Americans would neither give up their cars nor modify the use of these vehicles, regardless of the prospect of more expensive and possibly diminishing energy supplies. Clearly, too, Americans wanted improved air travel in terms of both greater frequency of flights and more choice of destination points. These preferences resulted in declining business for public carriers in long-distance ground transport and this decline stimulated government action in the form of subsidizing railroad passenger services and deregulating both the airlines and the buses. Public investment would underwrite a limited train service; competition might improve air service and breathe more life into a struggling bus industry.

The crisis in ground transportation emerged first on the trains, where freight had been cross-subsidizing passengers for years and where the railroads had been withdrawing from unprofitable passenger services whenever possible.[36] Concerned to ensure a minimum route network and to avoid rail nationalization, Congress intervened in 1970 and established the National Rail Passenger Corporation, better known as Amtrak, to run passenger operations. It was hoped that this corporation would need only one injection of government finance before becoming self-supporting. But while Amtrak improved train service, especially in the heavily populated Northeast corridor where passenger miles rose 33.3 per cent between 1972 and 1976, it continued to lose money. Passenger revenues covered only a third of operating costs and the federal government continued to provide subsidies estimated at 16 cents per passenger mile or $38 per passenger trip. Plans were discussed to reduce Amtrak routes and subsidies, but the energy problems of the late 1970s led to reductions in the proposed cuts.[37]

The bus industry was outraged by the creation of Amtrak and complained about unfair competition throughout the decade. With subsidized train fares which were now also unregulated by the ICC, bus carriers faced serious difficulties. Amtrak priced rail fares at or below bus fares and in the Northeast corridor especially, bus operators reduced ticket prices to avoid losing customers. Companies requested permission from the ICC to adjust fares at short notice, thereby responding to price competition. Major carriers deemed that it was necessary to maintain income from the high-density areas to help cross-subsidize unprofitable lightly-travelled rural routes. They also continued to improve special 'high quality' services to attract business commuters, and offered maximum one-way fares and discounts for midweek travel and travel on selected routes to encourage long-distance journeys. The viability of a national network was at stake. But their efforts were in vain. In the early 1970s the net operating revenue of Class I carriers, companies who had an average gross revenue of $1 million annually, showed a sharp drop, falling by 50 per cent to $44.2 million between 1971 and 1976. Operating profit margins declined from 12.4 per cent to 4.5 per cent in the same years. Had Amtrak not existed it is estimated that the bus industry might have experienced a 15–30 per cent increase in revenue passenger miles.[38]

But unfair competition from the revitalized railroads was not the only reason why the bus industry fared poorly in the 1970s. Airlines continued to increase their share of intermodal travel by public carrier, rising from 9.8 per cent of passenger miles in 1969 to 13.4 per cent a decade later (see table 2.1 on page 27). In part this rise was attributed to federal government subsidies to airways, air terminals and local service airlines. More significantly, however, the improved technology of jet propulsion and the wide-bodied plane increased speed and contributed generally to a relative price decline between air and bus fares, with even lower fares in many high-density markets. Then as the real incomes of Americans rose air travel became more affordable and many decided to fly because 'time was money'. Following deregulation of air transport in 1978 and intramodal competition between air companies, air fares dropped again. Commercial airlines were gaining a higher market share of intercity passengers, often at the expense of the buses.[39]

Though planes and trains threatened the viability of the bus industry in the 1970s, the chief competitor for all modes of public transport still remained the private automobile. The emergence of the interstate highway system and improvements in regional and local roads encouraged Americans both to increase the distances they drove and to acquire second cars. Car ownership rose markedly from 89.3 million in 1970 to 121.7 million a decade later. By 1977, 84 per cent of households possessed cars. In that same year 37 per cent of households owned two or more vehicles. Americans were committed to automobility. Energy crises, which made gasoline both more expensive and scarce, had only a temporary effect on personal travel habits in the USA. Once consumers had sunk money into buying an automobile it proved very difficult to persuade them to use public transport. Even when they travelled long distances by plane they drove themselves or were driven to the airport and then picked up a rental car at their destination.[40]

Intermodal competition, however, could not fully explain the precarious economic condition of the bus industry. The 1970s generally have been labelled 'the troubled economy', not only in the USA, but in much of the Western world. Stagflation, or poor economic performance marked by both high inflation rates and high unemployment, replaced the 'golden age' of post-war expansion. The USA was hurt in particular by her deteriorating position in the international market and by mounting rates of inflation. The former weakened confidence in the dollar and increased the price of primary products. The latter, which rose to double figures in the mid-1970s, contributed to escalating expenses and the erosion of profits. In the bus industry carriers found, as in the immediate post-war years, that increases in production costs were not matched by receipts. The revenue lag grew progressively worse from 1972 and bus fares could not be increased proportionately because of intermodal competition. The prospects for the industry looked dire.[41]

Why did the bus industry find high inflation rates in the 1970s so crippling? Carriers and economists offered both traditional and new explanations. Firstly, wages and employee benefits continued to rise as a result of new wage contracts and cost-of-living adjustments built into earlier agreements. Labour costs totalled some 60 per cent of operating costs in contrast to 45 per cent in 1951. Fuel prices, stimulated by the Arab oil embargo of 1973–1974, virtually quadrupled and then doubled later in the decade, following the revolution in Iran. The bus industry faced significant absolute and relative increases in gasoline costs and these were difficult to pass on to passengers. A 75 per cent increase in the price of buses created further and more complex problems for operators. Normally, capital set aside for depreciation from internally-generated cash flows paid for new equipment. High inflation now ruined this business strategy and outside investment funds were needed. Raising these through public flotation was difficult because investors perceived that the bus industry was struggling. Managers could delay replacing older vehicles until conditions improved but they were reluctant to do this. Technologically new buses cost less to run and maintain than older vehicles, and promotionally the industry wanted to present an 'upbeat' image. To achieve this, terminals and garages also needed to be replaced or at least modernized.[42]

Carriers were not lacking in enterprise in these difficult years. Having concluded that cutting expenditure on plant and equipment might have an adverse effect on passenger flows they sought greater efficiency within the industry and a more positive image. They examined increased labour productivity and devised more aggressive marketing programmes to boost business. At the same time, they attempted to improve the general terms of trade under which they operated by persuading the government to alter transport policy. The major carriers, the trade association, the American Bus Association (ABA), and the federal government discussed the possibility of both an injection of public money to alleviate the specific problems created by sharp inflation and the restructuring of the industry through new regulatory legislation. Both the bus executives and the government were aware that buses served some 15,000 communities in the USA and that buses were very important in rural life. It was thus in the public interest to have a healthy, profitable and effective bus service in the late twentieth century.[43]

Wages, salaries and associated labour costs like employee welfare benefits, social security taxes paid by employers, workmen's compensation, holiday entitlements, sick pay and the cost of meals and lodgings when absent from home, constituted the majority of bus companies' operating expenses. Could savings be made by freezing or cutting back on wages, by reducing fringe benefits or by increasing productivity? Wages generally were subject to negotiation between employer and employee. As many bus employees in large companies belonged to unions they took care to negotiate contracts which included cost-of-living increases and benefits. Operators in these companies did not wish to antagonize their workers by pressing wage cuts for fear of disruption, strike action and loss of skilled labour. They turned rather to increasing productivity rates among bus workers. Productivity in the bus industry had remained fairly static since the 1950s. There was little room for improvement among bus drivers, other than in changing work schedules, particularly after the 55 miles per hour speed limit was imposed in 1974. Technological advances in terminal facilities, alterations to all work schedules to respond to market demand and intramodal and intermodal cooperation in terminal use offered some savings, but these were limited. Use of cheaper labour suggested greater economies, but only the smaller companies followed this route prior to deregulation.[44]

Perhaps more user-friendly and upbeat marketing drives would reap greater benefits. Public attention was directed to bus travel by colourful presentations on television glamorized by movie stars such as Fred MacMurry, television stars such as Claude Atkins or singers such as Pearl Bailey. The visual media was an excellent way of widely publicizing new and refurbished terminals and restaurants and highlighting new coaches like the Americruiser with its automatic transmission, sophisticated air conditioning, roomier seating arrangements, concealed overhead lighting and plush carpets. It also demonstrated Greyhound's patriotism as its buses were painted in bold red, white and blue. More generally, buses were championed as a safe means of travel and were deemed to be the most fuel-efficient American passenger service, two important features in a crisis-ridden decade. Poster and leaflet campaigns supported the television commercials while the ABA lobbied for bus involvement in tourism through its new magazine, *Destinations*, and its forum, 'The American Bus Marketplace'. The American public was regularly informed that buses provided a modern, flexible, safe, convenient and economical method of both scheduled and recreational travel.[45]

Advertising was an essential facet of business endeavour, but it had to be directed at separate audiences if it was to be successful. The largest companies – Greyhound and Trailways which generated some 62 per cent of the industry's revenue in 1976 – canvassed passengers who used regular route service, a service which they dominated. Other Class I operators also relied on scheduled traffic for part of their income. The major carriers, however, found that they increasingly relied on special services which included small freight, charters and tours. Smaller, Class II and III carriers were much more dependent on special services for their livelihood. As their vehicles were not tied into scheduled routes they could adapt their business to local needs.[46]

Efforts to boost passenger usage on scheduled routes continued to target two distinct markets. The large companies still solicited business-class and upper-income clients who wanted fast and luxury travel. They advertised a quality service which operated in the major urban corridors between central business districts. Greyhound, for example, ran the Bus Plus service which featured specially customized buses, on-board hostesses and refreshments. Jefferson Lines operated a deluxe service known as the 'Fat Cats Service' between Des Moines and Kansas City. In addition to having luxury features this service was able to beat the air travel time from downtown to downtown – and at half the price. Carriers, however, knew that over 90 per cent of patrons travelled for private or family reasons and typically were older or younger persons, had modest incomes, were more likely to be female and might well have rural or small-community connections. New promotions appealing to this market or people on the edge of this market offered special fares to encourage passengers to travel more often. Both Greyhound and Trailways and their affiliates instituted two-month 'ride anywhere' passes in September 1972, Greyhound offering the Ameripass and Trailways the Eaglepass. Maximum one-way fares anywhere in the USA also attempted to stimulate long-distance travel while bargain rates were made available in low-volume periods like midweek, late night or the winter season. Yet these offers had only a small impact in increasing bus revenue because most customers travelled relatively short distances – between 111 and 145 miles. There was certainly a place in the national transport system for scheduled lines which served Americans without cars and those in rural communities, but it was debatable whether this service could be economically viable.[47]

To make their business profitable, bus operators therefore increasingly depended on special services. Travel and tourism, which by the late 1970s was the nation's third-largest industry, contributing some $130 billion annually to the gross national product, offered considerable potential. Small companies relied heavily on charters and tours for their livelihood. These family operations, which often started on a shoestring and built up their reputations, were always looking to offer new services to customers in their vicinity. Their charter work ranged from all-inclusive packaged motor-coach tours, through becoming a Gray Line Tours Operator, to serving university campuses, taking skiers to winter resorts, transporting visitors to theme parks or making connections between airports and downtown districts. Indeed, in 1976 Class II and III carriers had 39 per cent of the charter miles and earned 36 per cent of the charter revenue in the USA.[48]

When the volume of intercity regular route traffic declined in the 1970s, larger companies found that they needed to supplement their scheduled operations by building up their tourist services. Like their smaller counterparts they engaged in a variety of charter activities. Frequently establishing a separate tour division within their organization, they often paid more attention to advertising, linked into other leisure networks, and attracted foreign business. The two dominant companies, Greyhound and Trailways, also undertook charter work, but in differing proportions. In 1976 Greyhound obtained 10.9 per cent and Trailways 17.2 per cent of revenue from special passenger services, compared to the 16.3 per cent for all Class I carriers. Greyhound faced more difficulties in coordinating special passenger services with its extensive regular route commitments. Nevertheless, the company used its tour and charter division to seek out national and international opportunities both as part of its own multi-faceted transport offerings and as part of a conglomerate which had broad interests in leisure. The bus industry as a whole might not be able to shake off the general image of being the poor person's option for routine travel, but it could offer quality service, organization, flexibility and convenience for all classes of people seeking relaxation and vacations.[49]

The large carriers further added to their scheduled passenger income by increasing special freight services. Package express became a more significant source of income in the 1970s and in 1976 it provided 15.2 per cent of all Class I carriers' revenue, 16.2 per cent of Greyhound's and 19.9 per cent of Trailways'. For the large bus companies small freight was both convenient and profitable because it slotted into established routes and even cross-subsidized these services to communities whose passenger demand alone was inadequate to warrant service. For many of the 15 000 communities in the USA, buses provided a regular package service and one which could link up with airlines and which was cost competitive with alternatives like United Parcels Services (UPS), Federal Express and the USA Post Office. Indeed, package express started to look such a promising business that some buses were specially altered to accommodate larger shipments and there was even some talk about running separate vehicles for the movement of small freight.[50]

But it was of no avail for bus carriers to make plans to improve their economic standing unless these met with official approval. In the mid-1970s the federal government became concerned about the deteriorating financial condition of the bus industry and discussed external solutions to the problems in the context of a national transport policy. Fully aware of the role which the intercity bus industry fulfilled in supplying a service for small rural communities and lower-income citizens, it was necessary to see how the public interest could best be served. Two possibilities were considered – subsidizing companies within the existing transport structure and altering the *status quo* to allow more bus competition and thus stimulate greater efficiency.[51]

The bus industry initially favoured government subsidy as the way forward. In the middle of the economic squeeze of the mid-1970s, operators thought that they could pull through and move into a new phase of business growth if the

government provided some financial assistance. In the 1977 congressional
hearings on the financial condition of the bus industry, bus delegates proposed a
revitalization strategy which included capital grants for the construction and
improvement of bus terminals and other facilities, operating subsidies directed
primarily towards rural and small urban areas, tax concessions and regulatory
reform aimed in particular at rate flexibility. The Surface Transportation
Assistance Act of the following year authorized some help with terminal
development which facilitated intermodal transport, and operating assistance
was also provided for bus systems serving small rural communities. This
limited aid had only a temporary impact because most government representatives, their advisors, economists and some bus carriers themselves were more
interested in altering the regulatory system to promote the competition which
they hoped would bring efficiency and profitability.[52]

In an era of conservative politics and economics favouring the operation of
the free market and the rational allocation of resources, pressure was placed
on the government to move out of its managerial role in the transport sector.
It was argued that rather than protecting the public interest by ensuring a
balance between economic efficiency, reasonable rates, useful service, industry
viability, safety, protection of the environment and conservation of energy, the
government should let the pricing mechanism operate on the premise that
private enterprise could satisfy societal needs. Within the space of a few years
much of the nation's transport was partially deregulated. In 1978 the Airline
Deregulation Act gave airlines much freedom in pricing policies, and entry to
and exit from routes. In 1980 both trucks and railroads were substantially
deregulated and in 1982 these were followed by the buses. By then many bus
operators accepted that they would have to work in a more competitive
environment on both intramodal and intermodal levels.[53]

The Bus Regulatory Reform Act of 1982 did not completely deregulate the
industry, but it did markedly relax governmental authority. Entry into business
was liberalized by allowing any able carrier to start operating a route unless it
was contrary to the public interest. Price flexibility was granted on fares and
state regulations about exit from unprofitable routes were eased.[54] In providing
greater freedom within the bus industry to respond to competitive pressures, the
Act undermined cross-subsidies which had supported marginal routes and
lower intrastate fares, thereby bringing closures. Bus companies started to
operate over each others' routes if they were profitable, and engaged in price
warfare, thereby creating other financial difficulties. The industry, however,
was not only facing rivalry from within its own ranks. Competition from new
low-cost deregulated airlines for both passengers and freight, and from trucks
free to engage in package express, resulted in substantial revenue losses. As the
industry looked forward into the 1980s and the era of deregulation it faced
major readjustments if it was going to survive, let alone flourish.[55]

Conclusion

In the years following the Second World War the American bus industry faded from being a dynamic part of a national transport system to becoming a minor provider of regular route services for 'underprivileged groups'. Though this role was officially recognized as essential for the public interest it was limited. The continued and growing popularity of the individualistic car and the increasing attraction of high-speed air travel supported by car rentals undermined the vitality of slower public ground-transportation systems. On the ground, buses could provide a more flexible, accessible and cheaper means of scheduled travel than trains and they frequently gained passengers from their railroad rivals in these years but trains, too, faced a declining passenger trade. Motor-coach operators also offered charters and tours which tapped into the leisure market and this market displayed great potential.

Buses might have made more connections with passengers under different government regulations and they might have been a more successful means of travel if their public-relations managers had promoted a more-user friendly and 'upbeat' image. Their operators, however, were not conservative entrepreneurs unable to adjust to change. They innovated in bus technology and in business administration and did actively market their product, but they faced severe odds in a nation which has always been dedicated to individualism. Some connections may have been missed, both by carriers and the government, but other connections were impossible to make.

Notes

1. 'Report of National Association of Motor Bus Operators', (NAMBO), submitted by Edgar F. Zelle, at the 40th Annual Meeting of the American Automobile Association, Illinois, 20–21 November 1944, typescript, p. 2 in E.F. Zelle Records, Jefferson Lines Inc., Minneapolis (hereafter cited as EFZR); NAMBO *Proceedings*, **17**, (1946), p. 10 (hereafter cited as NAMBO *Procs*); Greyhound Corporation *Annual Report* (1942), p. 6 (hereafter cited as GC, *AR*); M. Walsh, 'Minnesota's Mr Bus: Edgar F. Zelle and the Jefferson Highway Transportation Company', (chapter 6), p. 117; NAMBO *The Intercity Bus Industry at War*, (1943), Washington, DC, pp. 11, 16; NAMBO *Intercity Buses at War*, (1944), Washington, DC, n.p.

2. *The Intercity Bus Industry at War*, pp. 20–21; *Intercity Buses at War*, n.p; Report of NAMBO submitted by E.F. Zelle, p. 2. *Bus Transportation*, **22**(8) (1943), pp. 38–40; **24**(1) (1945), p. 50; **25**(1) (1946), p. 64 (hereafter cited as *BT*). GC, *AR* (1943), p. 7.

3. GC, *AR*, (1942), pp. 9–10; (1944), p. 8. *The Intercity Bus Industry at War*, pp. 22–8; *Intercity Buses at War*, n.p.; *BT*, **21**(7) (1942), pp. 310–12, 368, 427–30, 550–52; **22**(1) (1943), p. 84. Letters and Memoranda from Greyhound Officials to General Motors, to NAMBO and to the War Production Board, July 1943 –

May 1944, file 2, Greyhound Corporate Records, American Heritage Center, University of Wyoming (hereafter cited as GCR); Report of NAMBO submitted by E.F. Zelle, pp. 2–4; M. Walsh, 'Not Rosie the Riveter: Women's Diverse Roles in the Making of the American Long-Distance Bus Industry', (chapter 9), pp. 179–80.

4. *Intercity Buses at War*, n.p.; *The Intercity Bus Industry at War*, pp. 17–20; *BT* **24**(2) (1945), pp. 42–3; NAMBO Minutes of the Board of Directors, 23–24 November 1942, pp. 1–2 American Heritage Center, University of Wyoming (hereafter cited as NAMBO Mins); Esther Bubbley, bus photographs, taken for Farm Security Administration-Office of War Information (FSA-OWI), (1943), Library of Congress, Prints and Photographs Division, FSA-OWI Collection; M. Walsh (1988), ' "See/Serve America Now". Advertising bus travel in the USA during the Second World War', *Journal of Advertising History*, **11**(1), published in association with the *European Journal of Marketing*, **22**(4), pp. 41–60.

5. NAMBO, *Procs*, **17** (1946), pp. 7–14; NAMBO, 'Scrapbook of Newspaper Publicity, 1945–1946', American Bus Association (ABA), Washington, DC; *BT*, **25**(5) (1946), pp. 42–4.

6. Interstate Commerce Commission (ICC) (1950), 'Investigation of Bus Fares', Docket No. MC–C–550, **1**, *Brief of Respondents*, Washington, DC; National Archives Record Group (hereafter cited as NARG) BMC–C–550, **23**, Washington National Records Center, Suitland, MD. For a summary of regulation and motor-carrier transport policy see C.A. Taff (1980), *Commercial Motor Transportation*, Centreville, MD, 6th edn, pp. 403–37, and for a broader and contemporary discussion of transport policy see C.L. Dearing and W. Owen (1949), *National Transportation Policy*, Washington, DC.

7. The ICC instituted this investigation on 1 July 1946. Pre-hearing conferences were held in October 1946 and January 1947. The commission denied a request by the National Bus Traffic Association Inc. (NBTA) made on behalf of 225 respondents that hearings be postponed until normal and stable conditions had returned to the bus industry. Regional hearings were held in 1947, 1948 and 1949 and bus representatives were given time to present evidence of their traffic and costs studies. A large part of the evidence, which would normally have been presented orally, was submitted in writing. Briefs were due and filed on 16 January 1950. National Archives Record Group (NARG) BMC–C–500 'Investigation of Bus Fares' contained several thousands of pages of transcript of these hearings as well as the printed (1949 and 1950), *Briefs of Respondents*, 3 vols, Washington, DC. Summaries of the testimony were found in the 'Proposed Report of Investigation of Bus Fares', typescript. See in particular, *Brief of Respondents*, **1**, (1950), Washington, DC, and 'Proposed Report of Investigation of Bus Fares'. During the ten-year period 1938–1947, income taxes of Class I operators approximated 60 per cent of net income. Taking the 255 bus respondents as a whole, their income taxes in 1948 were about 40 per cent of net operating income.

8. During the ten-year period 1938–1948, bus operating ratios varied considerably between years, between small and large and weak and strong carriers and in the three major districts, Eastern, Southern and Western. The commissioners decided that the war years were abnormal and should not be used in establishing a standard operating ratio. They therefore looked to figures in the late 1930s and in the post-war years. Operating ratios for bus respondents as a whole were 89 per cent in 1938, 88 per cent in 1946, 92 per cent in 1947 and 97 per cent in 1948. In 1947 a significant number of companies had ratios of 100 per cent and over and it was

estimated that some 40 per cent of the companies were in a precarious position. The 'official' pre-tax operating ratio of 85 per cent would produce an overall operating ratio of 93 after income taxes and this seemed adequate to provide funds to reinvest in the bus industry. The NBTA had contended that an operating ratio of slightly less than 80 would be more appropriate. ICC, *Brief of Respondents*, **1**, pp. 87–94; 'Proposed Report of Investigation of Bus Fares', pp. 130–34, 188–9.

9. B.J. Wattenburg, Intro. (1976), *The Statistical History of the USA: From Colonial Times to the Present*, New York, p. 716; ICC, *Brief of Respondents*, **1**, pp. 66–7; Taff (1951), *Commercial Motor Transportation*, Homewood, IL, 1st edn, pp. 22–51; Dearing and Owen, *National Transportation Policy*, pp. 105–20; J.B. Rae (1965), *The American Automobile. A Brief History*, Chicago, pp. 179–84, 186; R.E. Bilstein (1984), *Flight in America. From the Wrights to the Astronauts*, Baltimore, pp. 169–78, 227–39, 257–66.

10. Comparative bus and rail fares are difficult to obtain. ICC (1932), 'Coordination of Motor Transportation' *Report*, **182**, p. 316 concluded that bus rates ranged from 86 per cent of the rail rate at a distance of about 160 miles to 58 per cent at a distance from 475 to 1,140 miles. L.A. Rossman (1938), 'Memorandum Concerning Some Financial Aspects of Intercity Motor Bus Transportation', Grand Rapids, MN, p. 5, L.A. Rossman Records, Minnesota Historical Society, St Paul (hereafter cited as LARR), suggests that substantial price competition existed between a large diversified bus company, presumably Greyhound, and trains from 1931 to 1937. Prices on trains fell from 3.06 cents per passenger mile in 1931 to 1.95 cents in 1937. The respective figures for the bus company were 2.52 cents in 1931 and 1.54 cents in 1937. G.L. Thompson (1993), *The Passenger Train in the Motor Age. California's Rail and Bus Industries, 1910–41*, Columbus, OH, pp. 104, 176–81, 186, suggests that in 1933 in the West, buses charged higher prices than trains for short-distance traffic, but lower fares for long-distance traffic. In the East most bus fares were lower than train fares. ICC, *Brief of Respondents*, p. 67 and ICC, 'Proposed Report on Investigation of Bus Fares', pp. 135–40. Comparison of 7,025 bus fares between m ̣ points in six rate territories with corresponding rail fares between the same points, effective as on 1 September 1940 and 1 September 1948, show that the bus fares in 1940 averaged 78 per cent of the rail fares and that in 1948 this percentage had dropped to 64.

11. Tax apportionment was a problem which was particularly relevant to large operators. NAMBO (1945), 'Statement re National Transportation Inquiry', pp. 13–15; 'Report on State Legislation for NAMBO Meeting of Board of Directors, 6 April 1949, pp. 1–2; NAMBO, Mins, 16–17 January 1951, p. 18, 6 November 1951, p. 10, 24 January 1952, pp. 7–8; correspondence between L.A. Rossman, special consultant to the bus industry and Greyhound officials, 1948–1954 and L.A. Rossman (1951), draft booklet, 'Intercity Motor Bus Transportation, The Greyhound Lines and the Public', p. 15, both in LARR; Taff (1951), *Commercial Motor Transportation*, p. 355.

12. The issue of increased size and weight of buses was high on the agenda of most operators in the late 1940s and early 1950s. Correspondence between Greyhound officials, L.A. Rossman, NAMBO executives and AASHO executives, from 1945–1955, can be found in both LARR and in boxes 1 and 3, GCR; NAMBO, *Procs*, **18** (1947), pp. 10–11, 142–3; **20** (1949), pp. 20–21; **21** (1950), pp. 36–7. Motor Bus Lines of America (1966), *Modern Highways and How they Can Serve You Better*, Washington, DC, pp. 11–16 and 'Intercity Motor Bus Transportation, The Greyhound Lines and the Public', pp. 14–15, both in LARR; Taff (1951), *Commercial Motor Transportation*, pp. 353–5.

13. Normally one-seventh of Greyhound's fleet was replaced annually. Thanks to wartime restrictions and post-war delays orders of new equipment were bunched thereby creating higher depreciation charges. GC, *AR*, (1945), pp. 8–9; (1946), pp. 7, 9; (1947), pp. 8, 10; (1948), pp. 6, 10; (1949), pp. 5, 11–12. *BT*, **27**(2) (1948), pp. 56–7; **28**(2) (1949), pp. 60–1. *Rear View Mirror*, **13**(8) (1946), pp. 2, 7; **13**(12) (1946), p. 1 (hereafter cited as *RVM*). M. Walsh, 'Minnesota's Mr Bus: Edgar F. Zelle and the Jefferson Highway Transportation Company' (see chapter 6), p. 117–18.

14. NAMBO, *Procs*, **17**, (1946), pp. 12, 79, 80; **18** (1947), pp. 167–75. ICC, 'Brief of Respondents', **1**, p. 94.

15. GC, *AR*, (1946), p. 10; (1947), p. 11; (1948), p. 5; (1949), p. 12–13; (1950), pp. 7, 13–14. Jefferson Transportation Company, *Annual Report*, (1946), n.p.; (1947), n.p.; (1948), n.p.; (1949), n.p. *BT*, **25**(5) (1946), p. 40. For an explanation of American post-war inflation see H. Van Der Wee (1986), *Prosperity and Upheaval. The World Economy 1945–1980*, transl. edn Harmondsworth, pp. 36–7.

16. Taxes paid by Class I motor carriers rose from $16.1 million in 1941 to $77.7 million in 1942 and a peak of $119.7 million in 1944. They subsequently fell to $60.7 million in 1946 and $48.0 million in 1948. Class I carriers for the years 1939–1949 had annual revenues of $100,000 or more. Federal and state income taxes paid by Greyhound increased from $3.2 million in 1940 to $32.8 million in 1942 to $42.9 million in 1944 and fell to $18.8 in 1946. CG, *AR*, (1942), p. 12; (1944), p. 11; (1946), p. 11; (1948), p. 9. ICC, *Brief of Respondents*, **1**, pp. 61, 87–90 and ICC, Proposed Report on Investigation of Bus Fares', p. 94. *Bus Facts*, (1949), pp. 29, 34; (1952), p. 32 (hereafter cited as *BF*).

17. NAMBO, *Procs*, **18**, (1947), pp. 63–9; **20**, (1949), pp. 24–6. US Department of Labor (1946), 'Report and Recommendations of the Fact Finding Panel in the Greyhound Bus Dispute', Washington, DC, (ICC Library). *BF*, (1949), pp. 30–31, 38–9, 42–5, 48–9. *BT*, **25**(11) (1946), p. 71; **26**(5) (1947), pp. 40–41; **27**(1) (1948), pp. 44–5; **27**(5) (1948), pp. 87–9; **28**(5) (1949), pp. 56–7; **30**(9) (1951), pp. 56–7. GC, *AR*, (1945), pp. 9–10, (1946), p. 10, (1947), pp. 14–15, (1948), p. 14, (1949), pp. 5, 18; (1950), p. 15.

18. M. Walsh, ' "See This Amazing America". The long-distance bus industry's use of advertising in its first quarter century', (chapter 8), pp. 159, 161; Walsh, ' "Serve/See America Now" ', pp. 41–60; NAMBO, Mins, 26–27 October 1944, p. 11; 5 November 1947, pp. 5–6. NAMBO, *Procs*, **17** (1946), pp. 77–85; **18** (1947), pp. 15–16, 108–16, 167–85; **19**, (1948), pp. 170–78; **20** (1949), pp. 157–75. *RVM*, **13**(4) (1946), pp. 1, 6; **17**(2) (1950), p. 6. *BT*, **24**(8) (1945), pp. 54–5; **25**(11) (1946), p. 68; **26**(1) (1947), p. 43; **26**(3) (1947), pp. 56–8; **28**(2) (1949), pp. 43–4; **29**(3) (1950), pp. 42–3. GC, *AR*, (1947), pp. 30–31. NAMBO, 'Scrapbook of Newspaper Publicity, 1945–1946, ABA; (1948), 'A Memorandum Concerning activities to Increase Public Understanding of Intercity Motor Bus Transportation' and (1950), 'A Memorandum Concerning Greyhound Employees and Public Relations', both in LARR.

19. Bus officials negotiated a military agreement for the transportation of military personnel in July 1947. This was renewed and revised in 1949 and 1950. Partial mobilization of the armed forces following the outbreak of war in Korea increased military business, and though a change in policy brought some loss of traffic in 1951 bus operators continued to carry troops as part of their charter service. NAMBO, Mins, 5 November 1947 (Separate Memorandum), pp. 1–3; 5 May 1948, p. 9; 16–17 January 1951, pp. 4–5; 24 January 1952, pp. 3–4. NAMBO,

Procs, **18** (1947), p. 9; **19** (1948), pp. 16–18; **20**, (1949), pp. 13–14; **21** (1950), pp. 21–2; **22** (1951), pp. 56–62; **23** (1952), pp. 32–41. *BT*, **31**(1) (1952), p. 28; **32**(2) (1952), pp. 56–7. GC, *AR*, (1950), p. 7; (1951), pp. 9–10; (1952), p. 10; (1953), p. 7. When measured in terms of intercity passengers carried via public transport, a statistic which favours buses rather than trains or planes because bus passengers travel shorter distances, buses still declined, from 40.1 per cent of the total in 1950 to 33.5 per cent in 1955 and then to 31.9 per cent in 1959 or from an index of 100 in 1950 to 70 in 1955 and 56 in 1959. *BF*, (1965), pp. 6, 8; F.A. Smith (1986), *Transportation in America. Historical Compendium, 1939–85*, Washington, DC, pp. 12, 14–15.

20. *BT*, **27**(3) (1948), pp. 46–8; **28**(7) (1949), p. 47; **28**(10) (1949), p. 73; **29**(11) (1950), p. 35; **33**(5) (1954), p. 45; **33**(10) (1954), pp. 44–5, 60–61; **34**(5) (1955), pp. 44–5, 119; **35**(10) (1956), pp. 54–5, 59. *RVM*, **15**(3) (1948), pp. 6–7; **16**(4) (1950), pp. 8–11; **16**(6) (1949), p. 8; **17**(12) (1950), p. 2; **21**(6) (1954), p. 2. *Highway Traveler*, **20**(2) (1948), pp. 16–17, 46; **25**(1) (1953), pp. 23–5; **26**(3) (1954), pp. 40–41 (hereafter cited as *HT*). The Greyhound Corporation (1954), *The Scenicruiser. A New Milestone* …pamphlet, n.p., pp. 1–18, GCR. GC, *AR*, (1951), pp. 10–11; (1952), pp. 5, 11; (1953), pp. 12, 27–8; (1954), p. 12; (1955), pp. 7, 14; (1956), p. 22. Continental Trailways, *Annual Report*, (1953) p. 4; (1954), pp. 4–5; (1955), p. 3; (1956), p. 3 (hereafter cited as Cont., *AR*).

21. GC, *AR*, (1950), pp. 7, 13–14, 15, 18; (1951), pp. 11–12, 13; (1952), pp. 11–12, 13; (1953), pp. 12, 13; (1954), pp. 12, 13; (1955), pp. 14, 16. Cont., *AR*, (1953), pp. 4, 5; (1954), p. 5; (1955), p. 7; (1956), p. 3. *RVM*, **16**(3) (1949), pp. 3, 12; **16**(5) (1949), pp. 8, 9; **17**(1) (1950), p. 6; **17**(4) (1950), p. 6; **18**(4) (1951), pp. 6–7; **18**(11) (1951), pp. 8–9. *BT*, **28**(5) (1949), pp. 54, 74–5; **28**(9) (1949), pp. 73–4; **28**(11) (1950), p. 79; **29**(2) (1950), p. 93; **29**(3) (1950), p. 62; **29**(7) (1950), pp. 46–7; **30**(1) (1951), pp. 34–7; **30**(2) (1951), pp. 52–4; **31**(5) (1952), pp. 39–41; **32**(1) (1953), p. 56, **32**(3) (1953), pp. 28–9; **32**(11) (1953), p. 74; **34**(12) (1955), pp. 40–42; **35**(4) (1956), pp. 31–3; **35**(9) (1956), pp. 52–3. *HT*, **24**(3) (1952), pp. 27–8; *Greyhound News*, **14**(3) (1955), pp. 2–3.

22. NAMBO, *Procs*, **27** (1956), pp. 61–73; A.O. Olson to J.M. Budd, 22 September 1955, Presidents File, 11532, Great Northern Railway Company Records, Minnesota Historical Society. Cont., *AR*, (1953), pp. 5–6; (1954), pp. 3, 6; (1955), pp. 5, 7; (1956), p. 4. GC, *AR*, (1950), p. 10; (1951), p. 9; (1952), pp. 10–11; (1953), pp. 10–11; (1954), pp. 10–11; (1955), pp. 7–8. *BT*, **30**(1) (1951), pp. 27–30; **30**(12) (1951), p. 46; **31**(2) (1952), pp. 70–71; **31**(8) (1952), pp. 40–41; **32**(2) (1953), p. 59; **33**(12) (1954), pp. 50–51; **34**(4) (1955), pp. 30–32; **35**(4) (1956), pp. 24–7; **35**(7) (1956), pp. 34–5. *RVM*, **17**(2) (1950), p. 2; **17**(9) (1950), p. 10; **18**(1) (1951), p. 14; **18**(9) (1951), pp. 3, 10. *HT*, **23**(2) (1951), pp. 28–30; **23**(3) (1951), p. 21; **24**(3) (1952), p. 42; **25**(3) (1953), pp. 40–41; **26**(3) (1954), pp. 36–7; **27**(2) (1955), pp. 28–32. Walsh, ' "See This Amazing America", (chapter 8), pp. 158, 161.

23. ICC, *AR*, **68** (1954), pp. 13–14; **69** (1955), pp. 15–16. US Congress, Senate, Committee on Interstate and Foreign Commerce, 87 Cong., 1 Sess. (1961), *National Transportation Policy*, Committee Print, pp. 283–90, 348–9; *BT*, **35**(4) (1956), pp. 24, 28–30; *The Statistical History of the USA*, pp. 8, 716; J.B. Rae (1971), *The Road and the Car in American Life*, Cambridge, MA, pp. 104–6, 138–44.

24. NAMBO, *Procs*, **24** (1954), pp. 116–28; **26** (1955), pp. 118–123. *BT*, **34**(11) (1955), p. 54; **35**(4) (1956), p. 24; **35**(5) (1956), pp. 42–3. J.C. Nelson (1959), *Railroad Transportation and Public Policy*, Washington, DC, pp. 311–16; J.F.

Stover (1961), *American Railroads*, Chicago, (1968 edition), p. 239; Bilstein, *Flight in America*, pp. 232–9; R.E.G. Davies (1972), *Airlines of the USA since 1914*, London, (rev. ed., 1982), pp. 336–48.

25. GC, *AR*, (1956), pp. 6, 19. *Fleet Owner*, **52**(2) (1957), pp. 66–8; **55**(1) (1960), pp. 67–80 (hereafter cited as *FO*). *BT*, **34**(11) (1955), p. 65; *Greyhound News*, **14**(12) (1955), p. 2; *Time*, **72**(7) (1958), p. 76; A.S. Genet (1958), *'Profile of Greyhound'*. *The Greyhound Corporation*, pamphlet, New York, pp. 22–3. Arthur Genet, a railroad official, was brought in as president of Greyhound on 1 January 1956. He resigned, under pressure in August 1958.

26. GC, *AR*, (1956), p. 23; (1957), pp.16–19; (1958), pp. 7–8, 16. *FO*, **52**(2) (1957), p. 67; *Time*, **72**(7) (1958), p. 76; *BT*, **35**(11) (1956), p. 47. 'Lady Greyhound' materials, GCR; L.A. Rossman to A.S. Genet, 5 April 1956; A.S. Genet to L.A. Rossman, 17 April 1956; LARR. notes about Grey advertising for Greyhound c.1956, Walter B. Grosvenor Records; O. Schisgall (1985), *The Greyhound Story. From Hibbing to Everywhere*, Chicago, pp. 118–19.

27. US Department of Transportation (1975), *1974 National Transportation Report*, Washington, DC, pp. 288–94; Office of Transportation Analysis, ICC (1984), *The Intercity Bus Industry*, Washington, DC, pp. 24–7; US Congress, 95 Cong. 1 Sess. (1977), *Intercity Domestic Transportation System for Passengers and Freight*, (Committee Print), pp. 339, 345; Rae, *Road and the Car*, pp. 187–94; Taff (1969), *Commercial Motor Transportation*, Homewood, IL, 4th edn, pp. 19–24; Smith, *Transportation in America*, pp. 12, 14–15.

28. *Intercity Domestic Transportation System for Passengers and Freight*, p. 358; G.W. Hilton (1969), *The Transportation Act of 1958: A Decade of Experience*, Bloomington, IND, pp. 35–8; D.M. Itzkoff (1985), *Off the Track: The Decline of the Intercity Passenger Train in the USA*, Westport, CN, p. 58; Nelson, *Railroad Transportation and Public Policy* pp. 311–16; Stover, *American Railroads* pp. 238–45; Bilstein, *Flight in America* pp. 257–67; Davies, *Airlines of the USA*, pp. 517–31, 541–54, 568–70.

29. GC, *AR*, (1962), p. 6; (1963), p. 5; (1964), pp. 4, 8; (1965), pp. 4–5. Cont., *AR*, (1962), n.p.; (1964), pp. 4, 5; (1965), p. 4; (1967), p. 3. *FO*, **55**(1) (1960), pp. 70–71; **56**(9) (1961), p. 79; **57**(7) (1962), p. 41; **58**(12) (1963), p. 42; **60**(9) (1965), pp. 43–4. *Transportation in America* (1986), pp. 12–15; C. Jackson (1984), *Hounds of the Road. A History of the Greyhound Bus Company*, Bowling Green, OH, pp. 134, 135. Greyhound introduced the $99 fare for international travellers in mid-1961. Variations and extensions were added in 1962. The advertising phrase 'Go Greyhound and Leave the Driving to Us' was used mostly in the 1960s.

30. GC, *AR*, (1962), pp. 8, 11; (1963), pp. 2, 5, 8; (1964), pp. 8, 11; (1965), p. 5; (1966), p. 9; (1967), pp. 11–12; (1968), p. 10. Cont., *AR*, (1963), n.p.; (1964), p. 3; (1966), pp. 3, 5; (1967), pp. 6–7. *FO*, **58**(4) (1963), pp. 43–4; **58**(12) (1963), p. 42. *Greyhound Reporter*, **2**(4) (1962), p. 3; **4**(1) (1964), p. 1. New York World's Fair, 1963–1966, GCR; miscellaneous Greyhound brochures, 1960s, William A. Luke Records, Spokane, WA, (hereafter cited as WALR); (1978), *The Intercity Bus Industry. A Preliminary Study*, Washington, DC, pp. 46, 53.

31. *Go Greyhound*, **4**(4) (1969), pp. 8–11. Cont., *AR*, (1964), p. 4; (1965), p. 5; (1966), p. 6; (1967), p. 4. GC, *AR*, (1962), p. 7; (1963), p. 6; (1964), p. 7; (1967), p. 11. *BF*, (1962), p. 10; (1964), p. 17; (1965), pp. 5, 18, 27–8; (1966), p. 11. *Heart of America Purchaser*, **43**(1) (1961), pp. 26, outside back cover, GCR; *The Intercity Bus Industry*(1978), pp. 50–3; *Intercity Bus Industry* (1984), pp. 5–6; Taff (1969), *Commercial Motor Transportation*, pp. 434–5. In 1970 a Class I motor carrier had

an average gross operating revenue of $1 million or more. This definition had been changed, effective 1 January 1969. From 1950 to 1968 the revenue test for Class I carriers was $200,000. *BF*, (1972), p. 4.

32. *Go Greyhound*, **1**(1) (1966), pp. 16–25; **4**(1) (1969), pp. 9–10, 12–13; **4**(3) (1969), p. 16; **6**(3 & 4) (1971), pp. 11–17. *Greyhound West*, **2**(1) (1972), pp. 1–3 and *Greyhound Reporter*, **1**(3) (1961), p. 1; **2**(3) (1962), p. 3; **2**(4) (1962), p. 5, WALR. G.H. Trautman (1968), 'Greyhound, Yesterday, Today and Tomorrow', A Published Address, Chicago, pp. 1–12, GCR; Cont., *AR*, (1967), pp. 1, 8–10, 12; *Time*, **81**(17) (1963), pp. 82–3; *Business Week*, 16 November 1963, pp. 85–90; *The Intercity Bus Industry* (1978), pp. 86–8; Taff (1969), *Commercial Motor Transportation*, pp. 439–42.

33. *Corporate Report*, January, 1978, p. 47, WALR; *Bus Ride*, **7**(5) (1971), pp. 17–19; **9**(3) (1973), pp. 12–13; **24**(2) (1988), pp. 50–51 (hereafter cited as *BR*). *Motor Coach Age*, **21**(9) (1969), pp. 4–8; **35**(4) (1983), pp. 8, 11–12 (hereafter cited as *MCA*).

34. *BF*, (1962), p. 9; (1965), pp. 9–10; (1966), pp. 4, 5, 7. *The Intercity Bus Industry* (1978), p. 59. Most intercity bus companies were small businesses, with annual gross revenues of under $50,000 in the mid-1960s. They belonged to the Class III carriers as defined by the ICC. Class II carriers had an annual gross revenue of between $50,000 and $200,000, while Class I carriers had annual gross revenues of $200,000 or over. In 1965 there were 166 Class I carriers out of a total of 1,400 operating companies. These Class I carriers were dominated by Greyhound and Trailways. Some general information on small, family bus companies is available in *Bus Ride*, but most material would have to be gleaned from local newspapers.

35. *Intercity Domestic Transportation System for Passengers and Freight*.

36. Nelson, *Railroad Transportation and Public Policy*, pp. 311–16; Stover, *American Railroads*, p. 239; Itzkoff, *Off the Track*, p. 58; Hilton, *The Transportation Act of 1958: A Decade of Experience*, pp. 35–8; J.R. Meyer, C.V. Oster Jr, et al. (1987), *Deregulation and the Future of Intercity Passenger Travel*, Cambridge, MA, p. 165.

37. American Bus Association, *Annual Report*, (1979), pp. 10, 20 (hereafter cited as ABA, *AR*); *BR*, **8**(2) (1972), pp. 23–6; Meyer & Oster, *Deregulation and the Future*, pp. 167–9; *The Intercity Bus Industry* (1984), p. 31; *1974 National Transportation Report*, pp. 306–9.

38. NAMBO, *AR*, (1972), pp. 5, 6, 20; (1974), p. 7. ABA, *AR*, (1977), pp. 2, 10, 18–19; (1979), pp. 10, 20; (1980), pp. 4, 10; (1981), pp. 4, 6. NAMBO (1976), *1926–1976. One-Half Century of Service to America*, Washington, DC, pp. 6, 8, 10; *The Intercity Bus Industry* (1978), pp. 49, 50, 60, 61; F.D. Fravel (1990), *The Greyhound Story, 1979–90*, Bethesda, MD, p. 13; *1974 National Transportation Report*, pp. 306–9. *BR*, **8**(2) (1972), pp. 23–6; **11**(5) (1975), pp. 26, 27. Estimates of the lost revenue due to the subsidized Amtrak services vary. The ABA considered that since its beginning Amtrak had diverted $500 million from the bus industry by 1978 and $600 million by 1980. Net operating revenue is defined as operating revenues minus expenses.

39. *Intercity Domestic Transportation System for Passengers and Freight*, pp. 85, 87, 365–6; US Congress, 95 Cong. 2 Sess. (1978), *Intercity Bus Service in Small Communities*, Committee Print, pp. 13, 16–17; ABA, *AR*, (1977), pp. 18–19; Management Analysis Center Inc. (MAC) (1981), *Deregulation of the Intercity Bus Industry*, Washington, DC, pp. 10, 17, 18; C.F. Hitchcock (1981), 'Regulatory Reform in the Intercity Bus Industry', *Journal of Law Reform*, **15**(1), pp. 10–11; *Intercity Bus Industry* (1984), pp. 30–31; Fravel, *The Greyhound Story*, pp. 13, 15;

Bilstein, *Flight in America*, pp. 257–65, 285–90; Davies, *Airlines of the USA*, pp. 526–31, 568–77. The initial impact of airline deregulation was muted as fuel prices rose following the Iranian crisis, but by 1981 the bus industry was feeling increased competition from airlines.

40. F.A. Smith (1996), *Transportation in America. A Statistical Analysis of Transportation in the USA*, Lansdowne, VA, p. 63; (1984), *The Intercity Bus Industry*, pp. 25–6; *Intercity Bus Service in Small Communities*, pp. 12–3; *Intercity Domestic Transportation System for Passengers and Freight*, pp. 339–46; Meyer and Oster, *Deregulation and the Future*, pp. 178–81.

41. For general information on economic conditions in the 1970s see A. Maddison (1991), *Dynamic forces in Capitalist Development. A Long-Run Comparative View*, Oxford, pp. 128–166 and Van Der Wee, *Prosperity and Upheaval*, pp. 79–93. For more details on the USA see T. Kemp (1990), *The Climax of Capitalism*, London, pp. 177–203, and A.S. Campagna (1987), *US National Economic Policy, 1917–1985*, New York, pp. 343–481. For specific material on the bus industry see US Congress, 95 Cong. 1 Sess. (1977), *Financial Condition of the Intercity Bus Industry*, Serial No. 95–29, pp. 53–6.

42. *Intercity Bus Service in Small Communities*, pp. 13–5; *Financial Condition of the Intercity Bus Industry*, pp. 53–6; (1978), *The Intercity Bus Industry*, pp. 61–92; National Transportation Policy Study Commission (1979), *Intercity Bus Transportation*, Iowa City, IO, pp. 5–6; *BF*, (1952), p. 30. Sources vary in reporting wages as a proportion of total expenses – from 57 per cent to nearly two-thirds. Regardless of which figure is correct, wages comprised a larger part of expenses than in the post-war years. The cost of fuel rose rapidly from $38 million in 1974 (exclusive of taxes) to $75 million in 1979 and $113 million in 1980. *BF*, (1981), p. 13. See also Congressional Quarterly Inc. (1981), *Energy Policy*, Washington, DC, 2nd edn, pp. 14–23.

43. Two hearings before, and one report for the Senate Committee on Commerce, Science and Transportation (namely *Intercity Domestic Transportation System For passengers and Freight*, *Intercity Bus Services in Small Communities*, and *Financial Condition of the Intercity Bus Industry*) provide evidence of the problems of intercity bus operators in the 1970s. On 19 September 1977 the National Association of Motor Bus Owners changed its name to the American Bus Association. This trade association had experienced two earlier name changes from the National Motor Bus Association to the National Association of Motor Bus Operators and then to the National Association of Motor Bus Owners. ABA, *AR*, (1977), p. 31; *BR* **32**(7) (1996), p. 32.

44. ABA, *AR*, (1977), p. 24; (1979), p. 27. *1926–1976. One Half Century of Service to America*, p. 20. *BF*, (1972), p. 9; (1981), pp. 13, 15. *The Intercity Bus Industry* (1978), pp. 68–9, 70–72; *The Intercity Bus Industry* (1984), p. 55; *Financial Conditions of the Intercity Bus Industry*, p. 20; Meyer and Oster, *Deregulation and the Future*, p. 174.

45. NAMBO (1974), *The Intercity and Suburban Bus Industry, 1973–1974*, Washington, DC, pp. 4–7; *1926–1976, One Half Century of Service to America*, p. 22. ABA, *AR*, (1979), pp. 4, 11, 15; (1980), pp. 9, 12, 14, 18. Greyhound Lines Inc., *News*, **Spring** 1973, p. 4; **September** 1973, p. 6. *BR*, **8**(6) (1972), pp. 23–6, **9**(4) (1973), pp. 31–2; **9**(6) (1973), p. 25; **11**(4) (1975), p. 33; **11**(5) (1975), p. 29; **13**(4) (1977), pp. 28–9, 36–7; **15**(6) (1979), pp. 26–7. Schisgall, *The Greyhound Story*, p. 237.

46. *The Intercity Bus Industry* (1978), pp. 45–7, 50–55; MAC, *Deregulation of the Intercity Bus Industry*, pp. 15–16.

47. ABA, *AR*, (1979), p. 20. *BR*, **8**(6) (1972), pp. 23–6; **9**(4) (1973), pp. 2–3; **11**(5) (1975), p. 29. MAC, *Deregulation of the Intercity Bus Industry*, p. 13. *The Intercity Bus Industry*, (1978), pp. 26–36, 50; (1984), pp. 18–24. *Intercity Bus Service in Small Communities*, pp. 3–4; *Financial Conditions of the Intercity Bus Industry*, pp. 55, 56, 70, 77–8; A.E. Meier and J.P. Hoschek (1975), *Over the Road. A History of Intercity Bus Transportation in the USA*, Upper Montclair, NJ, p. 141.

48. *BR*, **6**(4) (1970), pp. 26–7; **9**(3) (1973), pp. 12–13; **13**(1) (1977), pp. 32–4; **15**(6) (1979), pp. 26–7; **24**(2) (1988), pp. 50–52; **27**(4) (1991), p. 44; **27**(5) (1991), pp. 42–3; **28**(3) (1992), pp. 44–6; **28**(6) (1992), pp. 54–5; **29**(7) (1993), pp. 26–7. ABA, *AR*, (1979), pp. 11, 14; (1980), pp. 16–18. MAC, *Deregulation of the Intercity Bus Industry*, p. 12; *Intercity Bus Transportation* (1979), p. 8; *Intercity Domestic Transportation System for Passengers and Freight*, p. 455.

49. *BR*, **7**(5) (1971), pp. 17–19; **11**(5) (1975), p. 29; **15**(6) (1979), pp. 26–7; **16**(5) (1980), pp. 30–32. *MCA*, **35**(4) (1983), pp. 8, 11–12; *BF* (1972), p. 14. ABA, *AR*, (1977), p. 2; (1979), pp. 11, 14; (1980), pp. 16–18; *The Intercity Bus Industry* (1984), p. 57; MAC, *Deregulation of the Intercity Bus Industry*, p. 12; *The Intercity Bus Industry* (1978), pp. 46–7, 53–4; *Intercity Domestic Transportation System for Passengers and Freight*, p. 455.

50. *BF*, (1972), p. 8; ABA, *AR*, (1979), pp. 18, 22, 26; *Intercity Bus Transportation* (1979), p. 8; *The Intercity Bus Industry* (1978), pp. 46–7, 50–53; ICC, (1979), *Report of the Bus Industry Study Group*, Washington, DC, pp. 57–8; *Intercity Bus Service in Small Communities*, pp. 1, 5–6, 17–19.

51. The 'public interest' has been defined differently over the course of American history and within the framework of government regulation. For an historical view see T.K. McGraw (1975), 'Regulation in America. A review article', *Business History Review*, **49**, pp. 159–83; for an economist's survey see P.W. MacAvoy (1979), *The Regulated Industries and the Economy*, New York, and for a legal approach see S.G. Breyer (1982), *Regulation and Its Reform*, Cambridge, MA. For an international comparison see D. Swann (1988), *The Retreat of the State. Deregulation and Privatisation in the UK and the US*, London. 'Public interest' as applied to the American intercity bus industry in the 1970s is examined in *Intercity Domestic Transportation System for Passengers and Freight*, pp. 5–43; MAC, *Deregulation of the Intercity Bus Industry*, pp. 21–6.

52. *Financial Conditions of the Intercity Bus Industry*, pp. 1–96; Transportation Research Board (1980), *Proceedings: Conference On Intercity Bus Transportation*, Washington, DC; MAC, *Deregulation of the Intercity Bus Industry*, pp. 1–28; *Report of the Bus Industry Study Group*, pp. 1–79; Greyhound Lines Inc. (1979), *A Proposal for Federal Legislative Deregulation of the Intercity Bus Industry*, Pheonix, AZ; Taff (1980), *Commercial Motor Transportation*, p. 506.

53. American Association of State Highway and Transportation Officials (AASHTO), (1983), *Deregulation of the Transportation Industry. Task Force Report*, Denver, CO; MAC, *Deregulation of the Intercity Bus Industry*, pp. 1–28; M.T. Farris (1983), 'Evolution of the Transport Regulatory Structure of the US', *International Journal of Transport Economics*, **10**, pp. 173–93; Meyer and Oster, *Deregulation and the Future*, pp. 1–5, 161–82; Swann, *The Retreat of the State*, pp. 32–41, 135–60.

54. 'Bus Regulatory Reform Act of 1981' (1981), *Congressional Record*, **127**(170) (*Proceedings and Debates*, of US Congress, 97th Cong. 1 Sess., H8581–H8602); M.T. Ferris and N.E. Daniel (1983), 'Bus Regulatory Reform Act of 1982',

Transportation Journal, **23**, pp. 4–15; E.A. Pinkston (1984), 'The Rise and Fall of Bus Regulation', *Regulation*, **8** (September/December), pp. 49–51.

55. Meyer and Oster, *Deregulation and the Future*, pp. 161–224; (1984), *The Intercity Bus Industry*, pp. 74–92; K.J. Button (1987), 'The Effects of Regulatory Reform in the US Intercity Bus Industry', *Transport Reviews*, **7**(2), pp. 145–65; Pinkston, 'The Rise and Fall of Bus Regulation', pp. 51–2; Fravel, *The Greyhound Story*, pp. 15, 17.

Fig. 1   Stretched out automobile (Dodge) of the early 1920s

Fig. 2   Downtown Hibbing, Minnesota, 1921. Buses on either side of 3rd Avenue with the bus stop on the left

Fig. 3 On the road near Zumbrota, Minnesota in 1926

Fig. 4   Connecting Union Pacific stages (buses) and Union Pacific trains, Eastside (East Los Angeles) Station in 1929

Fig. 5 Inside the Jefferson Lines' Mason City Bus Terminal about 1922. This is the Amber Room, reputed to be one of the best restaurants in Mason City at the time

Fig. 6 Trailways Bus Terminal St Joseph, Missouri, c. 1935

Fig. 7   Waiting outside the Pennsylvania Greyhound Terminal 33rd Street entrance –
1936. Looking east towards 7th Avenue with the Pennsylvania Railroad Station
on the right

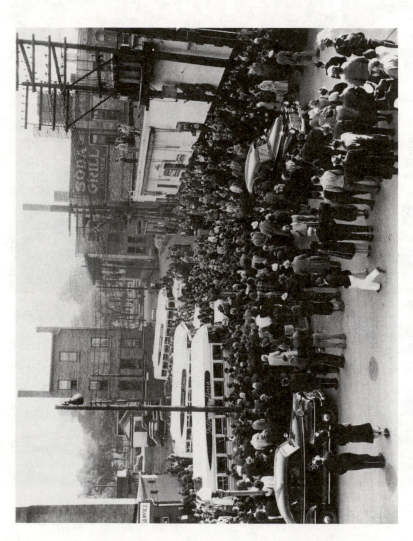

Fig. 8 122 draftees embarking for service via motor coaches, 23 May 1942, with over 2,000 people seeing them off, Mason City Iowa

Part Two

Regional Highways

4   Tracing the Hound:
The Minnesota Roots of the
Greyhound Bus Corporation

On Tuesday, 31 July 1984, the city of Hibbing in the Iron Range region of northern Minnesota's St Louis County celebrated Greyhound Bus Day. Commemorating the seventieth anniversary of the founding of the world's largest intercity passenger carrier, the Hibbing city council voted unanimously to rename that section of 3rd Avenue East from 17th Street to the Hull Rust Mine as 'Greyhound Boulevard'. Company officials from Phoenix, Dallas and Minneapolis, along with 184 retired bus drivers, travelled to Hibbing for a luncheon and the unveiling of a street sign complete with the blue greyhound, which has become the corporate symbol of the bus line. For not only did local officials claim that the Greyhound Bus Corporation could trace its roots back to Hibbing, but Frederick Dunikoski, then president of Greyhound Bus Lines, Inc., went on record as saying that Hibbing 'is our birthplace, it's like Plymouth Rock'.[1]

Many Americans and historians may be surprised to learn that the Greyhound Corporation has recognized this relatively small city – population 21,193 – known chiefly as the site of the world's largest open-cast iron mine, as its birthplace. Most people, whether bus travellers or not, associate Greyhound either with its recent base in Phoenix or with its earlier head office in Chicago. Most historians who are interested in modern transport developments would hesitate to focus on any specific location, suggesting instead that the nation's leading bus operation had diverse and multiple origins. To attribute the founding of a major corporation involved in the movement of passengers throughout the country to particular individuals in one place would give too much emphasis to specific entrepreneurs at a time when managerial capitalism called on a broad range of talents to ensure success.

The early years of long-distance bus transport in the USA offer some support for such a ubiquitous and almost anonymous approach to entrepreneurship. Intercity passenger travel originated in the second decade of the twentieth century when countless venturers throughout the country started up local 'jitney' services using auto sedans between nearby towns.[2] Newspaper reports from states as different and widespread as California, Minnesota, Georgia and Maine reveal a 'grass-roots' activity in which a variety of entrepreneurs who owned or could acquire vehicles were willing to chance their hand in a risk-taking business with a low initial investment. By capitalizing on the surge of mobility resulting from the mass production of automobiles, they hoped to create a new passenger transport boom.

What was the nature of these pioneer ventures? Many bus or 'jitney' owners ran competitive local services, frequently on a customer-demand basis with cash fares paid to the driver. There were no fixed timetables or routes, though some operators who transported men to work started and ended their journeys at either hotels or stores. Others, however, loaded anywhere along the street, often picking up passengers waiting for scheduled electric trains. Word-of-mouth or newspaper advertisements quickly announced the existence of the new service, but there was no guarantee of a regular commitment. If bus men did not get a payload, they might not operate. And those who travelled 'on rubber' rather than by rail had to be satisfied merely with arriving, instead of anticipating a safe and fast journey in comfort. As might be expected, many of these improvised – often one-man – ventures collapsed within a few months, even weeks, if begun in the winter. Competition from like-minded operators or lack of managerial skills usually meant either bankruptcy or sell-out.[3]

In the Iron Range country of northern Minnesota bus operators were both numerous and vigorous in the chaotic years prior to 1920. When Carl Eric Wickman, a former diamond driller, was unable to sell the first car shipped to his Hupmobile agency, he decided to run it as a 'jitney'. Acquiring two partners, Andrew G. Anderson and C.A.A. (Arvid) Heed, both of whom were also previously employed in diamond drilling, he built up a regular service to the nearby mining community of Alice. As business grew, profits were invested in more vehicles. When the partners ran into competition with another bus operator, Ralph Bogan, they decided to merge to form the Hibbing Transportation Company. Business continued to increase and a new corporation, the Mesaba Transportation Company, was formed on 17 December 1915. Acquiring more buses to accommodate a growing number of patrons, the company, now with six members, transported passengers and freight between Hibbing and nearby Alice, and Hibbing and Grand Rapids, taking in the intermediate points of Nashwauk, Marble, Coleraine and Bovey. Trade was prospering.[4]

By December 1917, the Mesaba Transportation Company was the largest bus concern in the Iron Range region. With its fleet of fourteen large buses, the company was able to maintain a half-hourly service to and from Alice, to make hourly trips to Nashwauk and all intermediate points, and to run two round trips daily between Hibbing and Grand Rapids. When roads were passable, the company made two trips a day to Bear River. To ensure that these services could be maintained, the concern had its own garage and repair shop, employing four mechanics to look after the vehicles. By 1918 the company had expanded to a fleet of eighteen buses operating in northern Minnesota. Wickman and his associates were notable entrepreneurs and were attracting regional attention, but they needed to make several business adjustments if they were to expand in the post-war years, for the bus industry was progressing out of its unorganized early stages.[5]

Throughout the nation, in the early and middle 1920s bus owners were bringing system and order to their expanding business. They were also responding to changing external conditions in the shape of regulations imposed by state governments. Within the industry itself, practical mechanical experience and competition among small bus operators, and increasingly among buses and electric and steam railroads brought significant improvements in motor-coaches and in business practices. On the design and technical side, the early sedan car and its successor, the elongated passenger car with one or more additional rows of seats, capable of carrying up to seventeen persons, were gradually replaced by specially-designed buses with better mechanical features and larger and more comfortable carrying capacity. Bus owners had experimented with building their own vehicles but soon found that they could purchase superior buses either from truck or automobile manufacturers.

As early as 1921, the Fageol concern of Oakland, California introduced the first vehicle specifically designed and built as a motor bus – the Fageol Safety Coach – a low-slung four-wheeler with sedan doors along the side, equipped with a powerful Hall-Scott aeroplane-type engine. The following year, the White Manufacturing Company of Cleveland began producing chassis designed for buses. Soon, other motor vehicle manufacturers like the Pierce Arrow Motor Car Company of Buffalo, New York, or Wilcox Trux of Minneapolis started to specialize in manufacturing buses. Still other companies like Eckland Brothers of Minneapolis, Hoover Body Company of York, Pennsylvania, and Champion Auto Equipment Company of Hammond, Indiana, developed an expertise in manufacturing bus bodies. By the mid-1920s new types of buses with more powerful engines, larger seating capacity, improved safety features such as air brakes, and amenities such as heating systems and inside baggage racks were readily available.[6]

Improved vehicles demanded higher investment, and this capital was likely to be available only if bus companies were well organized and were managed efficiently with systematic procedures. As early as the 1860s railroads had found that survival in a larger market required coordination and control of traffic flows, accurate cost accounting, and divisional lines of command. Sixty years later bus firms faced a similar situation. Routes had to be selected carefully and traffic flow analysed; simple and fast connections had to be available; well-trained drivers had to be at the right places at the correct times;

and adequate numbers of mechanics were essential to maintain buses in good running order. Garages were required for storing buses, and terminals were needed to provide waiting areas and ticket sales in the cities, while a network of agencies, frequently located in hotels, drugstores or other retail establishments, were necessary to build up business in rural areas. Furthermore, updated schedules and widespread advertising were indispensable if entrepreneurs were to retain trade, let alone expand it.[7]

Institutional pressures in the form of state regulations also stimulated changes in the early long-distance bus industry. The need for improved roads and the public demand for safety prompted several states, in the years up to 1919, to pass laws licensing vehicles and requiring driver insurance and competency. But, faced by the rapid growth of motor-vehicle transport after the First World War, more states undertook specific and stringent motor-carrier legislation and authorities increasingly became concerned with economic issues like competition and fares. Would-be operators now had to obtain certificates of public convenience and necessity and had to conform to specified financial and business practices and procedures. By 1925 three-quarters of the states, including Minnesota, required that bus companies meet some standards.[8]

Minnesota bus managers were well aware of the nationwide developments in both business organization and government regulations. In the northern Iron Range region, the Mesaba Transportation Company quickly moved into a more mature stage of operations. With the establishment of routes between Hibbing and Duluth and Virginia and Duluth, the company acquired new buses from leading manufacturers. A 45-horsepower White capable of a speed of 50 miles per hour, equipped with steel wheels, ventilators and other improvements was placed on the Duluth run. Soon the latest Fageol model, a twenty-passenger sedan with reclining seats, was added. As service increased not only on the longer routes but also to Grand Rapids and on the shorter routes between the mining locations, the Mesaba Transportation Company also built buses. Using its experience of running vehicles over poor roads in a harsh climate, managers hired local blacksmiths and mechanics to construct vehicles incorporating such special features as a unified heating system.[9]

The firm also formed a subsidiary manufacturing company – the Mesaba Motor Company – to build, repair and sell buses. Most contemporary and subsequent sources have failed to distinguish the Mesaba Transportation Company from the Mesaba Motor Company. The Mesaba Transportation Company was incorporated on 17 December 1915 by C.E. Wickman, R.A.L. Bogan, C.A.A. Heed and Andrew G. Anderson. Its first board of directors also included Dominick Bretto and Fred Lindberg. The Mesaba Motor Company, incorporated on 23 October 1919 by Wickman, Anderson and Edwin C. Eckstrom, was formed to build, repair, and make bus and automobile bodies;

from 1920 onward it also operated buses. In 1922 the interests and personnel of the two companies diverged. Anderson and Bogan purchased the interests of Wickman and Heed in the Mesaba Transportation Company and ceded their interest in the Mesaba Motor Company. Wickman and Heed then moved to Duluth and expanded from there.[10]

The establishment of new, longer routes and better service and the acquisition of new buses were by themselves insufficient to constitute significant changes in operating practices. Hibbing bus operators realized the importance of a well-developed bus infrastructure and took care to establish good mechanical services and passenger amenities. The Mesaba Motor Company's garage building in South Hibbing provided modern facilities, consisting of a repair shop capable of accommodating fifteen vehicles, a paint and main storage garage, reputed to be the best-equipped in northern Minnesota, and two suites of offices. Then, in 1923, to service the long-distance route, the Mesaba Transportation Company built a complex in Duluth, incorporating a garage with space for forty buses, a repair shop, and a body-building shop. They also had plans for waiting-rooms and general offices. Along with these facilities came widely advertised regular schedules. While the novelty of riding on rubber was still adequate to attract many passengers, Hibbing entrepreneurs realized that to build up and maintain a steady trade in the face of competition from automobiles and steam and electric trains, they had to run both an economical and an attractive service.[11]

Though Hibbing was soon recognized for the stability and efficiency of its bus transport, it was not alone. As yet there was nothing unique about either its character or its personnel. Other Minnesota communities also had successful track records. At Eveleth in the northeastern part of the state, the Range Rapid Transit operated by brothers John and Kent Fitzgerald served the eastern Mesabi Range and had good connections to Duluth, while the White Bus Lines, not to be confused with the Cleveland manufacturer, served the territory north of Lake Superior. In the southeastern part of the state the Jefferson Highway Transportation Company, under the leadership of E.L. Bryant and Rodney S. Dimmock, was steadily extending important routes toward points in Iowa and North Dakota. The Gopher Coach Lines operated between the Twin Cities and both Duluth and Mankato, while the Twin Cities & Southern pioneered bus operations from Minneapolis and St Paul to various points in Wisconsin. There were, indeed, several ambitious bus owners running sound business lines, each contributing to the carrying of 10 million passengers in the state in 1922. Even further afield, California and Ohio operators, carrying 14 million and nearly 12 million passengers respectively, also offered examples of industrious intercity bus managing.[12]

Why, then, should the major American bus corporation – Greyhound – choose to find its roots in northern Minnesota and in Hibbing in particular? The

answer lies in the merging of strong and thriving local companies into statewide
enterprises, the involvement of the railroads primarily as allies of bus operators
rather than competitors, further company amalgamations stimulated in part by
state regulations, and finally entrepreneurial drive by both bus managers and
investment financiers in the late 1920s.

Mergers, rather than neighbourly cooperation between small companies to
carry passengers long distances, were essential as bus men broadened their
horizons. Entrepreneurs could profitably extend and expand their business only
through more unified operating systems, with cost-effective route planning,
timetables and centralized management of vehicle and driver availability.
Competition could and did stimulate better services for both local and longer-
distance travellers. But with the growing popularity of bus transport and the
increasing consumer demands for quality service, companies had to sink
additional capital into both vehicles and permanent structures such as garages
and terminals. Such financial outlays demanded larger-scale ventures.[13]

Early mergers in Minnesota took place between 1923 and 1925. Late in
1922, Eric Wickman, still heading the Mesaba Motor Company, moved to
Duluth. He bought the White Bus Lines, which maintained routes from Duluth
to Grand Marais on the north shore, to Virginia on the eastern range, and to
Minneapolis. As northern Minnesota's most substantial bus concern, the firm
soon turned its ambitions southward. Wickman and others incorporated a
new company, Northland Transportation, on 20 December 1924; with this
transfusion of new capital, the young corporation shortly purchased the Mesaba
Motor Company. The Northland, under the presidency of Wickman, expanded
rapidly. In 1925 the most significant acquisition of routes took place when the
Jefferson Highway Transportation Company, recently acquired by Edgar Zelle,
sold its northern lines to the Northland. Zelle retained and expanded the
Jefferson's lines in central and southeastern Minnesota. The most important
acquisition of personnel took place when the Northland acquired the Superior-
White Company and its major entrepreneur, Orville S. Caesar. Caesar's
mechanical skills, business acumen and ambition would eventually lead him to
the presidency of the Greyhound Corporation. Minnesota bus operators were
prepared to launch into big business with the Northland.[14]

But in 1925 the impact of railroad activity and of state regulations had a
marked effect on the conduct and decisions of independent bus companies.
Already in the early 1920s electric and steam railroads generally were voicing
concern that bus services contributed to the decline in the number of their
passengers. In an attempt to curb motor-coach competition, several major
railroads cut their fares and agitated for more stringent regulations and
higher taxation of road vehicles. Other companies, taking a more positive
and constructive position, accepted the economic facts that motor coaches
offered advantages of greater flexibility and cheaper running costs, especially

for short- and intermediate-haul traffic, and decided to use buses as auxiliaries to or even in lieu of some trains. Their view was that cooperation was a more fruitful path to pursue than uneconomic competition or an attempt to curb transport technology by regulation.[15]

In Minnesota, the Great Northern, under its forward-looking president Ralph Budd, was one of these railroads. In May 1925, after much discussion and analysis of the problems and possibilities of a rate war with competing bus lines, Budd organized two subsidiary companies, capitalized at $2 million, to carry passengers and freight. While the Minnesota Railroad and Warehouse Commission was still considering whether to grant these companies certificates of convenience and necessity, the Great Northern management abandoned its plans to establish new motor companies in favour of buying into the major existing independent firm, the Northland. Now Budd, Wickman and Caesar used railroad capital and tapped new outside sources of finance to weld together a $2.5 million merger of eight independent lines, creating a huge operation dominating the region north and west of the Twin Cities of St Paul and Minneapolis. By the end of 1925 the Northland Transportation Company ran some 150 buses operating over 2,625 miles of rural route, and it dominated motor transport in those parts of Minnesota served by the Great Northern.[16]

Meanwhile, other railroad companies with routes in Minnesota were cutting rates in an attempt to retain passenger traffic. And in 1925, when the state government started to regulate motor carriers by licensing them, many railroads either petitioned the Railroad and Warehouse Commission for monopoly rights on their routes, on the grounds that there was insufficient public necessity for any proposed competing bus services, or they abandoned uneconomic lines. Other railroads accepted the presence of bus lines but argued that these should be taxed in the same way as the rail passenger services, which were losing money. When the regulatory commission had examined all the arguments, its decision to grant thirty-five bus licences while denying only four indicated that bus as well as rail transport was an essential part of the economy and was here to stay. New state rules about safety, facilities, accounts, rates and schedules were to create difficulties for undercapitalized and poorly-managed firms that wished to stay in business, but motor-coach operation was no longer an adventure. It was an organized and systematic business enterprise.[17]

Consolidation of independent bus companies, intervention by railroads in bus operations, and state regulation of motor carriers were common in many states. Even though Minnesota was one of the national leaders in long-distance bus activity, the genealogical linkage to the modern Greyhound Corporation still had to be forged more firmly during the next few years. The connections would be made through the Northland Transportation Company – indirectly through the entrepreneurial activity of the company's leading bus managers and then directly through a corporate reorganization – with the formation of

Northland Greyhound Lines, Incorporated, which became part of the emerging Greyhound system.

In Minnesota, the Northland strengthened its position as the dominant operator of passenger buses in the late 1920s. Great Northern ownership brought capital for investment in new routes and new equipment. In 1926, its first year of operation, Northland acquired six more bus companies with a route mileage of 1848 and expended $500,000 for new vehicles. In the following year the purchase of the Mesaba Railway Coach Company gave the Northland the bus line paralleling the electric line, soon to be abandoned, between Hibbing and Gilbert on the Iron Range. Route extensions provided better service from the Twin Cities to points in central and northern Minnesota and more buses were added to the existing large fleet.

The year 1928 brought further activity; the Northland bought a large share of the routes belonging to the Mesaba Transportation Company, the last major independent operator in the Iron Range country. For six years after 1922 this firm had been a partnership between Andrew Anderson and Ralph Bogan. When that partnership dissolved in 1928, Anderson bought Bogan's share but sold Bogan his share in an Indiana bus company. Northland thus acquired most of the Mesaba company's routes from Anderson, who continued to operate the North and South Hibbing bus line. Another $500,000 was spent on new vehicles. Northland was going from strength to strength; when duplicate routes had been eliminated, the system's lines extended over 3,000 miles from Minneapolis and St Paul to most major cities in Minnesota, except those in the southeastern section, and to cities in neighbouring Wisconsin, Canada and the Dakotas. During 1928 the fleet of 127 buses travelled 8,285,138 miles and carried 3,147,230 people. Other bus companies were active in Minnesota, but the Northland took pride of place.[18]

But the Northland was yet to become part of the Motor Transit Corporation, a consolidation that would form the basis of the Greyhound Corporation – and this bus giant still had to take on a strong Minnesotan leadership. Eric Wickman, president of the Northland, and Glenn W. Traer, of the Minneapolis investment securities firm of Lane, Piper & Jaffray, would provide the main managerial and financial links from Minnesota to the Motor Transit Corporation in Chicago. Two other successful bus operators, Edwin C. Eckstrom, one of Wickman's former Hibbing partners who had moved to Michigan and then to Chicago, and Orville Caesar who moved from the Northland headquarters in Minneapolis to Chicago in 1927, would provide the linkage back to Minnesota. The shared experiences of these men, together with the assistance of other Minnesotans – bus operator Ralph Bogan, banker Richard L. Griggs, Ivan Bowen, formerly of the Minnesota Railroad and Warehouse Commission, Christian Steen, formerly of Lane, Piper & Jaffray, and Minneapolis accountants E.M. Rumpf and R.B. Phillips, of Touche, Nevan

& Company – gave the emerging Greyhound Corporation its firm connections to the state.[19]

Wickman's experience in managing bus companies was not limited to Minnesota. As early as 1924 he had been involved in running lines in Michigan, Wisconsin, Illinois and Indiana. Clearly, he envisaged a strong future for bus transportation, but his expansionary plans required more capital than could be generated by his early business profits. Initially he had looked for and found financial support from local banks. Richard Griggs, vice-president of the Northern National Bank of Duluth and treasurer of the Northern Trust Company, was particularly helpful during the mid-1920s, but by that time the financing of bus operations on a statewide or regional scale required the services of specialized investment bankers. Here Wickman was fortunate in attracting the services of Glenn Traer. Impressed by the performance of bus firms in Minnesota and by their relatively harmonious relationships with the railroads, Traer took a decisive role in forming and in marketing the stock of existing companies like the Northland and in amalgamating lines.[20]

Following successful sales of Northland Transportation stock, Traer ambitiously turned to the regional scene with the capitalization of the Motor Transit Corporation. This concern had been organized in September 1926 as a $10 million holding company in the field of bus transportation, primarily in the Middle West. Motor Transit had been formed by acquiring Eckstrom's Safety Motor Coach Lines of Michigan and two other companies, the Interstate Stages Inc., operating from Chicago to Detroit, and the Transportation Securities Company, an equipment finance concern. Eckstrom had successfully built up a bus company in western Michigan, which he ran under the name of Greyhound Lines. When he moved to Chicago, he sought to acquire new routes by attracting both Chicago and Minneapolis money and skills. He relied partially on men in Minnesota because he had long-standing contacts there and he knew that bus transport in that northern state was in the forefront of technological and managerial developments. Wickman was to provide the business experience; Lane, Piper & Jaffray furnished investment services; and the Northern Trust Company of Duluth contributed some financial underwriting.[21]

Traer had marketed the early issue of Motor Transit Corporation stock in the spring of 1927. Expansion was rapid, and during the year the corporation extended the routes of its original bus subsidiaries. It purchased three lines running out of Chicago: the Royal Rapid Transit Company to Janesville, Wisconsin, the Mohawk Stage Lines to northern Illinois, and the Purple Swan Safety Coach Lines to St Louis and Kansas City. When Edwin Eckstrom withdrew from Motor Transit in July to run the Southland Greyhound lines in Texas, Orville Caesar, superintendent of the Northland Transportation Company in Minneapolis, moved to Chicago to become president of Motor

Transit. More capital was needed in 1928 to acquire further routes, to buy new vehicles, and to improve services and facilities.

Once again Motor Transit, which was now using the name Greyhound throughout the system, drew on the services of the Minneapolis investment firm. In the summer of 1928, at a meeting held to familiarize salesmen and investors with the new financing, Harry C. Piper, vice-president of Lane, Piper & Jaffray, stated that expansion had been faster than anticipated. Motor Transit had moved rapidly in order to hold its position and get into new territory before it was tied up by competing systems. He expected to build up revenues once the corporation had established its network.[22]

The acquisitions of the Motor Transit Corporation, or the Greyhound Corporation as it more frequently became known, were almost breathtaking. From a total motor-coach mileage of 5 million in 1927, the figures increased to 20 million in 1929. In 1928 the corporation acquired nine operating subsidiaries, most of which were east of Chicago. By the end of the year it controlled, through these acquisitions, a strong system of lines between Chicago and Pittsburgh.

In 1929, stimulated by the prospect of a national bus service, Greyhound started to buy substantial minority interests in bus companies and their subsidiaries in other parts of the USA. First purchasing the companies of the Pioneer Yelloway System, a large regional network whose owner, Wesley E. Travis, had inaugurated the first transcontinental bus service, Greyhound then set up a new company, Pacific Greyhound, on the West Coast. In the South, Greyhound acquired an interest in the Southland Transportation Company and in the East purchased the Gray Line and part of the Colonial Motor Coach company to form Eastern Greyhound Lines.

In the North, Greyhound bought into the Northland Transportation Company, which was then reorganized as Northland Greyhound Lines. The Great Northern Railway took, as part payment of its stock, a 30 per cent interest in the common stock of Northland Greyhound. The leading bus company in the Upper Midwest was now an integral part of a sprawling empire. Because Northland's managers had been influential in stimulating the nationwide merger and were to take an active role in national decisions in years to come, Greyhound thus looked north to its foundations.[23]

Minnesota contributions to the birth of this big intercity bus organization were strong. Within fifteen years, entrepreneurs in the Iron Range country had built up a steady and reliable transportation network. Similar developments took place elsewhere in the second decade of this century,[24] but by the early 1920s northern Minnesota bus executives exuded an air of confidence and stability which was evident in only a few other parts of the USA. They extended their dynamic entrepreneurial skills to forming a national consolidation. At the end of the twentieth century Greyhound Boulevard and the Greyhound Bus

Origin Museum both offered concrete testimony to the Iron Range origins of the national long-distance bus industry.

Notes

1. *Hibbing Daily Tribune*, 29 July, pp. 1, 10, 1 August, p. 1, both in 1984; *Go Greyhound*, **19**(2) (1984), p. 20.

2. In California auto owners pulled up at streetcar stops and offered rides for a 'jitney' or nickel. The name 'jitney' was frequently ascribed to the early passenger vehicles used before buses were designed; in 1915 the newly incorporated Mesaba Transportation Company was described as a 'jitney' company. *Hibbing Daily Tribune*, 17 December 1915, p. 4.

3. A.E. Meier and J.P. Hoschek (1975), *Over the Road: A History of Intercity Bus Transportation in the United States*, Upper Montclair, NJ, pp. 1–9; B.B. Crandall (1954), *The Growth of the Intercity Bus Industry*, Syracuse, NY, pp. 6–13; F.K. Edwards (1933), *Principles of Motor Transportation*, New York, pp. 5–9.

4. 'Statement of Mr Wickman in connection with his operation of the Northland Bus Company and predecessors of the Northland Bus Company', [15 May 1925], Northland Greyhound Lines, Inc. (Delaware), in Great Northern Railway Company Records, Minnesota Historical Society, (hereafter cited as GNR); F.H. Schultz (c. 1954), 'Greyhound, The Greatest Name on the Highway', thesis, pp. 5–7, and C.G. Schultz, 'Notes on Son's Thesis', folder 3, box 3, both in Greyhound Corporation Records, American Heritage Center Archives, University of Wyoming, Laramie, (hereafter cited as GCR); 'Jitney into Giant', *Fortune*, **10**(2) (1934), pp. 42–3, 110; H.V. Anderson (c. 1954), 'A History of the Beginnings of the Bus Industry with Grass Roots in St Louis County', unpublished manuscript, pp. 5–14; *Hibbing Daily Tribune*, 18 December 1915, p. 5; Minnesota, Articles of Incorporation, Book B–4, p. 22 in Secretary of State's office, St Paul. W. Van Brunt (1921), *Duluth and St Louis County, Minnesota*, Chicago and New York: **2**, p. 567; **3**, pp. 1059,1120.

5. 'Statement of Mr Wickman', [15 May 1925], GNR; Anderson, 'Beginnings of the Bus Industry', pp. 5–13; *Mesaba Ore and Hibbing News*, 21 December 1917, Sec. 2, p. 8.

6. *Bus Transportation*, **1–4** (1922–1925), (hereafter cited as *BT*), contains practical articles on various facets of bus construction as well as advertisements by manufacturers. Meier and Hoschek, *Over the Road*, pp. 17–25, provide general insights. Minnesota viewpoints can be found in a publication of the Minnesota Motor Bus Association, *Travel by Bus*, **1–3** (1924–1926), (hereafter cited as *TbB*), and in taped oral history interviews of retired bus drivers and old residents of the Iron Range region: A.B. Lennartson, 16 December 1974; P.D. Silliman, 18 June 1975; A. Tamadge, 24 October 1975; M. Hemphill, 7 June 1976 – all in Iron Range Research Center, Chisholm, MN.

7. A.D. Chandler, Jr (1977), *The Visible Hand: The Managerial Revolution in American Business*, Cambridge, MA, is the standard authority on the modernization of business practices. For the bus industry, see numerous articles in *BT*, **1–4** (1922–1925); by 1932 this periodical had compiled a specialized study, *Making Bus Operations Pay*, New York. Some technical manuals like P. White (1923), *Motor Transportation of Merchandise and Passengers*, New York, pp. 278–362, also offer guidance.

8. General discussions of the state regulation of motor carriers can be found in Crandall, *Intercity Bus Industry*, pp. 38–97; S. Szto (1934), *Federal and State Regulation of Motor Carrier Rates and Services*, Philadelphia, pp. 9–189; J.J. George (1929), *Motor Carrier Regulation in the United States*, Spartanburg, SC, pp. 1–213. More detailed information is available in *BT*, **1–4** (1922–1925), and *Railway Age*, **70–79** (1921–1925), (hereafter cited as *RA*); Minnesota, *Laws*, 1925, pp. 178–85. For a more detailed discussion of state regulation see chapter 7, 'The Motor Carrier Act of 1935: The Origins and Establishment of Federal Regulation of the Interstate Bus Industry in the United States', pp. 138–40.

9. *Hibbing Daily Tribune*, 21 May, p. 5; 3 June, pp. 1, 8; 23 September, p. 3, all in 1921; 21 January, p. 8; 15 February, p. 1; 14 March, p. 8; 29 April, p. 2; 13 June, p. 2; 9 August, p. 4; 21 September, p. 1; 29 December, p. 7, all in 1922. *The Truck And Bus Owner*, **June** (1923), p. 7; **August** (1923), p. 9 (hereafter cited as *T&BO*).

10. Articles of Incorporation, book B–4, p. 22 and book H–4, p. 584; 'History', c. 1927, Northland Transportation Company in GNR; *Hibbing Daily Tribune*, 21 September 1922, p. 1; *T&BO*, **February** (1923), p. 8.

11. *Hibbing Daily Tribune*, 20 April, p. 23; 23 September, p. 3, both in 1921; 29 April, p. 2; 21 September, p. 1, both in 1922; 7 April, pp. 1 and 3; 13 July, p. 1; 30 August, p. 2, all in 1923.

12. *Hibbing Daily Tribune*, 9 August, p. 4; 21 September, p. 1, both in 1922; 13 February, p. 3; 23 October, p. 2, both in 1923. *Minneapolis Journal*, 3 February 1924, sec. 3; 'Statement of Issue of Stock for The Jefferson Highway Transportation Company, 1923', and *Jefferson Highway Transportation Company* (c. 1921), both in E.F. Zelle Records, Jefferson Lines Inc., Minneapolis. *T&BO*, **December** (1922), p. 23; **January** (1923), p. 8; **February** (1923), pp. 8, 9; **April** (1923), p. 7; **June** (1923), pp. 6, 7, 8; **September** (1923), p. 5. *BT*, **2**(1) (1923), pp. 58; **2**(3) (1923), p. 163; **3** (1924), pp. 435, 439. *The Northland Greyhound Lines* (1929), p. 5 in Northland Greyhound Lines Inc. (Delaware), GNR; L.A. Rossman (1940), *A Romance of Transportation*, Grand Rapids, MN, pp. 4–7.

13. *BT*, **4**(1) (1925), pp. 25, 47, 48; **4**(2) (1925), p. 64; **4**(3) (1925), p. 147; **4**(6) (1925), p. 261. Crandall, *Intercity Bus Industry*, pp. 88–94. Bus routes increased from 179,415 miles in 1924, the first year statistics are available, to 250,391 in 1925; National Association of Motor Bus Operators (NAMBO) (1927), *Bus Facts for 1927*, Washington, DC, p. 3.

14. A.L. Janes, Assistant General Council, to R. Budd, President, 9, 20 June 1925, President's Subject File 11532 and 'History', c. 1927, Northland Transportation Company (Minnesota), both in GNR; Articles of Incorporation, book Q–4, p. 795. *Hibbing Daily Tribune*, 13 February 1923, p. 3; 1 February, p. 1; 31 May, p. 12; 18 November, p. 2 all in 1924. *Minneapolis Journal*, Travel and Resort Sec., 1 June, p. 1; General News Sec., 7 December, p. 1, both in 1924; 13 May 1925, pp. 1, 7. *T&BO*, **1–2** (1922–1924); *TbB*, **1–2** (1924–5); Rossman, *Romance of Transportation*, p. 11; A.S. Genet (1958), 'Profile of Greyhound!' *The Greyhound Corporation*, New York, pp. 13,14. More information on the Jefferson Highway Transportation Company is available in chapter 6, 'Minnesota's "Mr Bus": Edgar F. Zelle and the Jefferson Highway Transportation Company', pp. 107–10.

15. *RA*, **72–85** (1921–1927), contains lengthy discussions of the attitudes of particular railroads to bus transport. There was also considerable private discussion among railroad officials; see, for example, a circular letter from the General Superintendent of the Illinois Central Railroad to twelve railroads,

18 January 1926, together with a memorandum, 'Suggestions for the Committee on How To Meet Motor Truck and Motor Bus Competition', President's Subject File 11532, GNR.

16. Memorandum from G.H. Hess, Jr, comptroller, concerning the Great Northern's involvement with the Northland Transportation Company, 29 December 1925; S.O. Dunn, editor of *Railway Age*, to Budd, 27 November, 8 December, both 1925; Budd to Dunn, 2 December 1925; S.M. Felton, president of Chicago Great Western Railroad Company, to Budd, 26 September 1925; *Canadian Railway and Marine World*, **September** (1926), p. 493 – all in President's Subject File 11532, GNR; Van Brunt, *Duluth*, **1**, p. 460. *Minneapolis Journal*, 21 May, p. 1; 11 June, p. 26; 15 June, p. 1; 19 June, p. 1; 1 November, pp. 1, 4, all in 1925; 7 February 1926, Auto Sec., p. 7. *RA*, **80**(25) (1926), p. 1401; *BT*, **5**(6) (1926), p. 313. More information on the relationship of the Great Northern Railway to independent bus companies can be found in M. Walsh, 'Coordination, Cooperation or Competition: The Great Northern Railway and Bus Transportation in the 1920s' in R. Cameron and L.F. Schnore (eds) (1991), *Cities and Markets. Studies in the Organization of Human Space*, Lanham, MD, p. 163–99.

17. Budd to M. Thorpe, editor of *The Nation's Business*, 8 December 1925, President's Subject File 11532, GNR. *Minneapolis Journal*, 19 May, p. 17; 14 July, p. 1; 15 July, p. 15; 16 July, p. 13; 31 July, pp. 1, 8; 16 August, p. 1; 5 September, p. 1; 20 September, pp. 1, 6; 4 October, pp. 1, 8; 19 October, p. 2; 22 October, pp. 1, 4; 26 October, p. 21; 3 November, p. 4; 6 December, Sec. 2, p. 2, all in 1925; 7 February, Auto Sec., p. 7; 13 June, p. 3, both 1926. Minnesota, Railroad and Warehouse Commission, Auto Transportation Company Division, *Biennial Report*, (1926), p. 167 (hereafter cited as MR&WC, ATCD, *BR*).

18. Northland Greyhound Lines, Inc., 'Acquisition of Routes by Purchase', and 'Issue of Stock Notice', August 1929, both in Northland Greyhound Lines, Inc., (Delaware), GNC; 'The Motor Bus and Commercial Transportation', abstract of an address by L.A. Rossman to the Iowa Electric Railway Association, Cedar Rapids, 8 November 1928, and 'Northland Transportation Company', a memorandum by C.E. Wickman, April, 1927, President's Subject File 11532, GNC. *BT*, **6**(3) (1927), pp. 176; **6**(5) (1927), p. 291; **7**(3) (1927), p. 174. MR&WC, ATCD, *BR*, (1928), pp. 160, 307, 308, 319; *Hibbing Daily Tribune*, 1 February, p. 8; 3 February, p. 13, both in 1928.

19. 'Statement of Mr Wickman', [15 May 1925]; W.R. Fowler, Jr, advertising department of Motor Transit Corporation, to C.E. Doherty, 10 September 1925, includes a proposed newspaper article, in correspondence file, 1927–1928, GCR; *Minneapolis Journal*, City Life sec., 1 July 1928, p. 3; *Mesabi Daily News*, 15 February 1962, in 'Bus Lines', clippings file, Northeast Minnesota Historical Center, Duluth. *The Greyhound Traveler*, **June** (1929), p. 10, 11, 28; **February** (1930), pp. 16, 17, 29; *Motor Bus Traveler*, **April** (1930), p. 22, 23, 40; *BT*, **6**(8) (1927), p. 465.

20. Lane, Piper & Jaffray, Inc., *Business Survey*, 20 October 1927, copy in President's Subject File 11532, GNR; 'Greyhound Bus – Motor Transit', 'Banking', in Richard L. Griggs Papers, Northeast Minnesota Historical Center; interviews with Harry Piper, Jr, and Ruth Cranston, 1983, oral history transcripts in offices of Pine and Mundale, Inc. (1986), authors of *Ticker Tape Tales: Piper, Jaffray & Hopwood, 1895–1985*, Minneapolis. *Hibbing Daily Tribune*, 31 May, p. 12; 18 November, p. 2, both in 1924. *Greyhound Traveler*, **June** (1929), pp. 10, 11, 28; *Encyclopedia of American Biography*, new series, New York, **31** (1961), pp. 7, 8; *Duluth City Directory*, (1925), p. 291.

21. 'Corporate History of the Greyhound Corporation and Affiliated Companies', 26 September 1930, and Report of Sales Meeting, 30 April 1927, Miscellaneous File, both in GCR; Schultz, 'Greyhound, The Greatest Name', pp. 8–10; *BT*, **5**(12) (1926), p. 707; **6**(8) (1927), p. 465. 'Jitney into Giant', *Fortune*, **10**(2) (1934), pp. 110, 113.
22. Motor Transit Corporation, 'Issue of Stock Notice', 20 April 1927, President's Subject File 11532, GNR; 'Corporate History of Greyhound' and 'Sales Meeting, Motor Transit Corporation', being procedures of a meeting to discuss motor transit financing, Summer, 1928, both in Miscellaneous File, GCR. *BT*, **6**(8) (1927), p. 465; 7(2) (1928), p. 81. *Minneapolis City Directory* (1928), p. 1942.
23. 'Corporate History of Greyhound'; Greyhound Corporation, 'New Issue of Stock Notification' and 'Accompanying Letter', March, 1930, and 'Supplementary Information for Salesmen: The Greyhound Corporation', 27 February 1930, GCR; Stock Issue, Certificate of Incorporation, 1929, Northland Greyhound Lines, Inc. (Delaware), GNR; *The Greyhound Limited*, **September** (1929), p. 1, in President's Subject File 11532, GNR. *BT*, **8**(3) (1929), pp. 168; **8**(6) (1929), pp. 350–52; **8**(9) (1929), p. 509. J.B. Walker (1930), 'Selling More Rides' in *RA*, **88**(12), pp. 725–8; Schultz, 'Greyhound, The Greatest Name', pp. 10–15.
24. California was the other leading pioneer state in long-distance bus travel. Here, too, companies merged and then became part of the Greyhound Corporation. Gregory Thompson has undertaken extensive work on bus and rail competition and cooperation in California. See G.L. Thompson, *The Passenger Train in the Motor Age. California's Rail and Bus Industries 1910–1941*, Columbus, OH, and G.L. Thompson, 'Planning Beats the Market: The Case of Pacific Greyhound Lines in the 1930s', *Journal of Planning Education and Research*, **13** (1993), pp. 33–49. Thompson, like myself, was very fortunate in obtaining access to several private collections, one of which, Railroad Commission of California (1938), *Santa Fe Case*, he used to great effect.

5   Iowa's Bus Queen:
Helen M. Schultz and the Red Ball Transportation Company

Bus transport emerged in the USA in the 1910s and 1920s primarily as a small-scale, often family,enterprise. That has made its early history difficult to trace. The few narratives that have been published so far suggest that those who entered the bus business during its early years faced fierce competition, poor trade prospects, inadequate vehicles, bad roads and daredevil attitudes. Bus pioneers were usually men. Of the few women who did take up the challenge, the majority inherited their businesses from their husbands or their fathers and continued to run the undertakings as local ventures. Only occasionally did a female entrepreneur set up a bus company in her own right and experience the rough-and-tumble from the start.[1] Among the most prominent of those pioneers was an Iowa woman who came to be known nationally at the time as 'Iowa's Bus Queen'.

Helen Schultz and the Red Ball Transportation Company, which she established in 1922, encountered a number of challenges in the pioneering era in bus transport. First, she had to secure capital in the face of several obstacles. Then there was the battle with the state legislature and regulatory commission over the licensing of routes and other rules. Finally, operating conditions and competition from regional carriers created continuing financial stress and eventually induced her to sell her business to a regional competitor. Schultz confronted each of these obstacles in her own indomitable manner. Having established her own company, she relished the fight to keep it going. She even found ways to turn her gender, which in some ways was an entrepreneurial liability, into a public relations asset.

Helen Mary Schultz was born on 12 February 1898, the second child and elder daughter of Joseph and Mary Schultz who farmed near Nashua, Iowa, and Shell Lake, Wisconsin. She was always a strong-willed and dominant member of the family. After completing her education in local schools, she left home to attend business college in Duluth, then to earn her living as a stenographer, a respectable occupation for a young single woman in the early years of the twentieth century.[2]

The series of temporary positions Schultz held in northern Minnesota and then in California proved fortuitous for her later career. In northern Minnesota she worked for the Butler Brothers, building contractors, where she encountered a future supporter in Emmett Butler. At the offices of the Duluth, South Shore & Atlantic Railroad Company she picked up rudimentary knowledge about rail transport. Moving on to California, reputedly to visit a girl friend from college, she 'temped' at yet another rail company office, the Santa Fe in Stockton, and then for the Cunard Steamship Lines in San Francisco. These jobs not only exposed her to the established world of transportation, but also to the emergence of the new motor services provided by pioneer bus companies. The Iron Range country in northern Minnesota and the Stockton–San Francisco Bay corridor in northern California were renowned in the contemporary press for the early development of bus transport.[3]

By 1921 Helen Schultz had travelled widely and had gained valuable work experience. She was now eager to be her own boss. As an observant and outgoing person she had witnessed the adventure and the potential of burgeoning bus lines. Although most bus companies were operated by men, conventions were not yet firmly established in this new arena. Here was an opportunity to be seized. She could start her business in northern Iowa where she would have family support and where there were few, if any, bus rivals.[4]

The opportunity was real, but Schultz faced several obstacles to realizing her dream. She would have to establish routes in a state notorious for its impassable mud roads during frequent bouts of bad weather; and the established modes of transport, namely the electric and steam railroads, were unlikely to accept buses without a fight. If the bus business did begin to look viable, rival bus companies were likely to emerge. There was much to be considered. But first, before she could establish a bus company, she needed to secure capital.

Schultz needed a capital sum of $500 for a vehicle, a reserve to cover the monthly payments on the bus and some cash to pay her drivers, to advertise in the local newspapers and to rent an office and depot.[5] She hoped the line would quickly return some income from which she could furnish her subsequent running costs. Where could she get capital for a speculative business in a period when women were rarely financially independent and were not seen as a good economic risk?

Schultz's male contemporaries in the 1910s and 1920s often started up in a bus business by acquiring a second-hand auto and then operating a taxi-like service. If they got sufficient trade they then placed a deposit on a larger, stretched-out vehicle or acquired another second-hand vehicle to run on a different short-distance route. These men had either used their small savings to acquire their initial vehicle or had persuaded a male friend or possibly a local bank manager to make them a loan. They then drove and maintained their autos themselves. Their modest operating costs consisted mainly of spare parts, especially tyres, and gasoline. They paid for such costs out of the income generated by their bus service. If they were successful, they could expand.[6]

Schultz herself had some savings from her employment as a stenographer, but these were not adequate to start a business. Stenographers generally earned from $17.50 to $35.00 per week, but living expenses incurred in both Minnesota and California had eaten into her wages. Her father owned land in Iowa and Wisconsin, but his capital was locked up in his farms so he was more likely to offer emotional than financial support. Banks generally were reluctant to loan money to single women or for untried new ventures. Schultz needed a private backer. Fortunately, she had impressed Emmett Butler, the building contractor for whom she had worked in northern Minnesota. He was able to offer risk capital both at the onset of her bus venture and in its early years when further financing was needed for expansion.[7]

With the necessary capital secured, Schultz incorporated the Red Ball Transportation Company, optimistically named after the Red Ball Route, now Highway 218, a 600-mile route that started in St Paul, Minnesota and ended up in St Louis, Missouri. She then purchased a vehicle from White Manufacturers, who had welded a bus body on to a truck chassis, a normal practice in a period when specialized bus manufacturers were rare. Relying on word-of-mouth publicity, Schultz started local operation in April 1922 with two round trips daily between Charles City and Waterloo. Her bus picked up passengers not only from stated points but also when flagged down.[8]

Within days of making the first run, Schultz was in trouble. Heavy rain broke up the dirt road leaving her only bus stranded for two weeks halfway between Charles City and Nashua, in mud up to the axles. Meanwhile, her driver, her brother Magnus, quit the risky venture in despair. Schultz remained at the depot in Charles City, parrying questions about the future of her bus line. She was determined to continue. She had both her self-respect and her capital investment to salvage.[9]

When the weather allowed the bus to be rescued she hired a driver to help make the bus runs, and she gradually built up a clientele that included women shoppers and travelling salesmen. But traffic was not large enough to provide a sound income. She needed to open a route to Mason City, the manufacturing and trading centre, to attract more customers. As an additional incentive there was a concrete road from Mason City to the summer resort of Clear Lake, and a paved road under construction to Charles City. Such roads would eliminate many obstacles and delays. But Schultz needed another bus. Fortunately, the sales representative from the White Company was anxious to sell more vehicles and offered a contract on a second bus. As business grew she acquired a third vehicle later that year for the evening express run from Mason City to Waterloo. By that time her brother Magnus felt confident enough about the prospects of the company to re-enter the business as her partner.[10]

Schultz may have emerged from the mud to establish her business, but she was by no means secure in 1922. The Speedway Motor Coach Company soon provided fierce competition. Operated by a Chicago entrepreneur who also recognized Mason City's potential as a bus entrepôt, that company quickly established a route to Charles City. It attempted to squeeze out the Red Ball Company by running its buses on a slightly earlier schedule – a tactic that led to several altercations between the bus drivers of the two companies and occasional overnight jail visits. Such competition was 'like a nightmare' to Helen Schultz, but, she later recalled, 'my jaw was set and my drivers were loyal'. She moved her main office from Charles City to Mason City, thereby providing a convenient bus depot as well as a headquarters from which she could orchestrate a publicity campaign. She quickly demonstrated the advantages of better motor vehicles and her longer through services to Waterloo. The out-of-town bus company retired temporarily, only to return later in the year with faster and better vehicles. By then, however, Schultz had acquired more buses, was offering more frequent service, and had started a new route from Mason City to Des Moines. She was building a reputation for reliability, and her presence as a local entrepreneur enabled her to outmanoeuvre interlopers.[11]

Helen Schultz had managed to fend off an intercity bus rival during her first year of business, but competition was not her only operating problem. She still faced considerable difficulties in establishing the legitimacy of her business in some of the towns she served. When she started her company, bus operations in Iowa were not regulated. Using local ordinances, town and city governments decided whether to impose a tax or a license fee or whether to allow buses free use of the urban streets. A few cities, such as Waterloo, welcomed the new mode of transport as a means of enhancing their economic position, but most towns were worried about the expenses involved and demanded some user fee. Schultz was prepared to pay a vehicle tax, but she was not prepared to pay several local taxes of varying amounts. She became caught up in legal cases contesting local ordinances that imposed fees. She was not alone in this struggle. For example, two of her rivals, the Speedway Company and the Star Transportation Company, both of Mason City, had carried out successful challenges to local licence fees. By the end of 1922 it became apparent that the state needed motor-carrier legislation that would apply uniformly throughout Iowa and would be monitored by a state government authority.[12]

In April 1923 the Iowa General Assembly vested the Iowa Board of Railroad Commissioners with the power to prescribe regulations for the operation of motor-carrier lines. Like the railroads, motor-carriers would be subject to rules established in the public interest. All intercity bus lines would have to have a certificate authorizing their business and they would have to provide information on their schedules and their property. They would also have to keep records of their business and pay the required taxes. Schultz was entitled to operate under this new law because she had 'grandfather rights', but in order to obtain her certificate she needed to show that she was already in business before the law went into effect. She could do that in most places, but she also had to establish that her routes were 'convenient'. That would be more difficult.[13]

When Schultz had started her bus line in 1922 there was already a viable transport network in northeastern Iowa. Steam railroads, electric interurbans and the automobile offered residents mobility over both short and longer distances. For example, Mason City had six passenger-carrying railroads, Waterloo four and Charles City three. To connect with these lines, and for travelling from one local community to another, rural Iowans were turning from the farm buggy to the automobile, especially Ford's Model T. Better roads enabled such auto usage to become more reliable.[14] The 'convenience' of the Red Ball Transportation Company would be challenged on the grounds that it was stealing established passenger business.

The initial challenge came from the electric interurban, the Mason City and Clear Lake which charged that the Red Ball Transportation Company had not been operating in good faith on a specific route between Mason City and Clear Lake prior to 14 April 1923 when the motor-vehicle legislation went into effect. Helen Schultz and her brother needed to prove to the satisfaction of the Iowa Board of Railroad Commissioners that they had established that service. The issue turned on the bus company's frequent and special service to the summer resort of Clear Lake during the summer of 1923 (after the 14 April cut-off date). If the electric railway company opposed that service because adequate provision already existed, then the Red Ball line could lose the route. If, however, either the Mason City–Clear Lake section of the bus company's longer route from Mason City to Algona or its brief special service of September 1922 between the two points was recognized as legitimate, then its right to the route would be allowed.[15]

The majority decision of two to one, with Chairman Fred Woodruff dissenting, disallowed the Red Ball Company's special summer service, although it did authorize the company's regular service between Mason City and Algona, making a stop at Clear Lake. The initial legal battle at the state level demonstrated that buses could not operate wherever their owners wanted. Schultz tried again the following year to obtain permission to use Clear Lake as a regular terminal. She fought throughout the summer to establish the route and both she and her drivers faced arrest, jail and fines. She later claimed that on 4 July 1924, she wrote 'thirty two $100.00 checks to free my drivers each time they were jailed' for their attempts to take vacation-makers to and from Clear Lake. Her efforts were in vain; the route belonged to the railway company. She had to be content with establishing a new service between Clear Lake and

Bayside, another lake resort where there was no other competing public land transport.[16]

The legal contest over the Mason City–Clear Lake route was a preliminary skirmish for the longer and larger battle with the more powerful steam railroads. They also contested several bus routes on the grounds that a convenient service was already available for Iowans. Schultz requested that the hearings on these routes scheduled for September be postponed until 23 October so that she could better prepare her case. Although heavily in debt, she was still committed to further expansion. By the autumn of 1923 she had eleven large twenty-four seater coaches, some of which were up-to-date models costing $11,000 each. To acquire these she had managed to borrow some capital from local banks. If she were forbidden from operating over some routes, then her financial viability would be threatened. Not only was her livelihood at stake; the consequences of the struggle had broader implications. The Red Ball Transportation Company was the leading bus enterprise in Iowa. Even though it was capable of providing faster and better service than some of the railroads, the future development of the new mode of transport in the region would be threatened if Schultz's company could not succeed in establishing its routes.[17]

Schultz was convinced that she was legally entitled to run her business, but she knew that this confidence was not enough to keep her company in operation. She needed evidence of 'convenience'. To obtain that evidence, she had to demonstrate grass-roots support. She, her family, her employees and her friends proceeded to gather lists of signatures from patrons testifying that the bus service was both advantageous and essential. Such documentation was designed to impress on the Board of Railroad Commissioners the positive and popular response to buses.[18]

As she began buckling on the gauntlets for the biggest fight of her meteoric business career, Schultz also recognized that she needed a wider promotional effort. She began to capitalize on her newsworthy image as an attractive and plucky young woman fighting the mighty railroad corporations. 'The railroads and interurban companies are determined to "get" me if they can', she told one reporter. 'Well I'm not going to be gotten unless I have to be. And if they put me out of business here, well I'll just simply take my little buses some place else and start a few new lines.'[19] Well before the hearings began, the *Des Moines Register* named her the 'Iowa Bus Queen'. This title stuck as did her age; she was perennially twenty-four years old, the age at which she had started the Red Ball Transportation Company in 1922. Newspapers in other parts of the USA reported similar struggles of male bus pioneers to maintain their routes against railroad pressures, but rarely were these struggles so dramatic or even romantic. Such a good story could not be neglected by either Schultz or the media.

The three members of the Board of Railroad Commissioners were aware of the growing publicity in favour of the Iowa Bus Queen. Their duty, however, was to serve the public interest. They knew that the electric and steam railroads were not alone in opposing buses. Commercial clubs, such as those in Northwood, Manly and Kensett, thought that bus companies did not pay taxes commensurate with the capital involved in their business. Farmers and county supervisors claimed that the heavy vehicles ruined the road surfaces, and many residents were worried about the speed of the buses and the danger of road accidents.[20]

The commissioners also had to take into account motor-carrier legislation in other states. By the end of 1922, nineteen states had made legal provision for intercity buses and the issue was being discussed in five other states in addition to Iowa in 1923.[21] Even though buses were gaining legitimacy elsewhere, Schultz knew that at least one of the commissioners, Charles Webster, was firmly opposed to bus lines. She would need to make a strong case.

At the October hearings in Des Moines, two of the five routes of the Red Ball Transportation Company were contested: the one between Mason City and Des Moines and the one from Mason City to the Iowa–Minnesota state line. These routes were opposed by five steam railroads – the Chicago and Northwestern, the Minneapolis and St Louis, the Chicago Great Western, the Chicago, Rock Island and Pacific, and the Chicago, Milwaukee and St Paul – by one electric interurban (the Fort Dodge, Des Moines and Southern), by the supervisors of various counties through which the routes passed, and by some local commercial interests, including farmers. Initially, the Jefferson Highway Transportation Company, another ambitious bus firm that wanted to extend its routes through northern Iowa to Des Moines, had been in contention with the Red Ball Company. After consultation, however, the two bus firms decided to resolve their differences and stand together against the railway in order to protect the infant bus industry in Iowa.[22]

In making their decision, the Railroad Commissioners considered the issues of damage to the highways, harm to the railroads' business, danger to the public and the efficiency of the company's operations. For example, they deliberated whether the establishment of bus routes would so cripple rail services that these would not be able to operate, but decided that it was not in their brief to speculate on future developments. The commissioners also decided not to surmise whether the railroads would suffer 'a gross injustice' because they were taxed more heavily than motor vehicles. In the end, their decision turned on their interpretation of their charge to promote 'the public convenience'. After hearing many Iowans testify that buses were useful, the commissioners agreed to grant permits to the Red Ball Company because it provided a convenient service. The Iowa Bus Queen had won her fight to establish a new mode of transport that was competitive with existing modes.[23]

Her victory, however, had its downside. Both Commissioner Lewis and Chairman Woodruff thought that motor carriers should pay adequately for highway use and that, like the railroads, they should be subject to regulation. Commissioner Webster was worried about the excessive speed of buses and their destructive impact on gravel roads. The commissioners thus insisted that bus schedules should not compete directly with those of existing companies, that buses should not exceed the speed limit of 25 miles per hour and that all passengers should pay the stated fares. Failure to comply with these provisions would bring a loss of licence.[24] Schultz declared that she was satisfied with the judgement. Her buses already operated within the speed limit, she claimed, and she did not like giving out free passes as incentives because these undermined the economic viability of her company. She had got what she wanted – the right to stay in business. In a statement to the trade magazine *Bus Transportation*, she said: 'I am naturally very happy over the outcome of my petitions ... My bus business is the pride of my life and I love my buses'.[25]

The Iowa Bus Queen now looked forward to building up her bus line. Difficulties abounded, however. Like other bus pioneers, she found that it was a constant struggle to provide regular, comfortable and economic service. The weather and the poor road conditions often interfered with schedules. Investment capital remained scarce, while increased operating costs cut into profit margins. Furthermore, the 1923 legislation made it difficult to open up new routes. Schultz also faced managerial problems that could not always be resolved by the direct and often confrontational style which she had adopted. It might well be acceptable for her to drive one of her own buses, but engaging in verbal and physical showdowns with officials and rivals and being arrested for failing to comply with the law did not necessarily gain more passengers. Schultz had used her gender and her youth to advantage, but they had less impact as the bus industry matured and became more conventional.

In the face of such operational problems in the mid-1920s, Schultz, never content to delegate responsibility to lieutenants, took personal charge. When heavy snow blocked the roads out of Mason City in February 1924 she did not wait patiently for county officials to act or for nature to take its course. She recruited a gang of eighteen men and personally superintended the clearing of the snow on three highways. Hoping to make the most of the good publicity both for herself and her business, she then announced to the press that she would experiment with motor snow ploughs herself. The weather would not defeat her.[26]

Vehicle breakdowns, often caused by punctured tyres, were a more common problem. Drivers always travelled with a spare tyre and a repair kit, and passengers knew that delays were possible on any trip. Schultz, herself capable of repairing and changing tyres, became annoyed when punctures caused interruptions to her schedules. On one occasion, after a lengthy breakdown, she is reputed to have been so incensed that she threw a hammer through the windscreen when the bus did arrive. Fortunately, the driver ducked.[27] He knew that the Bus Queen could be irascible if all did not go smoothly. She wanted to show the world that she was capable of running a reliable business in an arena dominated by men.

That business was becoming one of consolidation rather than expansion in the middle and late 1920s. Having won her fight with the railroads, Schultz had hoped to enlarge the Red Ball Company either by opening new routes or by purchasing existing routes from rivals. Already in possession of routes stretching from Des Moines north to the state line, from Mason City west to Spirit Lake and Algona, east to Charles City and then south to Waterloo, she found that she could only make minor alterations to her established business in northern Iowa, and there were few opportunities to move further afield. Her application for a route between Waterloo and Cedar Rapids, for example, was denied, not only because the railroads claimed that adequate service already existed, but because motor-bus service was also available. Now that the state motor-carrier legislation was in force, the competition between bus lines as well as with railroads was regulated in the public interest. It was more important to provide adequate and reliable service than to increase the number of new routes.[28]

Perhaps it was just as well that Schultz's expansion plans were restricted because venture capital was scarce. By the mid-1920s the cost of new 'state-of-the-art' vehicles ranged between $8,000 and $14,000 each.[29] Deposits for the purchase of these vehicles required loans. Schultz had already used up her personal savings and had borrowed from family and friends. Local banks had offered some assistance but they resisted more, partly because they themselves were in difficulties and partly because of prejudice against bus operators and against women entrepreneurs. Ideally, the Red Ball Company should have been generating sufficient profit to reinvest in the business, but by 1927 it was running at a loss. That year there was a deficit of $7,419 and losses continued in subsequent years. Incoming revenue was insufficient to cover expenses, let alone to finance the purchase of modern equipment.[30]

The Iowa Bus Queen's financial troubles were not uncommon. Several other large bus companies in Iowa ran deficits in the late 1920s.[31] A combination of factors – economic conditions in rural Iowa, burdensome taxes and increasing competition among bus companies – contributed to their plight.

Iowa's economic condition in the middle to late 1920s was not as prosperous as it had been earlier in the century – a period often called the 'golden age of agriculture'.[32] During that period of prosperity, farmers had increased their output, productivity and investment, but in the 1920s they faced diminishing demand and falling prices. Their distress, in turn, depressed the rural economy.

In such a situation bus traffic might have declined or stagnated. But this did not seem to be the case for all large carriers. Official statistics show a 90 per cent increase in passengers for companies with annual revenues of $30,000 or more, rising from 1,446,407 passengers in 1927 to 2,747,557 in 1929, while the Red Ball Transportation Company saw its number of passengers decline by 4 per cent in those years.[33] A weak rural economy may have impeded local bus expansion, but it could not account for all poor performances.

State taxes added to the difficulties of Iowa bus entrepreneurs. All motor vehicles needed a licence and after 1925 all owners or operators paid a gasoline tax. A wheelage or ton-mile tax was levied on motor carriers beginning in 1923. That controversial tax was based on a bus's full capacity regardless of how many passengers were carried. When the Iowa legislature doubled the tax rate in 1925, the Iowa Motor Vehicle Association, of which Schultz was secretary, challenged the constitutionality of the law on the grounds that it was discriminatory. An injunction restrained the state commission from collecting the tax until the law was validated, and the association set aside money to pay the tax if and when it became necessary.[34]

All motor carriers claimed that the wheelage tax was unfair because it did not apply to irregular operators such as transfer, dray and taxicab companies whose daily business was to different points. Many thought legislators had been influenced by the railroad lobby, which sought to cripple the emerging bus industry. Certainly, in the mid-1920s the Iowa tax on buses was one of the highest in the USA, and it caused considerable difficulties for any company operating below average seating capacity. For Schultz the tax was a nightmare, costing her some $1,700 a month. When the Iowa Supreme Court upheld the constitutionality of the ton-mile tax law, late in 1928, the Red Ball Bus Company was reputed to owe the state nearly $50,000 in taxes.[35] Schultz might have been able to face that tax bill with more equanimity had she not been confronted with the more serious challenge of regional bus competition.

By the late 1920s the structure of the infant bus industry was changing. Intercity operations were consolidating at the regional level, and long-distance interstate lines were emerging to offer through bus transport across the continent. Iowa's location on east–west routes from Chicago to the West Coast and on north–south routes from the Canadian border through the Twin Cities to Kansas City made it attractive to ambitious interstate companies, which sought to take over local companies with legal rights to key routes. The Red Ball Transportation Company held rights to routes in central and eastern Iowa which could form part of a major north–south link.[36]

Schultz had experienced mixed success in attempting to consolidate her position in Iowa. In 1926 she joined with steam and electric railroads and motor-bus operators to defeat the application of Hawkeye Stages of Des Moines for some routes across central Iowa. The following year, however, she failed to prevent the Waterloo, Cedar Falls and Northern Railway Company from establishing a route between Waterloo and Mason City. In 1929 she failed again to obtain permission to open a line between Waterloo and Cedar Rapids because there was already a rail passenger service and bus service over part of the route. Despite such failures she was still well placed to withstand the competition of local Iowa firms.[37] She could not, however, take on stronger bus competition in the form of the Minnesota-based Jefferson Highway Transportation Company.

Headed by Edgar F. Zelle, this company wanted to establish routes in Iowa in order to reach St Louis or Kansas City. The company had operated to Mason City for several years, using both interline connections with the Red Ball Company at Albert Lea and its own through route. But Zelle needed more connections and other routes. In 1927 he opened direct runs from Austin, Minnesota to Charles City and from Rochester, Minnesota to Decorah. The following year he extended the Decorah service to Cedar Rapids and Independence, the Charles City service to Waterloo, and most significantly, he reached Des Moines via Garner and Ames. In 1929 he successfully gained access to Kansas City by the central Iowa route through Des Moines and Osceola to the state line and then through Missouri.[38]

The Jefferson's expansion programme did not go unopposed. In 1923 Schultz had agreed with the previous owners of the company to share the Albert Lea, Minnesota, to Mason City route only so that the bus companies could present a united bus front against the railroads. In 1928 when Edgar Zelle sought to establish first interstate and then intrastate lines to Cedar Rapids, he met resistance not only from the railroads, but also from Schultz. In moving southward through Iowa to Kansas City he was again opposed by the railroads who were joined by the emerging bus giant Pickwick-Greyhound Lines of Chicago. The search for mid-continental bus routes that could be linked into a regional or a national network required the acquisition of established Iowa companies.[39]

Edgar Zelle had decided to build a strong regional bus company, but his progress in realising this ambition increasingly depended on merging his lines with Schultz's. He knew that he was unlikely to obtain a permit to duplicate her key routes, so he proposed either coordinating schedules or preferably buying her out.[40] Initially, Schultz preferred coordination, but by early 1930 she was contemplating selling. Competition was no longer small scale, and many local operators were under financial pressure to sell out at a profit. Pickwick-Greyhound Lines, a part of the Motor Transit Company, which would shortly become the Greyhound Corporation, was interested in the north–south through route. Two other giants, the Yelloway System, through its subsidiary, Pioneer Stages of Oakland, California, and Interstate Transit Lines of Omaha, part of the Union Pacific Railway Company, were interested in the east–west routes. Although the mergers that would create the transcontinental bus systems were not clear in 1929 and 1930, local Iowa bus owners could see the advantages of selling their routes to well-financed out-of-state corporations.[41] When Edgar

Zelle, owner of the smallest of those companies, offered to buy out Schultz in June 1930 for $200,000, she decided to retire from the bus business.[42]

It was a wise decision. She probably could not have survived the emerging competition. She was already in financial difficulties because her company was not profitable. The accumulated wheelage tax of some $50,000 was a drain on her financial resources. Furthermore, she needed to invest capital in both motor coaches and buildings. Of the eleven buses in service in 1929 only four were reputed to be in sound condition. Ticket offices, waiting rooms and garages needed to be modernized and more staff were required to manage particular facets of the operation such as advertising, legal affairs, accounting and bus scheduling. She did not have the capital, nor was she likely to be able to borrow it, to carry out such improvements. Moreover, her style was not bureaucratic. She was accustomed to taking direct action when competitors stood in her way: she had tongue-lashed railroad attorneys and government officials who opposed her bus lines and she had defied the law, risking fines and imprisonment for contempt of court. Such a feisty fighter would not take kindly to a more administrative role.[43]

Neither Helen Schultz nor the routes of the Red Ball Transportation Company faded away when she left the bus business. The Jefferson Highway Transportation Company developed its newly acquired Iowa routes as part of a strong Midwestern operation. The Minneapolis-based company weathered the difficult years of the Great Depression, enjoyed increased trade during the Second World War and then successfully adjusted to the competition from other modes of transport in the post-war years. It still remains a sound company.[44]

Schultz used part of the profits from the sale of the Red Ball Company to move laterally in motor transport. She invested in a one-stop automobile service station and Firestone tyre agency, the Brewer Tyre and Battery Company. Once again she was featured in local headlines in several court cases involving the running of the business and the payment of taxes. She continued to fight corporations and the law in the same confrontational manner she had adopted while running her bus line. She and her husband, Donald Brewer, whom she had married secretly in Omaha in 1925, did not remain long in the new business before moving to the Twin Cities. They later moved back to Iowa to live either in Mason City or on the family farm near Nashua, where Donald Brewer reluctantly became a farmer. On the death of her father in 1946, Helen Schultz inherited his 400-acre property. She gained title after a legal suit involving her brother Magnus and then sold the farm at a profit in 1950. She continued to assert her strong will in whatever venture she undertook until her death in 1974, even though she did not always win her fights and the strain of fighting took its toll.[45]

Helen Schultz is one of the small number of bus pioneers, let alone female bus pioneers, who have a recoverable past. She gained her reputation as a forceful woman in a man's world. She may have hoped to establish a sound business with long-term prospects, or she may have been searching for adventure or personal fulfilment. Her ability to remain in operation for eight years in a period when women were not welcome in business circles and when men systematically excluded women from entry to the professions was a remarkable achievement.

Notes

1. Little is known about American bus pioneers. Their endeavours are buried in the memories of their children and grandchildren, in folders buries in attics or basements, or in snippets in local newspapers. Some information about men who founded companies with long lifespans or with national reputations is available in M. Walsh, 'From Jitney to Giant. The Early Growth of Long-Distance Bus Transport in the United States', (chapter 2), pp. 17–31; M. Walsh, 'Tracing the Hound: The Minnesota Roots of the Greyhound Bus Corporation', (chapter 4), pp. 75–88; C. Gohres, 'History of Pacific Greyhound Lines', (chapter 1), 'Auto Stage Development in California', pp. 1–3, Greyhound Corporate Records, American Heritage Center, University of Wyoming, Laramie (hereafter cited as GCR); A.E. Meier and J.P. Hoschek (1975), *Over the Road. A History of Intercity Bus Transportation in the United States*, Upper Montclair, NJ, pp. 1–9; B.B. Crandall (1954), *The Growth of the Intercity Bus Industry*, Syracuse, NY, pp. 6–13.
2. Interview with M. Martin by M.Walsh and A. Fischbeck, Mason City, 20 May 1991; telephone interview with M. Martin by M. Walsh, 15 October 1993; United States Bureau of the Census, Manuscript Schedules, 12th Census of the United States, 1900, Riverton Township, Floyd county, Iowa; 13th Census of the United States, 1910, Riverton Township, Floyd county, Iowa; 14th Census of the United States, 1920, Sarona Township, Washburn County, Wisconsin; *Bus Transportation* 2(5) (1923), p. 262 (hereafter cited as *BT*); newspaper clippings, private collection of Mary Martin (daughter of Helen Schultz), Mankato, Minnesota. All newspaper clippings are in the M. Martin Collection unless otherwise stated. Copies of this material are available in the Mason City Public Library. Helen M. Schultz will be referred to throughout by her maiden name, the name under which she started the Red Ball Transportation Company, rather than her married name, Helen Schultz Brewer or Helen M. Brewer.
3. Helen Schultz Brewer, 'Autobiographical Account', p. 1, M. Martin collection; M. Martin interview; M. Martin telephone interview; newspaper clippings; Walsh, 'From Jitney to Giant', (chapter 2), pp. 18–19; Meier and Hoschek, *Over the Road*, pp. 1–9.
4. For a general discussion of women's proper role and women's ability to enter specific occupations in the early twentieth century see A. Kessler-Harris (1982), *Out to Work. A History of Wage-Earning Women in the United States*, New York, pp. 217–49. V. Scharff (1991), examines women's early engagement with the automobile in *Taking the Wheel. Women and the Coming of the Motor Age*, New York, and T.J. Morain (1981), looks more particularly at women in Greene County, Iowa in *Prairie Grass Roots. An Iowa Small Town in the Early Twentieth Century*, Ames, IO, pp. 126, 131.

5. 'Autobiographical Account', pp. 1–2.
6. Walsh, 'From Jitney to Giant', (chapter 2), pp. 18–19; Walsh, 'Tracing the Hound', (chapter 4), pp. 76–9; Gohres, 'Pacific Greyhound Lines', (chapter 1), 'Auto Stage Development in California', pp. 1–3; Meier and Hoschek, *Over the Road*, pp. 1–9; Crandall, *The Growth of the Intercity Bus Industry*, pp. 6–13.
7. 'Autobiographical Account', pp. 1–2; unidentified statement of Helen Schultz, n.d., M. Martin Collection; newspaper clippings, c. 1923 and 1947; *Opportunity for 1924*, p. 10 (M. Martin Collection); M. Martin interview. *St Paul City Directory*, **54** (1918), p. 119; **56** (1920), pp. 22, 303; **61** (1925), pp. 91, 274; **68** (1932), pp. 65, 232. T. Christianson (1935), *Minnesota. The Land of Sky-Tinted Waters*, 3, *Minnesota Biography*, Chicago, pp. 69–70; S.H. Strom (1992), *Beyond the Typewriter. Gender, Class and the Origins of Modern American Office Work, 1900–1930*, Urbana, IL, p. 208.
8. 'Autobiographical Account', pp. 1–3; newspaper clippings c. March, 1947; 'Iowa Registered Highway Routes, 1914–1925', an insert map in W.H. Thompson (1989), *Transportation in Iowa. A Historical Summary*, Ames, IO; Walsh, 'Tracing the Hound', (chapter 4), p. 77 ; M. Walsh, 'Minnesota's Mr Bus: Edgar F. Zelle and the Jefferson Highway Transportation Company', (chapter 6), p. 107.
9. 'Autobiographical Account', pp. 1–3; newspaper clippings, c. March 1947.
10. 'Autobiographical Account', pp. 4–5; newspaper clipping; *Concrete Highway Magazine*, **10**(April) (1926), pp. 81–3. *Mason City Globe Gazette*, 1 June 1953; 1 June. J.H. Wheeler (1910), (comp. and ed.) *History of Cerro Gordo County, Iowa*, Chicago, pp. 337–41; *WPA Guide to 1930s Iowa* (1938), (repr. Ames IO, 1986), pp. 285–7.
11. 'Autobiographical Account', pp. 4–10; newspaper clippings, c. March 1947; Red Ball Transportation Company 'Time-Table' (1922), effective 2 October (M. Martin Collection).
12. 'Autobiographical Account', pp. 11–13. *BT*, **2**(4) (1923), p. 204; **2**(5) (1923), p. 260.
13. *Laws of Iowa* (1923), pp. 90–5; Iowa Board of Railroad Commissioners, *Annual Report* 46 (1923), pp. 96–101 (hereafter cited as IBRC, *AR*); Interstate Commerce Commission (ICC), 'Coordination of Motor Transportation', Docket 23400, *Reports* 182 (1932), Appendix F, pp. 410–13. Iowa legislation initially required only the promotion of public convenience by motor carriers whereas other state legislatures approved necessity and convenience statutes. Contemporary legal opinion suggested that Iowa lawmakers nevertheless intended to control the competition of public utilities. They thought that the sole word 'convenience' covered the requirements. See W.S. Ingram and M.S. Breckenridge, (1923–1924), 'Motor Bus Competition With Established Carriers,' *Iowa Law Bulletin*, **9**, pp. 268–90.
14. For general information on transport in Iowa, see Thompson, *Transportation in Iowa*, pp. 83–165. For information on specific modes of transport see K.L. Bryant, Jr (ed.) (1988), *Railroads in the Age of Regulation, 1900–1980*, New York; G.W. Hilton and J.F. Due (1960), *The Electric Railways in America*, Stanford, CA, and J.F. Rae (1971), *The Road and the Car in American Life*, Cambridge, MA. For more specific information on the impact of transport on rural life in Iowa see Morain, *Prairie Grass Roots*, pp. 109–40. The passenger-carrier railroads running into Mason City were the Chicago and North Western, the Chicago Great Western, the Chicago, Milwaukee, St Paul and Pacific (the Milwaukee Road), the Chicago, Rock Island and Pacific, the Milwaukee and St Louis and the Mason City and Clear Lake; those running into Waterloo were the

Chicago Great Western, the Chicago, Rock Island and Pacific, the Illinois Central and the Waterloo, Cedar Falls and Northern; those running into Charles City were the Illinois Central, the Milwaukee Road and the Charles City Western.

15. IBRC, *AR*, **46** (1923), pp. 110–12; *Des Moines Register*, 24 October 1923; newspaper clipping c. November 1923.

16. IBRC, *AR*, **47** (1924), pp. 198–200; *Mason City Globe Gazette*, 4 July 1924; H.M. Schultz, 'True Facts Regarding the Adjoining Write-Up', typescript in M. Martin collection.

17. 'Autobiographical Account', pp. 19–24; Fageol Motor Company (1924), *It's Always 'Fare Weather'*, M. Martin collection; newspaper clipping c. November 1923; *Opportunity for 1924*, p. 10; M. Martin interview; 'First National Bank of Mason City', typescript, p. 2, Mason City Public Library.

18. 'Autobiographical Account', pp. 14–20; newspaper clipping c. October 1923.

19. Newspaper clipping, c. 1923; *Opportunity For 1924*, pp. 10–11, 44–5; M. Martin interview.

20. IBRC, *AR*, **46** (1923), pp. 115–19; *Des Moines Register*, 24, 25 October 1923; newspaper clipping, c. 1923.

21. ICC, 'Coordination of Motor Transportation', Appendix F, pp. 410–13.

22. IBRC, *AR*, **46** (1923), pp. 104, 105, 112, 113; *Des Moines Register*, 23, 24 October 1923.

23. IBRC, *AR*, **46** (1923), pp. 114–19; *Des Moines Register*, 24 October, 22 November 1923; *BT*, **2**(12) (1923), p. 599.

24. IBRC, *AR*, **46** (1923), pp. 114–19; *Laws of Iowa*, p. 95; *Des Moines Register*, 22 November 1923.

25. *Des Moines Register*, 22 November 1923; *BT*, **2** (1923), p. 599.

26. *BT*, **3**(2) (1924), p. 93.

27. Interview with R. Tracy, by M. Walsh, St Paul, Minnesota, 2 October 1985; *BT*, **5**(3) (1926), p. 169; Walsh, 'Minnesota's Mr Bus', (chapter 6), pp. 110–11; M. Martin, telephone interview. Some of the best information about the problems of driving early buses can be found in oral interviews with pioneer drivers. See, for example, A.B. Lennartson, 16 December 1974; P.D. Silliman, 18 June 1975; A. Tamadge, 24 October 1975; M. Hemphill, 7 June 1976 – all in Iron Range Research Center, Chisholm, Minnesota.

28. IBRC, *AR*, **50** (1927), pp. 101, 103, 114, 116, 123, 124, 125, 132; **51** (1928), p. 136; **52** (1929), pp. 90–91, 106–7, 110, 135. *Des Moines Register*, 9 November 1924; Red Ball Transportation Company, 'Bus Schedule', n.d. [c. mid-1920s] M. Martin Collection; *Concrete Highway Magazine*, **10**(April) (1926), pp. 81–3; *BT*, **5**(8) (1926), p. 458.

29. *Des Moines Sunday Register*, 9 November 1924; newspaper clipping, c. 1927; *BT*, **5**(10) (1926), p. 591; E.F. Zelle and Northland Transportation Company, 'Agreement', exhibit no. 1, 11 July 1925, Edgar F. Zelle Records, Jefferson Lines, Minneapolis (hereafter cited as EFZR).

30. 'Autobiographical Account', pp. 20–24. IBRC, *AR*, **50** (1927), p. 422; **51** (1928), p. 397; **52** (1929), p. 427; **53** (1930), p. 315; **54** (1931), p. 338.

31. In 1927 six of the ten Class I carriers – those with an annual gross revenue of $30,000 or more – operated at a loss. In 1928 and 1929 the respective figures were five out of fifteen and six out of twelve. The 1926 figures were classified differently. Then the Class A Motor Passenger Carriers had an annual operating revenue above $50,000 and two of the five companies, including the Red Ball Transportation Company, were in deficit. IBRC, *AR*, **50** (1927), pp. 421–2, **51** (1928), pp. 395–7; **52** (1929), pp. 426–7; **53** (1930), p. 314.

32. For a general overview of the farm conditions in the region, see T. Saloutos and J.D. Hicks (1951), *Agricultural Discontent in the Middle West, 1900–1939*, Madison, WI. For Iowa see L.L. Sage (1983), 'Rural Iowa in the 1920s and 1930s: Roots of the Farm Depression,' *Annals of Iowa*, **47**, pp. 91–103; J.F. Wall (1983), 'The Iowa Farmer in Crisis, 1920–1936,' *Annals of Iowa*, **47**, pp. 116–27 and Morain, *Prairie Grass Roots*, pp. 212–46.

33. How much of the overall increase came from out-of-state passengers is unclear. Operators with only or primarily Iowa passengers showed mixed records. The Fort Dodge, Des Moines and Southern Transportation Company had a passenger increase of 76 per cent, while the Motor Coach Division of the Waterloo, Cedar Falls and Northern Railway Company and the Red Ball Transportation Company had passenger decreases of 1 and 4 per cent in those years. IBRC, *AR*, **51** (1928), pp. 396–7; **52** (1929), p. 447; **53** (1930), p. 324; **54** (1931), p. 347; **55** (1932), p. 355. Before 1930, the statistics in the IBRC, *AR*, do not differentiate between revenue passengers within and without the state of Iowa. Companies that listed high percentages of passengers as out-of-state, namely Interstate Transit Lines, Northland Transportation Company, Burlington Transportation Company and Jefferson Transportation Company, were responsible for an increasing percentage of passengers after 1928.

34. The tax amounted to one-eighth of one cent per ton mile of travel on vehicles with pneumatic tyres and double this amount for those with solid tyres. For buses, the full seating capacity was multiplied, by 150 pounds per passenger, together and added to the weight of the bus, the driver and any supplies. *Laws of Iowa* (1923), pp. 90–95. *BT*, **4**(1) (1925), p. 44; **4**(2) (1925), p. 97; **4**(5) (1925), p. 217; **5**(2) (1926), p. 111; **6**(2) (1927), p. 117; **7**(1) (1928), p. 52. *Truck and Bus Owner*, **2**(November) (1923), p. 6; *Mason City Globe-Gazette*, 7 January 1929; newspaper clippings; G.S. May (1965), 'The Good Roads Movement in Iowa', *The Palimpsest*, **46**, pp. 102–4.

35. IBRC, *AR*, **50** (1927), p. 422; **51** (1928), p. 397; **52** (1929), p. 442; **53** (1930), p. 326. *BT*, **6**(2) (1927), p. 115; **7**(1) (1928), pp. 52; (11) (1928), p. 644. *Mason City Globe Gazette*, 7 January 1929; newspaper clippings; Memo, 'Bus Mileage and Passengers', President's Subject File 11532, Great Northern Railway Company Records, Minnesota Historical Society, St Paul.

36. *BT*, **7**(5) (1928), pp. 251–4; **7**(10) (1928), pp. 523–6.

37. 'Autobiographical Account', pp. 14–15, 18–19; IBRC, *AR*, **49** (1926), pp. 116–18; **50** (1927), pp. 114–16; **52** (1929), pp. 90–91, 106–7. *Des Moines Evening Tribune*, 4 March 1926; *Mason City Globe Gazette*, 14 December 1928, 23, 27 February 1929; newspaper clippings, c. 1927.

38. IBRC, *AR*, **50** (1927), pp. 117, 133, 139; **51**(1928), pp. 70, 75, 78–81, 101–3, 114, 117, 123, 137, 141, 142; **52** (1929), pp. 88, 90–91, 93, 99, 100–104, 106–7, 108, 140, 141, 142. Minnesota Railroad and Warehouse Commission, Auto Transportation Company Division, *Biennial Report*, (1926), pp. 66, 68–72, 162; (1928), pp. 121–2, 175–7, 291–2; (1930), pp. 197–8; Jefferson Transportation Company, *Timetables* (1926–1929); Walsh, 'Minnesota's Mr Bus', (chapter 6), pp. 110, 111–12.

39. IBRC, *AR*, **46** (1923), pp. 104, 105, 112, 113; **50** (1927), pp. 78–81; **51** (1928), pp. 101–3; **52** (1929), pp. 90–91, 99–104, 106–7. *Des Moines Register*, 23, 24 October 1923; *Mason City Globe-Gazette*, 23 February 1929.

40. E.F. Zelle to H.M. Brewer, 7, 30 August 1929; H.M. Brewer to E.F. Zelle, 3, 24 August 1929, EFZ Records. Jefferson Transportation Company, *Timetables* (1924–1929); *Mason City Globe-Gazette*, 13 June 1930.

41. IBRC, *AR*, **52–4** (1929–1931); 'The Greyhound Corporation', typescript, GCR; 'Corporate History of Interstate Transit Lines', typescript, Union Pacific Railroad Company Collection, Nebraska State Historical Society, Lincoln; *BT*, **8** (1929), pp. 168–9, 350–52; *Mason City Globe-Gazette*, 16, 31 October 1929.

42. 'Articles of Agreement for the Sale of the Red Ball Transportation Company to the Jefferson Transportation Company', 16 June 1930, EFZ Records; *Mason City Globe-Gazette*, 13, 17 June 1930; *Des Moines Tribune*, 13 June 1930.

43. IBRC, *AR*, **50–54** (1927–1931); newspaper clippings; M. Martin interview; interview with R. Tracy, former Red Ball and Jefferson Company driver, by M. Walsh, M. Martin and A. Fischbeck, 20 May 1991, Mason City.

44. Walsh, 'Minnesota's Mr Bus', (chapter 6), pp. 113–19.

45. M. Martin, interview; M. Martin phone interview; miscellaneous newspaper clippings, 1927, 1930s and 1940s, M. Martin Collection and Mason City Public Library collection; *BT*, **6**(2) (1927), p. 124. Helen Schultz was able to continue as active head of the Red Ball Company after her marriage because her sister Margaret kept house and looked after her son Donald and her daughter Mary. Helen Schultz died in Cascade, Iowa, 8 March 1974, *Dubuque Telegraph-Herald*, 10 March 1974.

6 Minnesota's 'Mr Bus': Edgar F. Zelle and the Jefferson Highway Transportation Company

In March 1944 Edgar F. Zelle, President of the Jefferson Transportation Company, Minneapolis, resigned as associate director of the Office of Defense Transportation's Division of Local Transport, where he directed the administration of regulations and policies affecting intercity and school buses. This onerous and responsible wartime appointment recognized Zelle as both a major intercity bus operator and one of the industry's most respected leaders. On returning to Minneapolis, he continued for several years to manage the independent regional company to which he had devoted almost a quarter of a century.[1]

Edgar Frederick Zelle was born in 1890 in Havana, Illinois, to Lydia and Charles Zelle. Five years later the family moved to New Ulm. There young Zelle progressed through 'grade' and high school, helping in his parents' shoe store and thereby gaining some knowledge of small-scale business. While in high school he learned shorthand from a neighbour who was court reporter for Brown County. With this skill the sixteen-year-old obtained a position as a stenographer at the Eagle Roller Mills Company. Within two years he became personal secretary to its president. Yet Zelle wanted more than a routine job in New Ulm and decided to see what possibilities lay in the Twin Cities of Minneapolis-St Paul. On reading a University of Minnesota bulletin, he realized that higher education could open doors to success, and he calculated that if he used his savings of two years and found a part-time job, he could finance a degree course. Going early to inquire about registration, he talked himself into a job on the payroll of the busy university registrar's office. He was, in the early fall of 1909, set on new directions.[2]

Four years later he received his BA degree, attaining the scholastic honour of Phi Beta Kappa. A degree, however, was not the only achievement of his undergraduate career. He supported himself by his afternoon secretarial work for the registrar and for private firms, occasionally as a court reporter, and by selling his class notes, which he had typed and copied. Indeed, he was so well known for his entrepreneurial skills that he became business manager of the

1913 Gopher, the annual yearbook published by the junior (third year) class. He also found new activities in the university environment. Debating became his forte, an interest that would serve him well as a public figure. He joined the debating squad as a sophomore (second year student) and in his junior (third) year became a member of the intercollegiate team. He also belonged to the Forum Literary Society, the social fraternity Alpha Delta Phi, and the legal organization Phi Delta Phi. He was developing the versatility that gained him the presidency of the senior (fourth year) class and later carried him into civic service and several business directorships. Not least, he met his future wife, Lillian Nippert, another member of the class of 1913 and a talented violinist. Through her, he became involved in a range of musical and cultural activities.[3]

On graduation Edgar Zelle turned not to the law, as he might have done, but to the business world. He was immediately offered a position as secretary of Wilcox Motor Truck Company, a manufacturing firm in Minneapolis. There he gained considerable experience in an emerging part of the motor-vehicle industry. In 1913 few trucks were being used, partly because they were innovative and partly because servicing them was a difficult task, usually done at the factory. Such a situation was often not convenient for owners. Recognizing a business opportunity, Zelle decided to organize a company that would lease trucks to the contractors who were constructing Minnesota highways and to other local wholesale and manufacturing firms. But where and how would he raise the capital to begin? He persuaded his home-town banker in New Ulm to loan part of the money. His friend Cavour L. Truesdale, who was similarly impressed by the growth in road transport, also invested in the venture. In 1915, the year he married, Zelle formed the Motor Truck Service Company, locating in Minneapolis's St Anthony Main neighbourhood. Shortly thereafter he decided to build and run a gasoline station to provide for the new company's needs. Buying in bulk from the Sinclair Oil Company, he then supplied nearby industrial plants.[4]

Once the truck company was doing well, Zelle decided to enter another motor-vehicle business: buses. This was not a difficult feat. In these pioneering years the construction of the two vehicles was similar. A bus could be built on a truck chassis, and Wilcox could manufacture both. Several entrepreneurs were operating bus services both within the Twin Cities and to towns in southern and central Minnesota; in addition, there was a flourishing business in the Iron Range country of northern Minnesota. Watching the growing popularity of the automobile, made all the more enticing by the expansion of the road network, Zelle and Truesdale decided to capitalize on Minnesotans' desire to increase their mobility. In 1918 they started the Red Bus Line running north to St Cloud.[5]

The Red Bus Line was one of the several services out of the Twin Cities, but Zelle was more ambitious and a better manager than most of his counterparts. Gradually, he pushed his line north through Little Falls to Brainerd and west through Sauk Centre to Wadena, gaining passengers and a good reputation through reliable service and reasonable fares. In 1923, for example, travellers bound for Minneapolis paid $1.00 from St Cloud, $1.50 from Little Falls, and $2.00 from Brainerd. Competition in these unregulated years was stiff, not least from the Jefferson Highway Transportation Company, itself a merger of several small, owner-operator concerns. Rate warfare, both among the rival bus lines and between the buses and the trains, provided local residents with cheap travel but brought financial headaches to the operators. Railroad managers complained vociferously about their loss of passengers and petitioned the Minnesota Railroad and Warehouse Commission, a regulatory agency founded in the nineteenth century, to discontinue some services. Recently-formed bus companies with little or no financial reserves faced bankruptcy or reorganization. The Red Bus Line weathered the storms, however, posting a net profit of $20,000 in 1924.[6]

The Jefferson Highway Transportation Company, on the other hand, was in poor shape by that time. Co-partners Emery L. Bryant and Ivan D. Ansell had founded the firm in September 1919, operating their first bus between Minneapolis and nearby Osseo. Chartered by the Minnesota State Securities Commission on 23 March 1920, the company gradually built up its equipment and routes so that by mid-1922 it had nine buses and lines extending to St Cloud, Aitkin and Mora. That same year it absorbed Rodney S. Dimmick's Touring Car Bus Company, running between Minneapolis and Rochester, and incorporated under the laws of Delaware. Ambitious plans were circulating early in 1923. If sufficient capital was forthcoming from the sale of stock, Jefferson would purchase new buses and extend its lines to Sauk Centre, Brainerd, Bemidji, Grand Rapids, and Fargo, North Dakota. Clifford G. Schultz, a Minneapolis attorney, worked with that city's Phoenix Corporation on the stock flotation issue.[7]

Like many other operators and would-be operators on both proved and untried routes in these heady, unregulated years, the directors of the Jefferson Company were hoping to make a profit quickly. In 1923 they more than doubled their vehicles, going from seventeen to forty-eight. Yet despite having some of the best routes in the most heavily populated southern parts of the state, these men were losing money. Management was poor. In the financial year ending in August 1924, competition and rate-slashing meant lower revenue, yet expenses remained high. The need to purchase extra snow-clearing equipment as well as buses, and the requirement to set aside a fund to replace obsolete vehicles, brought the embarrassing result of no stock dividends. By 1925 the company could not hide its mounting difficulties. Debts were estimated at $300,000 by midyear, at which time post-dated cheques were written to take care of liabilities. The officers were looking to a rescue package from the Phoenix Corporation, but another option soon proved more effective.[8]

The year 1925 might be regarded as a turning point for Minnesota's bus industry. The state ranked second in the nation in bus mileage. In its northern parts, the Northland Transportation Company, a merger of several smaller firms, was becoming a dominant force. It was aided and partly financed by the Great Northern Railway, one of the few such lines to work with, rather than against, bus companies at that time. In the southern and central regions of Minnesota, the Jefferson Highway Transportation Company, despite its financial problems, was the major operator. Smaller concerns like the Red Bus, Boulevard Transportation, and Interstate Transportation Companies offered alternative and parallel routes. Lawmakers were well aware of activity in other states and felt considerable pressure from the railroads to enact regulation. In April 1925 the state legislature passed 'an act providing for supervision and regulation of transportation of persons and property for hire as common carriers on any public highway in this state, by motor vehicles ... subjecting such transportation to the jurisdiction and control of the Railroad and Warehouse Commission'. Bus companies would have to prove the convenience and necessity of their service in order to receive a licence and continue operating. They would have to conform to certain standards, such as having adequate public liability and indemnity insurance, providing all-year continuous service, and keeping financial records that could be scrutinized. The commission would determine schedules and rates, which could not be changed without permission. Some bus companies could not meet such standards. Those that could, also wanted to purchase the routes of weaker competitors.[9]

Edgar Zelle and the officers of the Jefferson Highway Transportation Company were able to help each other in 1925. The latter, with a gross earning capacity of some $700,000 annually, sorely needed a good manager. The former, running the Red Bus Line at a net profit, clearly had business acumen. Zelle, however, wanted a free hand, and he had neither the capital nor the desire to organize a large firm or become part of a national network. He did, however, have the credibility to obtain partial financing. Borrowing money from the First National Bank of Minneapolis, he purchased the Jefferson's common voting stock. He was thus able to obtain a ninety-day option during which time he ran the company. Zelle then proceeded to negotiate with the Northland Transportation Company and the Great Northern Railway to sell all the lines north of Minneapolis, leaving himself with the southern routes between the Twin Cities and Rochester and between the Twin Cities, Owatonna and Albert Lea. The money from this deal and the sale of the Red Bus Line to the Northland financed his purchase of the Jefferson Highway Transportation Company.[10]

The two leading bus companies in Minnesota thereby reached a satisfactory agreement, apparently dividing their territory. Northland then consolidated its position by purchasing other, smaller lines in the northern and north-central parts of the state, paralleling the routes of the Great Northern Railway. Within a few years it would become part of the national Greyhound network. Zelle, at the head of a much slimmed-down but financially sounder Jefferson Highway Transportation Company, could concentrate on developing the more profitable southern lines. He removed most of the previous directors and took on a capable staff, most notably Lester P. Wakefield, who began as a bookkeeper and became Zelle's right-hand man.[11]

During late 1925 and early 1926 Zelle concentrated his attention on defending his newly acquired bus business. Four major railroads opposed his routes from Minneapolis to Rochester and to Albert Lea. In response, he organized his patrons to petition and testify as to the public convenience and necessity of his buses at the Minnesota Railroad and Warehouse Commission's hearings in Rochester. This approach succeeded, and once his charter rights were secured in March 1926, the Twin Cities entrepreneur began developing routes through the prosperous southern Minnesota farmlands into neighbouring Iowa. By June 1927 he had extended the Albert Lea run to Mason City, Iowa, rather than relying on interline connections. The Jefferson also began a direct route from Owatonna to Austin and to Charles City, Iowa. Later that year Zelle pushed across Decorah, Iowa, and then to Independence, Iowa. In 1928 this service reached Cedar Rapids, while the Charles City line went on to Waterloo, Iowa. In the same year Zelle also bought some of the operating rights of a rival company, the Van Tassel Bus Line, between Rochester and Lanesboro and Rochester and Austin. He was building a sound rural bus network that had the possibility of becoming a mainline regional route.[12]

He was also building up a sound grass-roots bus service. Most of the Jefferson company's passengers were intrastate and local rather than interstate and regional. These travellers were concerned about day-to-day issues like reasonable costs and reliable services. Thanks to state regulation, customers would no longer benefit from the cheap fares produced by the rate wars of the early 1920s. Zelle was eager in the mid-1920s to gain a reputation for giving value for money. He wanted his rates to be competitive with those of the railroads, and he favoured round-trip saver fares, which encouraged regular patronage.

Zelle was also concerned with reliability, particularly in the winter when snow and ice were major hazards. The railroads often talked derisively about fair-weather lines, and Zelle wished to avoid such slurs, both against his company and the industry. Like many other bus operators, he aided the state highway department in snow removal. The Jefferson company kept a fleet of snowploughs, both the large, heavy Caterpillars and the small Fordsons used for clearing road shoulders. Indeed, southern Minnesota residents reputedly remembered this wintertime service as a sign of Jefferson dependability.

Attention to equipment was another, albeit less visible, contribution to dependability. In the late 1920s the company often retained older buses in working condition to replace ones that got stuck when flooding followed a quick spring thaw or when heavy rains caused mud-slides. In addition, drivers were expected to use their standard tool and spare-parts kits to make roadside repairs, especially on flat tyres. Jefferson buses were known to be customer friendly.[13]

Like several other bus entrepreneurs in the USA, Zelle also experimented with supplementing his service with an airline. On 5 May 1928, he and his board of directors established Jefferson Airways Incorporated as a division of the Jefferson Transportation System. A 45-minute, twice-daily flight between the Twin Cities and Rochester began on 13 July, and the twelve-seater Ford Tri-motor offered local sightseeing trips to raise extra money. During the summer and autumn of 1928, some fifty to sixty passengers flew in and out of the St Paul Municipal Airport weekly, along with about 400 local sightseers.

Such trade, however, was insufficient to form the basis of a sound business, and in December Zelle discontinued his air service. Sightseeing continued intermittently during the winter when the weather was favourable, with the pilot even using frozen Lake Superior as a landing strip after aerial tours of Duluth. But there were no more regular runs. The plane was sold in April 1929, and Jefferson Airways Incorporated was liquidated in July. The air venture was perhaps more romantic than practical. With scheduled fares significantly higher than those for bus or rail, and given the extra time needed to travel to and from the airports, local flights were prestigious rather than economical.[14]

Thereafter, Zelle concentrated on consolidating his bus operations and making them part of a viable long-distance network. By early 1929 his company was making southward connections to Kansas City, Missouri, using a route through Garner, Ames and Des Moines, Iowa, and Bethany and St Joseph, Missouri. The acquisition of routes and rolling stock, together with the expenditure on the short-lived airline, however, stretched his financial resources. New injections of capital were needed. Zelle responded by reorganizing, releasing some of the common stock, and issuing preferred stock, which he himself carefully monitored. He wanted the Jefferson Highway Transportation Company to remain a family-type operation, and so he offered small investments to a group of conservative bankers and businessmen whom he knew personally or by reputation. He wanted his company to be locally owned and financed, and he rejected any involvement with the speculative activity then rampant on the major stock markets.[15]

With the finance at hand, Zelle secured the Kansas City destination, which he regarded as an important gateway at the terminus of a well-patronized route. He had experimented with St Louis as a gateway, but abandoned the Des Moines, Iowa, to St Louis, Missouri, route in the autumn of 1929 in favour of obtaining local operations in Iowa and then on to Kansas City. The most important of these operations was the Red Ball Transportation Company. Zelle had wanted to purchase this independent Iowa firm for some time. Its owner, Helen Schultz, the 'Iowa Bus Queen', was a pioneer in transport, like Zelle himself. She had fought hard to establish her routes. In June 1930, perhaps realizing that her company could not compete successfully with larger and interstate operators, perhaps for personal reasons, she sold her routes, buses and other equipment to Zelle for $200,000. The Jefferson Highway Transportation Company then had three Iowa routes as well as good east–west connections with Interstate Transit Lines at Ames and Cedar Rapids. At Kansas City, Jefferson passengers could make connections with Pickwick Greyhound Lines for St Louis; Dallas, Texas; Phoenix, Arizona; and even Los Angeles, California. The company was now in a much stronger position for both local and long-distance business.[16]

Though busy with the operation and growth of the Jefferson Company, Edgar Zelle was also active on other fronts. From 1924 to 1930 he served as president of the Minnesota Motor Bus Association. Among other tasks he lobbied against restrictive motor-vehicle legislation, struggled to place the bus industry in a positive light by establishing rules of efficiency, courtesy and safety for the association's code of principles and publicized the development and value of bus transport. For such propaganda, he needed both a public presence and a good database. His undergraduate debating experience had provided sound training for public speaking, and his education, common sense and eye for economic affairs enabled him to make coherent arguments. For example, he presented a lucid case for buses when applying to the Minnesota Railroad and Warehouse Commission for the rights to the Jefferson Company's routes. And he was equally persuasive at the Interstate Commerce Commission's motor-bus and truck investigation hearings, when discussing the competition between Minnesota buses and trains. Zelle collected and retained information on bus activities in Minnesota and the nation. He was also able to acquire extra data from Laurence A. Rossman, editor of the *Grand Rapids Herald Review*, another eloquent bus spokesperson.[17]

Perhaps Zelle's most important public-relations task of the decade had come in 1925, when he appeared before the Minnesota State House Committee on Railroads and Motor Buses, hoping to counteract the rail lobby's demands for restrictive legislation. Though disappointed by the outcome that gave the railroads, in the shape of the Minnesota Railroad and Warehouse Commission, control over commercial road transport, Zelle had scored some important points. He notified legislators and Minnesotans alike that bus operators did not oppose fair regulation and that railroads were shortsighted in failing to consider the business that motor traffic could bring their way.[18]

Zelle regularly spoke at gatherings ranging from local chambers of commerce and Kiwanis clubs to the Minnesota Surveyors and Engineering

Society and the Transportation Club of St Paul. Furthermore, he presented annual statements to the press about the growth of bus lines in Minnesota. On request, he even wrote special features on such topics as how bus companies kept the roads open in winter. Such publicity was important in developing Minnesotans' awareness and appreciation of bus services.[19]

By 1930 the state's bus companies were well established, having carried more than 14 million passengers in the previous year. The majority rode local and intrastate lines, indicating that bus travel was essentially short distance. But two firms were looking to an interstate market in these still-early years of commercial road traffic: the Jefferson Highway Transportation Company and the Northland Transportation Company. The Jefferson was by far the smaller organization with thirty-three buses, 363,127 fare-paying passengers, and a total investment of $582,676. The Northland, with its 196 vehicles, 3,330,320 fare payers, and investment of $4,993,061, was already recognized as the leading bus line in the Upper Midwest; it was now part of the nationwide Greyhound empire, consisting of some 41,000 miles of highway. The paths of the two leading Minnesota bus companies had divided in 1925, but there would soon be an attempt to join them again.[20]

The Northland directors had not abandoned hope of obtaining the prosperous routes in southern Minnesota. The stumbling block to buying them in 1925 had been the financial involvement of the Great Northern Railway and the prospect that, through its bus subsidiary, it would be competing with the Chicago Great Western Railroad. Now Northland was part of Greyhound, and the Great Northern had become only a 30 per cent stockholder in an operating subsidiary of the national bus organization. Greyhound's president, Eric Wickman, and his backers were interested in acquiring the Jefferson company to control the through-franchises of the important routes in and out of the Twin Cities. Negotiations came to a head in March 1931 with a merger plan on the basis of a stock exchange and partial cash purchase. After consulting his stockholders and examining the proposal, Zelle rejected the offer. Questions of whether some investors would have to pay income tax if they took cash rather than Northland preferred stock may have raised some technical problems in closing the deal. But more than that, Zelle wanted to protect his employees and investors. He insisted that the workers be taken care of properly in the proposed larger Northland organization, and he was worried about his friends and colleagues who had invested in the Jefferson company primarily because they knew him. When he could get no definite assurances about his employees, he opted to retain his company rather than become part of a more impersonal unit.[21]

As an independent operator, Edgar Zelle needed to consolidate his position in order to withstand competition from major interstate carriers like Northland Greyhound Lines, Pickwick Greyhound Lines and Interstate Transit Lines;

from the large, Iowa-based Crandic Stages, Incorporated, and from small, intrastate companies. By December 1930 the Jefferson's lines extended to Dubuque in eastern Iowa, and in May 1931 Zelle purchased the routes of the La Crosse and Southeastern Transportation Company to connect points in southeastern Minnesota to that Wisconsin city. New depots, opened in the summer of 1931, demonstrated a commitment to developing the bus industry in Iowa. In Mason City, the Jefferson company's own bus depot included a restaurant, The Amber Room, and barbershop in addition to a ticket office, waiting rooms, and two restrooms. All were decorated, heated, and lit to high standards. Nearby, a well-equipped garage and workshop enabled Mason City to become the main southern servicing centre for Jefferson buses, complementing the Minneapolis maintenance facility. At Des Moines, an important bus junction, the Jefferson company joined with other major operators in the new Union Station.

Subsequent plans for additions to terminals and equipment, however, had to be put on the back burner; in the second half of 1931, the economic depression was making a marked impact on the company's financial position. In October Zelle asked all his employees to take a 25 per cent pay cut in the hope of avoiding dismissals and schedule reductions. The company's operating revenue, which had risen by $113,001 or 16 per cent in the financial year ending July 1931, fell by $137,634 or 16 per cent the following year. It would fall again for the year ending July 1933 – by $172,944, or 25 per cent. By 1932 it was time to retrench in order to stay in business.[22]

Poor economic conditions were not the only element contributing to the deteriorating balance sheet. Iowa tonnage taxes were another problem. Though the Jefferson's headquarters remained in Minneapolis, much of the business had become concentrated in Iowa. In 1932 the company served one point in Wisconsin, eighteen in Missouri, forty-three in Minnesota, and eighty-three in Iowa. This meant 421,200 bus miles or 13 per cent of the total in Missouri, 1,280,232 or 38 per cent in Minnesota, and 1,654,239 or 49 per cent in Iowa. That state's ton-mile tax of two and one-half mills (0.025 cents) on passenger buses was a burden in addition to a licence fee and gasoline tax. Jefferson paid $41,478 in tonnage taxes in 1932 representing 17 per cent of its gross Iowa revenue, or more than half of its Iowa loss of $78,824 in that year. Nearby Minnesota and Illinois had no such tonnage tax, while Wisconsin's was approximately one mill. Yet even if Iowa had not levied the tax, the Jefferson's operations there would have lost money, partly because of the prevalence of private automobiles and partly because of the economic depression. Zelle was disappointed but not totally dismayed. Unlike some of his Iowa counterparts who were also losing money, he did not abandon his business.[23]

Zelle decided to campaign for a change in legislation. Drawing on his Minnesota experiences in public relations, he appealed to both the Iowa state government and the public. During a seven-week stay in Des Moines in the spring of 1933, he lobbied senators and congressmen with correspondence and personal visits, and he got other interested parties – bus operators, retailers, bankers, and passengers – to follow suit. Such efforts paid dividends. In 1933 Iowa reduced the tonnage tax by one-half mill. That, coupled with a 21 per cent overall decline in bus revenue, lowered the company's tax bill to $27,671 – a 33.3 per cent drop. Lower taxes offered hope of staying in business, and Zelle planned to work for an additional reduction.[24]

This constructive approach to problem-solving was also visible in the internal management of the bus company. Business was at its lowest in the early 1930s, picking up slightly in 1936 and becoming more acceptable at decade's end. During the difficult years, Zelle shared much of the daily, routine work with his trusted lieutenant, Lester Wakefield, who had progressed through virtually all aspects of the bus business to become company treasurer. When Zelle was in Minneapolis, he came to the office every day; when out of town, he stayed in regular contact by mail and phone.[25]

Zelle and his staff devoted time and meticulous care to the maintenance and replacement of vehicles. Recognizing the link between efficiency and economy, for example, they devised a new system to maintain brake material. Since buying new motor coaches was a major financial outlay, the company also saved by rebuilding older ones and acquiring second-hand vehicles. These were spruced up and advertised as large, modern, luxurious buses. In 1939 the trade journal, *Bus Transportation*, recognized this dedication to service with its maintenance award for intercity bus operators having between twenty-five and fifty vehicles.

Labour relations also claimed much of Zelle's attention. It was a time for 'making do', and Jefferson employees were anxious to pull their weight. Despite wage cuts, they were still employed. Many had worked for Zelle for several years and knew that he was a man of integrity. Zelle treated his workers with courtesy and believed in keeping them well informed. Jefferson employees cooperated with a management that treated them well – for instance, giving them a bonus in 1937 when business picked up. When employees raised the question of a union that same year, Zelle publicly supported them, believing that unionism was not a threat, either to him personally or to the company's welfare. The Jefferson benefited from such an open-minded stance. Unlike some larger bus lines, it did not face worker antagonism and strike action.[26]

During the 1930s Edgar Zelle was also committed to improving conditions in the bus industry as a whole. He early became involved in the affairs of the American Automobile Association's bus division, which in 1929 was reorganized as the National Association of Motor Bus Operators (NAMBO). As Zelle well knew, the young industry needed to promote itself as an economical and comfortable means of travelling nationwide, and it needed protection from the railroads and restrictive federal legislation. Like many pioneer bus operators, Zelle had considerable experience with these issues at a state level; unlike many others, he was prepared to give considerable time to NAMBO. As a member of the board of directors during this crucial decade, he was involved in discussions of important issues like the National Recovery Administration's Motor Bus Code, adopted in October 1933, federal regulation before and after the Motor Carrier Act of 1935, rate competition between railroads and buses, national publicity, the size and weight of motor vehicles and troop transportation by bus. He served on committees, compiled reports and gave papers. Though the board of directors might meet only three or four times a year, the committees were convened more often and could generate large amounts of paperwork. As a board director, Zelle was also a spokesperson; for example, he testified at the USA Senate's Interstate Commerce Committee hearings on the regulation of motor carriers in March 1932 and at the Interstate Commerce Commission's hearings on motor-carrier safety regulations in February 1939. He also appeared as a witness in individual cases of national interest, as when he spoke before California's Railroad Commission on behalf of Pacific Greyhound Lines, which was applying for permission to charge lower fares for long-distance points. Edgar Zelle was a true servant of the bus industry.[27]

The busman continued his public service to the nation as well as to the industry during the Second World War. In June 1941, Zelle was appointed a consultant of the transportation division of the Office for Emergency Management. After the Office of Defense Transportation was established in December, he worked for six months as a member of the advisory committee of the local field office of the division of motor transport. Then in February 1943 he took up his most important government position: associate director of the Office of Defense Transportation's division of local transport.[28]

During the wartime crisis, when the demand for intercity bus service outstripped the supply, it was critical that the industry be represented on official bodies. With the scarcity of cars, intercity buses carried more than twice their 1940 numbers of passengers throughout the war. Yet the industry faced severe shortages of equipment, parts, gasoline and, finally, manpower. Speed restrictions also impaired efficiency. The permanent members of the NAMBO staff, located in Washington, DC, met frequently with government officials, but they were not always able to argue for intercity service. Thus the job fell to Edgar Zelle, who fought effectively to establish the importance of intercity buses – as distinct from local transit – in the motor-transport network. Such service required some changes at the Jefferson company. While a consultant or a member of the local field committee, Zelle did not need to leave his own business, but when he worked in Washington, Lester Wakefield ran the company, which was headed by Lillian Zelle.[29]

The war certainly brought additional business to the Jefferson company. The number of intercity passengers more than doubled between 1941 and 1943, rising from 651,091 to 1,370,130 and reaching a peak of 1,609,336 in the next two years. In 1943 the load factor (ratio of seats to occupancy) was 75 per cent, compared to the 44 per cent level of the years 1936 to 1940. Total revenue also more than doubled and then rose more gradually over the next three years to reach the highest ever experienced in 1946. But gross figures were somewhat misleading. Expenses were also increasing, leaving the company with a relatively smaller net income. All running costs had risen, most notable among them employee wages and pension provisions. Income-tax payments were also considerably higher.[30]

The most difficult problem for Jefferson managers in these years was to run schedules according to government guidelines, in the face of equipment and parts shortages. Only twelve additional buses were acquired from 1942 to 1945. Fortunately, Jefferson employees, who in 1941 had won *Bus Transportation*'s annual maintenance award for the third consecutive year, were experienced in repair work. Even so, bus accidents and old age necessitated the purchase of spare parts, and long delays in obtaining them were frustrating. Manpower shortages became more crucial in the later stages of the war. Twenty-one experienced drivers and maintenance workers served in the military in 1943, some 14 per cent of a work force of 154. More were called up in the next year. Old employees helped to train new ones, but the shortage of drivers, men likely to be under the age of thirty-eight, made for severe problems. Overwork strained labour relations in the wartime years. Here Lillian Zelle played an important role, both because of her friendly temperament and because a Zelle presence helped maintain morale. The Jefferson company emerged from the war as a viable and profitable operation, but one that would have to plan carefully to survive the changing peacetime economy of the late 1940s.[31]

Improved service and a better image were required throughout the industry if bus operators aimed to retain any of their extra passengers after the war. Americans were anxious to return to the individual freedom of their autos, but the slow production of new parts and vehicles impeded their move away from public transport. Here was an opportunity. Bus companies might thrive if they could obtain and then promote larger and more comfortable buses running on modern highways, using well-equipped terminals, and catering to a variety of regular and leisure travellers. Such improvements, however, demanded both entrepreneurial initiatives and the ability to obtain the necessary equipment and materials.[32]

As early as 1944, Zelle was negotiating for new coaches. He was well aware that his buses were old, some having done 1.5 million miles apiece. Purchases, however, were slow. Significant numbers of new vehicles were delivered in 1947, including limousine cars for the reservation service between the Twin

Cities and Rochester. Yet it was not until 1949 that the fleet acquired enough buses, including some powered by diesel, to retire veteran coaches. By this time a modern passenger terminal at Rochester was also open. This, however, was not purpose-built, as originally planned. It was a conversion of the Chicago Great Western station, which the Jefferson shared with that railway company and other bus lines. Given the need to add to the Minneapolis garage, to modernize the interior of the Mason City terminal, and to assist commission agents at small, intermediate points in upgrading their facilities – especially their restrooms – Jefferson directors could not finance a modern, independent terminal at Rochester. Building costs had risen dramatically.[33]

Post-war inflation also meant higher labour costs. Bus operators generally thought that wage and pension provisions had increased disproportionately, threatening their livelihood. Jefferson managers, though well disposed to their workers, were certainly concerned about the rise. In 1946, labour costs accounted for 48 per cent of total operating costs and consumed 38 cents of every dollar of gross operating revenue; they continued to rise throughout the decade. There was no clear way to reduce labour costs or, indeed, any other part of operating expenses. Neither was there any sign of an increase in income to offset them.

In 1946 and 1947 passengers rode the Jefferson buses because they wanted short-distance mobility and because they did not have access to autos. By 1949, however, they were drifting away in significant numbers. Those who remained expected high standards and better schedules at no added expense. In fact, fares were slow to rise and very nearly declined. Bus operators in 1947 and 1948 spent considerable time and money justifying their existing interstate rates to government authorities. As for intrastate fare increases, the Jefferson company did not file application for these in Missouri, Iowa and Minnesota until 1949. Additional revenue was certainly required to pay for rising operating costs, but managers sought a delicate balance between enticing and deterring passengers. A better image might justify higher prices. Yet despite advertising and greater publicity, the company still retained the negative wartime profile of standing room only, long ticket lines, and old, overworked buses. Neither modernization nor reasonable fares were sufficient to stop the decline in passengers in the early 1950s.[34]

The Jefferson Company was not alone in its struggle for a viable existence in post-war America. As a NAMBO director, Zelle saw that the entire bus industry needed to readjust. Like fellow Minnesotan Laurence Rossman in Grand Rapids, he thought that better public relations would both inform Americans about regular activities and market bus travel as an exciting commodity. There were legislative issues as well. Government authorities would have to be more flexible about the maximum size of buses and differential scales of charges if business was to grow. Another goal was state apportionment of motor-vehicle taxation, allowing bus companies to pay one tax, to be divided among the states through which their lines travelled, rather than being taxed in each state.[35]

While Zelle continued to contribute to the national bus debates in the late 1940s, he increasingly preferred to involve himself in Minnesota or midwestern affairs. He had always been active in the local business community and before the end of the war had become a director of the First National Bank of Minneapolis, the Russell Miller Milling Company, and the Northwestern Fire & Marine Insurance Company. In the late 1940s and early 1950s he accepted more directorships, including those of the First Bank Stock Corporation and the Federal Reserve Bank of Minneapolis. His most time-consuming appointment, however, came in 1944, when he was named a trustee of the bankrupt Wisconsin Central Railway Company. It was ironic that a man who had spent most of his working life developing a bus company should spend part of his mature years running a railroad. Yet it was also satisfying that he should be deemed suitable for the task. Edgar Zelle enjoyed this local diversification because he had more than contributed his share to the bus business. In 1950 he retired from the presidency of the Jefferson Transportation Company to become chairman of the board, a position he retained until 1964. Here he acted primarily as an advisor, while Lester Wakefield assumed the presidency. In this position Wakefield was assisted by Edgar's son, Louis, much as he had assisted Edgar Zelle.[36]

Edgar Zelle had been in the driver's seat for more than thirty-five years and at the head of the Jefferson Company for more than a quarter of a century. He had seen the bus industry emerge from its boisterous pioneering days to become a responsible and essential link in the country's transport network. With national giants like Greyhound and Trailways at one end of the spectrum and hundreds of small, independent companies linking thousands of communities at the other, the industry had adapted to the needs of a mobile population in the early twentieth century. Zelle's own route as an independent regional operator had travelled the middle ground. He emerged from the early days as a well-respected man who developed his business through careful planning and attention to detail. He chose not to become part of a large organization, preferring to run a compact, family-style company, over which he had control. He made a remarkable national contribution in the councils of the National Association of Motor Bus Operators, through government service in wartime, and as a public spokesperson for the industry at large. He always remained a gentleman who commanded widespread respect, both in the Minnesota community and throughout the bus industry.[37]

Notes

1. Office of Defense Transportation, press release, 15 February 1943, E.F. Zelle to L.P. Wakefield, 18 March 1944, and Jefferson Transportation Company, *Annual Report*, (1949), n.p. (hereafter cited as JTC, *AR*) – all in E.F. Zelle Records, Jefferson Lines, Inc., Minneapolis; *Bus Ride*, 3(4) (1967), p. 12. Unless otherwise noted, all archival material in this chapter, including clippings, is in the Zelle Records and all towns and cities mentioned are in Minnesota.

2. 'Resumé of E. Zelle's Life', incomplete typescript of an interview, n.d., p. 1; 'Edgar F. Zelle', typescript, 10 January 1951; *New Ulm Review* (1926), clipping.

3. 'Resume', p. 2; 'Edgar F. Zelle'; *New Ulm Review* (1926); *Minnesota Alumni Weekly* (1927), clipping; 'Biographical Fact Sheet, F. & M. Trustees, Past Presidents, Minnesota Alumni Association' (1967); *Minneapolis Tribune*, 2 March 1980, p. 4F; interview with L.N. Zelle (E.F. Zelle's son) by M. Walsh, Minneapolis, 8 October 1990.

4. 'Edgar F. Zelle'; [L.P. Wakefield], (1982), Comments on 'History of the Jefferson Company', typescript, 22 September 1982, pp. 1–2; 'The Past is Prologue', History of St Anthony Main, December 1982, n.p.; Order Notice Concerning the Share Holdings of the Motor Truck Service Co., 11 December 1919; *Minneapolis Tribune*, 7 August 1949, Upper Midwest Sec., p. 5; L. Zelle interview; W.R. Childs (1985), *Trucking and the Public Interest: The Emergence of Federal Regulation, 1914–1940*, Knoxville, TN, pp. 7–24.

5. [Wakefield], Comments, pp. 1–2; 'Past is Prologue'; L. Zelle interview; *Minneapolis Tribune*, 7 August 1949, Upper Midwest Sec., p. 5; Interstate Commerce Commission (ICC), (1926), 'Motor Bus and Truck Operations', docket 18300, Hearings, **5**, pp. 824–5, formerly ICC Records, ICC storage repository, Washington, DC; M. Walsh, 'Tracing the Hound: The Minnesota Roots of The Greyhound Bus Corporation', (chapter 4), pp. 76–7. *Truck and Bus Owner* **1–2** (1922–1924), (hereafter cited as *T&BO*), contains short descriptions of several Minnesota bus companies. Sources disagree about the formation date of the Red Bus Line: some give 1918, others 1921. Incorporation may have post-dated the actual operation.

6. 'Past is Prologue'; newspaper clipping scrapbook, 1923–1924, including: *St Cloud Daily Journal Press*, 22 January, 2 May, 13 June, 11 July, 28 July, 25 October, all in 1923, 20 February, ? October, both in 1924; *Little Falls Daily Transcript*, 9 March, 20 November, both in 1923; *Pierz Journal*, 26 April, 31 May, 8 November, all in 1923; *Minneapolis Tribune*, 20 July 1923, p. 4; *Long Prairie Leader*, 27 September, 1 November, both 1923; *Brainerd Dispatch*, 1, 2 and 10 November 1923; and *Pillager Herald*, 24 October 1924. A.L. Janes to R. Budd, 9 June 1925, President's Subject File 11532, Great Northern Railway Company Records, Minnesota Historical Society (MHS), (hereafter cited as GNR); Red Bus Line, *Timetables*, 15 October, 27 December both 1923, W.A. Luke Records, Spokane (hereafter cited as WALR). *T&BO*, **January** (1923), p. 7; **February** (1923), pp. 8, 9; **May** (1923), pp. 13–15; **June** (1923), pp. 6–7; **November** (1923), pp. 11–13. For examples of routes and service, see *Travel by Bus*, (the Minnesota Motor Bus Association's magazine with schedules), 15 July, 15 August, both 1924, 25 June, 1 August, and December, all 1925 (hereafter cited as *TbB*); *Bus Age*, **2**(June) (1922), pp. 20–23.

7. 'Jefferson Highway Transportation Co. Incorporated', (hereafter cited as JHTC), booklet published in conjunction with a stock flotation issue, [September 1921];

'$60,000 Class 'A' Common Stock ... JHTC', leaflet, and typescript financial statement, both released in conjunction with a stock flotation issue, February 1923; JHTC Certificate of Incorporation, 24 July 1922; 'Salesmen's Information Sheet', 1923. *Minneapolis Journal*, 22 April 1923, General News Sec., p. 19; and 3 February 1924, 5th Auto. Sec., p. 2. *Bus Age*, **2**(June) (1922), pp. 20–23. *Bus Transportation*, **2**(1) (1923), pp. 58–9; **2**(3) (1923), p. 163 (hereafter cited as *BT*).

8. 'To All Stockholders', in JHTC bulletin no. 9, 3 October 1924; [Wakefield], Comments, p. 2; A.L. Janes to R. Budd, 9 June 1925, GNR; ICC, 'Motor Bus and Truck Operations', exhibit 65; *Minneapolis Journal*, 3 February 1924, 2nd Auto. Sec., p. 7; *TbB*, 15 July 1924, p. 6; L. Zelle interview; *BT*, **2**(4) (1923), pp. 186–9.

9. A.L. Janes to R. Budd, 9 June 1925, GNR; *Laws of the State of Minnesota Relating to the Railroad and Warehouse Commission*, **1** (1925), pp. 161–7; ICC, 'Motor Bus and Truck Operations', **5**, pp. 852, 853; *Minneapolis Journal*, 2 August, p. 1; 27 October, p. 17 both 1925. *BT*, **4**(12) (1925), pp. 609, 610; Walsh, 'Tracing the Hound', (chapter 4), p. 81; M. Walsh, 'The Motor Carrier Act of 1935: The Origins and Establishment of Federal Regulation of the Interstate Bus Industry in the United States', (chapter 7), p. 139.

10. A.L. Janes to R, Budd, 9 June, 20 June, both 1925, GNR; Contract of Sale of JHTC Class C. Voting Stock to E.F. Zelle, 29 June 1925; E.F. Zelle and Northland Transportation Company, Agreement for purchase of 'certain property, busses and rights of the JHTC', 11 July 1925; [Wakefield], Comments, p. 2; L. Zelle interview. *Minneapolis Journal*, 2 August, pp. 1, 4; 3 August, p. 1, both 1925.

11. E.F. Zelle to the Stockholders of the JHTC, 24 August 1925, President's Subject File 11532, and 'Acquisition of Routes by Purchase', Northland Greyhound Lines, Inc. (Delaware), Memoranda and Instructions, undated, folder 4, both GNR. *Minneapolis Tribune*, 1 February, Auto Sec., p. 10, 14 July both in 1925; *Minneapolis Journal*, 13 July 1925, and assorted Twin Cities newspaper clippings c. 1925 in Bus Events folder. ICC, 'Investigation of Bus Fares', docket no. MC–C–550, stenographic minutes of proceedings, **13** (1948), pp. 3187, 3189, National Archives Record Group (hereafter cited as NARG), BMC–C–550, Washington National Records Center, Suitland, MD. Wakefield retired from his final position, chairman of the board, in 1973; 'History of the Jefferson Co.', n.p.

12. *Minneapolis Tribune*, 18 March; *Rochester* ?, 18 March; *Wanamingo Progress*, 25 March; *Owatonna Chronicle*, 26 March, all in 1926 clippings file. 'History of the Jefferson Co'. *Minneapolis Journal*, 27 October 1925, p. 17; 26 May, p. 2; 13 June, City Life Sec. p. 2, both 1926. JTC, *Timetables* (1926–1928), MHS. Minnesota, Railroad and Warehouse Commission, Auto Transportation Company Divison, *Biennial Report*, (1926), pp. 66, 68–72; (1928), pp. 175–7, 291, 292 (hereafter cited as MRWC, ATCD, *BR*). *Motor Coach Age*, **8**(September) (1956), pp. 3–4. The opposing railroads were the Chicago Great Western; Chicago, Milwaukee and St Paul; Chicago, Rock Island and Pacific; and the Minneapolis, Northfield, and Southern.

13. 'History of the Jefferson Company'. *Wanamingo Progress*, 17 December 1925; *Northfield Independent*, 14 January 1926; *Minneapolis Tribune*, 21 March 1926, clippings file. *Minneapolis Journal*, 4 December 1925, p. 38; 19 March, p. 25; 17 November, p. 1; 17 December, p. 39 – all 1926. *Minneapolis Tribune*, 7 February 1926, 6th Sec., p. 1 and 2nd Auto Sec., p. 4; ICC, 'Motor Bus and Truck Operations', **5**, pp. 874–5, ICC Records; *TbB*, **February** (1926), back cover. *BT*, **2**(8) (1923), pp. 372–4; **3**(9) (1924), pp. 393–5; **4**(1) (1925), p. 22 and **7**(6) (1928), pp. 314–16.

14. Certificate of Incorporation, Jefferson Airways Inc., 5 May 1928; Jefferson

Airways Board of Directors, Minutes, Special Meeting, 10 April, 30 July 1929; W.W. Quaintance to Jefferson Airways Depots, 28 November 1928; E.F. Zelle to J.W. Carnes, 3 December 1928; E.F Zelle to G.H. Hoppin, 14 January 1929; E.F. Zelle to City Editor, *St Paul Pioneer Press*, 15 March 1929; clippings from *Air Transportation*, June 1928 – January 1929; *Minneapolis Tribune*, 7 July 1928, p. 1; *Jefferson Bus and Airplane Timetables*, (1928), WALR. *BT*, **7**(11) (1928), p. 640; **8**(1) (1929), pp. 19–20; **8**(6) (1929), p. 353; G.N. Sandvick (1986), 'Enterprise in the Skies: The Early Years of Air Commerce in Minnesota', *Minnesota History* **50**(Fall), pp. 95–6.

15. 'History of the Jefferson Company'; JHTC Board of Directors, Minutes, Special Meeting, 20 August 1929, p. 94–7, bound in Corporate Records Book; E.F. Zelle to C.L. Truesdale, 8, 26, 30 October, 1929; E.F. Zelle to T. Albrecht, 22 October 1929; E.F. Zelle to R. Hastings, 21 March 1930; *Minnesota Motor Bus Schedules*, **January** (1929), pp. 2, 4, MHS.

16. E.F. Zelle to C.L. Truesdale, 8, 30 October, 1929; Articles of Agreement for the Sale of the Red Ball Transportation Company to the Jefferson Transportation Company, 16 June 1930. *Mason City Globe Gazette*, 13 June 1930, 30 June 1931; and *Des Moines Tribune*, 13 June 1930, clippings file. Mary Martin (Helen Schutz Brewer's daughter), interview with M. Walsh and A. Fishbeck, Mason City, 20 May 1991, and [H.S. Brewer], 'Autobiographical Account', typescript, copies of each in Mason City Public Library; JTC, 'AR', manuscript, 1930; JTC, *Timetable* 1 December 1930; ICC, 'Investigation of Bus Fares', **13** (1948), p. 3190, NARG BMC–C–550. For more information on Helen Schultz Brewer and the Red Ball Transportation Company, see 'Iowa's Bus Queen' (chapter 5), pp. 89–105.

17. 'Edgar F. Zelle'; L.A. Rossman to E.F. Zelle, 13 February 1925; 'Code of Principles of the Minnesota Motor Bus Association', (1924), WALR; *Commercial West*, 19 September 1925, p. 11. *BT*, **3**(10) (1924), pp. 482–4; **4**(3) (1925), p. 131. ICC, 'Motor Bus and Truck Operations', **5**, pp. 824–91, ICC Records. Rossman early became identified with the industry through his friendship with the Iron Range bus pioneers. He used his newspaper as a forum to argue the case for buses and his printing facilities to publish pamphlets as well as the early consolidated bus timetable, *Travel by Bus*. He gathered facts on the industry, became a consultant to the Greyhound Corporation, and sat on committees of the National Association of Motor Bus Operators (hereafter cited as NAMBO) – see Laurence A. Rossman Papers now in MHS Library, St Paul.

18. *St Paul Dispatch*, 19 February; *St Cloud Daily Times*, 23 April, 8 June; *Brainerd Daily Dispatch*, 25 April; *St Cloud Daily Journal Press*, 27 April; *Little Falls Transcript*, 22 May; *Little Falls Herald*, 29 May, and others, all 1925, in clippings file.

19. *Minneapolis Journal*, 4 January 1925, p. 6; 7 February 1926, 2nd Auto Sec., p. 4; 6 February 1927, 3rd Auto Sec., p. 4; 5 February 1928, 5th Auto Sec., p. 8; 3 February 1929, Northwest Auto Show Sec., p. 8; and 2 February 1930, Northwest Auto Show Sec., p. 10. *Minneapolis Tribune*, 1 February, Auto Sec., pp. 5, 10; and 7 February, 6th Sec., p. 1, both in 1926.

20. *Bus Facts*, (1930), pp. 6, 7; 'Brief History of Operation and Corporate History'(1939) , Northland Greyhound Lines, Inc. (Delaware), History, folder 1, GNR. 'Railroad Affiliations of the Greyhound Lines', pp. 1–3; and Greyhound Corporation, *Annual Report*, (1930), n.p., both in Greyhound Corporation Records, American Heritage Center, University of Wyoming, Laramie. Walsh, 'Tracing the Hound', (chapter 4), p. 84; MRWC, ATCD, *BR*, (1930), facing p. 342. The Northland Transportation Company and Northland Greyhound Lines list

separate statistics for 1929, but they were part of the same system and are treated here as one entity.

21. L.W. Hill to R. Budd, 16 March 1931, and E.F. Zelle to C.E. Wickman, 19 March 1931, both President's Subject File 11532, GNR; E.F. Zelle to H.R. Wiesner, to S.G. Palmer, to F.A. Chamberlain, and to C.L. Truesdale, all 12 March 1931; E.F. Zelle to A.F. Wagner, 13 and 17 March 1931; E.F. Zelle to G.N. Dayton, 14 March 1931; A.F. Wagner to E.F. Zelle, 14 March 1931; S.G. Palmer to E.F. Zelle, 18 March 1931; E.F. Zelle to S.G. Palmer, 25 March 1931. *Minneapolis Star*, 13 March; *Minneapolis Journal*, 13 March; *Mason City Globe Gazette*, 10 March – all 1931, clippings file. L. Zelle interview; *BT*, **10**(4) (1931), p. 209.

22. *Minneapolis Tribune*, 12 July 1930, pp. 1, 2. *Elkader Register* (Iowa), 2 October 1930; *Guttenberg Press* (Iowa), 27 November 1930; *Nevada Journal* (Iowa), 7 January 1931; *St Paul Dispatch*, 19 May 1931, clippings file. *Mason City Globe Gazette*, 30 June 1931, pp. 11, 12, 13; *Des Moines Register*, 19 July 1931, Bus Depot Sec. 8A, advertisement; E.F. Zelle to All Employees, 23 October 1931, in Minute Book, 1925 – December 1934, p. 159; JTC, manuscript and published Annual Reports, (AR) (1930–1933).

23. E.F. Zelle to R.J. Walsh, 19 January 1933; Dubuque Automobile Club to Governor C.H. Herring, 3 February 1933; E.F. Zelle to Our Iowa Friends, 20 February, 9 March, 1933; E.F. Zelle to R. Budd, 28 February 1933; 'List of bus companies doing business in Iowa in 1932 and their losses', 16 March 1933; 'Memorandum from E.F. Zelle re the burden of Iowa tonnage tax', 22 March 1933; 'Memorandum comparing ton-mile costs in Iowa of private passenger automobiles with the common carrier bus', [1933?]. Iowa Board of Railroad Commissioners, *Annual Report*, (1932), p. 354; (1933), pp. 394–5; (1934), pp. 392–3; (1935), p. 441 (hereafter cited as IBRC, *AR*).

24. E.F. Zelle to Crandic Stages Inc., to Our Iowa Friends, both 20 February 1933; E.F. Zelle to A.C. Bising, 1 March 1933; R.P. Smith to E.F. Zelle, 18 March, 25 March and 1 April 1933; E.F. Zelle to I. Bowen, 20 March 1933; J.W. Wrape to E.F. Zelle, 21 March 1933; E.F. Zelle to A.J. Ahlers, 17 April 1933; R.J. Walsh to E.F. Zelle, 20 April 1933; J.C. Davis, Jr, to R.J. Walsh, 26 April 1933; E.F. Zelle to J.M. Meighan, 11 May 1933; J.C. Davis, Jr to E.F. Zelle, 21 February 1935; JTC, Iowa Motor Bus Operating Expense Tax-Revenue Data, (1932–1934).

25. JTC, manuscript and published AR, (1930–1941); L. Zelle interview; 'History of the Jefferson Company'.

26. 'To All Employees', JHTC general bulletin nos 275 and 277, 27 May, 15 July 1937; E.F. Zelle to –?–, 16 December 1937; E.F. Zelle to C.L. Truesdale, 21 October 1937; *Mason City Globe Gazette*, 29 January, 31 December 1935, clippings; JTC, manuscript and published AR, (1930–1941); ICC, 'Investigation of Bus Fares', **13** (1948), p. 3187–8, NARG BMC–C–550; L. Zelle interview; NAMBO, *Proceedings*, **6** (1932), pp. 92–5 (hereafter cited as NAMBO, *Procs*); *BT*, **18**(11) (1939), p. 555. For a report of a strike against Greyhound, see *Minneapolis Tribune*, 26 November 1937, p. 4.

27. E.A. Bagby to E.F. Zelle, 4 August 1938; E.F. Zelle to J.F. Selb, 29 August 1938; 'Biographical Fact Sheet, F. & M. Trustees'; NAMBO, *Procs*, **1–15** (1927–1941); NAMBO Board of Directors, Minutes, (1927–1941), NAMBO Collection, American Heritage Center, University of Wyoming, Laramie (hereafter cited as NAMBO, Mins); US Congress, 72nd Cong., 1 Sess. (1932), *Hearings before the Senate Committee on Interstate Commerce*, part 3, pp. 480–5.

28. Office for Emergency Management, 'Statement of Acceptance', 23 June 1941;

Advisory Commission to the Council of National Defense, Memorandum to Members of Central and Regional Committees, 26 December 1941; E.F. Zelle to H.H. Kelly, 30 December 1941; J.L. Rogers to E.F. Zelle, 24 January, 25 February 1942; E.F. Zelle to J.L. Rogers, 24 August, 1942; Office of Defense Transportation, press release, 15 February, 21 December 1943.

29. R.C. Hoffman, Jr, to E.F. Zelle, 13 March 1944; G.A. Richardson to E.F. Zelle, 13 April 1944; E.F. Zelle to L.P. Wakefield, 11, 14, 18, 24 March 1944; E.F. Zelle to Our Stockholders, May 1944; E.F. Zelle to Lt Commander T.E. Pearson, 14 November 1944; L. Zelle interview. NAMBO Mins: 8 April 1941, pp. 1–3; 5 February, pp. 2–3; 2 April, pp. 1–3; 23–4 July, pp. 1–3; 23–4 November, pp. 2–3 – all 1942; 13 May 1943, pp. 3–7; 24–5 February, 1944, pp. 2–5; 26–7 October, 1944, pp. 4–6. E.F. Zelle, 'Highway Passenger Transportation by Bus in Wartime', NAMBO report to the 40th meeting of the American Automobile Association, 20–21 November 1944, NAMBO Collection; NAMBO, *Procs*, **16** (1942), pp. 10–14, 44, 45–6, 59–70, and **17** (1946), p. 11; *Bus Facts*, (1940), p. 7.

30. ICC, Bureau of Transport Economics and Statistics, 'Revenue, Expenses, Other Income and Statistics of Class I Motor Carriers of Passengers, Statement Q750' (Annual and Quarterly), (1940–1946), formerly ICC Departmental Library, Washington, DC, now Surface Transportation Board; JTC, *AR* (1940–1946); ICC, 'Investigation of Bus Fares', **13** (1948), pp. 3199–201, NARG BMC–C– 550. Revenues reached $1,855,030.76 in 1946, a figure that was not attained again until 1958, by which time inflation had affected the value of the dollar.

31. 'Statement of E.F. Zelle', 1 April 1942; E.F. Zelle to Arch [A.F. Wagner?], 17 June 1942; L.P. Wakefield to E.F. Zelle, 8 March 1944; E.F. Zelle to L.P. Wakefield, 11, 14, 18, 24 March 1944; E.F. Zelle to Our Stockholders, May 1944; E.F. Zelle to T.E. Pearson, 14 November 1944; JTC, *AR* (1940–1946); L. Zelle interview; ICC, 'Investigation of Bus Fares', **13**, pp. 3199–201, NARG BMC–C–550; *BT*, **21**(12) (1942), p. 562.

32. L. Zelle interview; interview with W.A. Luke, then editor of *Bus Ride*, with M. Walsh, Spokane, 22 October 1990; M. Walsh, 'The Intercity Bus and Its Competitors in the United States in the Mid-Twentieth Century' in C. Wrigley and J. Shepherd (eds) (1991), *On The Move: Essays in Labour and Transport History Presented to Philip Bagwell*, London, pp. 244–8.

33. E.F. Zelle to T.E. Pearson, 14 November 1944; E.F. Zelle to JTC Employees, 27 December 1946; E.F. Zelle to L.P. Wakefield, 30 April, 2 May 1947; E.F. Zelle to A.N. Kelting, 17 February 1948; J.B. Greeninger to Mr and Mrs Zelle, 10 March 1948; 'Instructions for Jefferson Transportation Limousine Service', 4 March 1948; JTC, *AR*, (1945–1952); Jefferson Lines, *Motor Bus Timetables*, (1946), (1947), MHS; ICC, 'Investigation of Bus Fares', **13** (1948), pp. 3190–92, NARG BMC–C–550.

34. E.F. Zelle to L.A. Rossman, 11 July 1945, 28 December 1946; L.A. Rossman to E.F. Zelle, 13 July 1945; L.A. Rossman to I. Bowen, 28 December 1946; 'Statement of E.F. Zelle re passenger rates', 28 December 1946; JTC, *AR*, (1945–52); L. Zelle interview; ICC, Statement Q750, (1940–1952), ICC library, and 'Investigation of Bus Fares', **13** (1948), p. 3200–201, NARG BMC–C–550; 'Excerpt from NAMBO, Procs, **18**, re The Bus Rate Case', NAMBO Collection; ICC, Docket no MC–C–550, *Investigation of Bus Fares*, **1–3** (1950), Washington, DC; NAMBO, *Procs*, **17** (1946), pp. 13–14.

35. L.A. Rossman to E.F. Zelle, 23, 27 May 1942; E.F. Zelle to L.A. Rossman, 29 May 1942, 11 July 1945; E.F. Zelle to A.W. Koehler, 4 January 1946; NAMBO

Board, Mins, (1945–1953), NAMBO Collection; L. Zelle interview; W.A. Luke interview; M. Walsh, 'The Intercity Bus', pp. 244–6.

36. 'Biographical Fact Sheet, F.& M. Trustees'; 'Edgar F. Zelle'; [Wakefield], Comments; *Who's Who in Minnesota* (1958), p. 233; *Minneapolis Tribune*, 7 August 1949, Upper Midwest Sec., p. 5; *Minneapolis Star*, 2 November 1951, p. 25. Wakefield became chairman of the board in 1964, at which time L. Zelle moved up to the presidency. He, in turn, became board chairman in 1978. His son, Charles A., is the current president of the Jefferson Lines, Inc.

37. L. Zelle interview; W.A. Luke interview; M. Wnek (1987), 'Edgar Frederick Zelle, A Shaper of the Industry', *Destinations*, March 1987, pp. 62–3. Zelle eased out of his business activities as he had eased out of the bus industry. Even in retirement, he remained busy with civic and cultural engagements. He died in Minneapolis on 28 August 1978, after several years of poor health.

YOU SAVE MONEY WHEN YOU TRAVEL BY GREYHOUND BUS

A message of economy...
to all who pay money for
TRAVEL

AT lowest costs in history you can travel almost anywhere in America today. Reaching out over the scenic highways, motor buses of the Greyhound Lines, and "Yelloway" system, touch at a thousand places from coast to coast and border to border.

In dollars New York is drawn closer to Pittsburgh; Philadelphia to Jacksonville; Chicago to Los Angeles; Denver to Baltimore. Glorious overland trips are now well within your means. Today you can afford to travel.

Through Greyhound Lines, places before accessible but once a day now enjoy two to five daily buses along each important highway. Between larger travel centers there are Greyhound buses almost every hour of the day and night. Here is new convenience, new and better service, in transportation. Your comfort and safe arrival are guarded by the largest, most responsible of motor bus systems. You are piloted by drivers not only highly skilled but selected carefully for character. Buses, of modern, all-steel construction, are fitted with every comfort and safety device.

Modern Transportation

Learn the economy of transportation that measures fuel in light weight gallons, that carries far more passengers per ton of vehicle weight, that is powered by the modern gasoline motor.

Learn, too, the pleasure of Greyhound travel—the thrill of the open road, of valley and vista seen from the bending highways.

Fares to local and long distance points from your city, together with time tables and interesting circle trip information, are yours upon request. Consult your local bus depot or write *Motor Transit Management Company, 1157 So. Wabash Ave., Chicago.*

NEW YORK · LOS ANGELES · JACKSONVILLE · CHICAGO · PHILADELPHIA · CLEVELAND · DETROIT · CINCINNATI · BALTIMORE
WASHINGTON · PITTSBURGH · INDIANAPOLIS · ST. LOUIS · SAN FRANCISCO · DENVER · ATLANTA · NEW ORLEANS

Fig. 9   Greyhound Advertisement reprinted in *Saturday Evening Post*, 14 September 1929, p. 224

"WE'RE A *two-car* FAMILY, NOW!

Our own auto for trips around-town
GREYHOUND for trips out-of-town
– saving us time, fatigue and money! "

GONE ARE THE DAYS when only a wealthy family could afford two cars! Today, any one owning a private automobile can have a *second car* without extra cost—one of the finest and smoothest-riding in the world.

This second car will deeply cut your yearly travel bill, instead of increasing it. Its cost will be about one-third as much as operating a private auto—although an expert driver (one of the world's safest and best) goes with it.

We're talking about Greyhound, of course. In what other "out-of-town car" can you find such riding ease, such security, such low cost? If you want economy and scenic enjoyment mixed with your travel, here is the ideal plan: Use the faithful family auto around town, on business or pleasure, for a thousand and one short trips.

But don't wear it out (and weary yourself) with long highway trips. Let Greyhound carry you—swiftly, safely, on the most convenient of all public transportation schedules.

A dozen authentic tests show that private car driving expense averages 4½ cents per mile, or more, *excluding* age depreciation. Greyhound round trips between principal American cities average from 1 cent to 1½ cents per mile—even less, on certain routes. Just compare these rates with *any* fares for *any* transportation!

So let this "second car" save dollars on each trip—save fatigue, repair bills, parking worries, traffic strain. Ride with Greyhound to business appointments, football games, Thanksgiving and Christmas reunions—or to the sunshine zones of Florida, Gulf Coast, California.

FREE—THIS FASCINATING PICTORIAL BOOKLET OF STRANGE AND UNBELIEVABLE PLACES

PRINCIPAL GREYHOUND INFORMATION OFFICES

Mail this coupon to nearest information office (listed at left) for an absorbing 24-page booklet, picturing and describing America's most amazing things and places. Paste coupon on a penny postcard if you wish. If you want rates and route information on any special trip, jot down destination on line below.

Information on trip to _____

Name _____

Address _____

Fig. 10 Greyhound Advertisement reprinted in *Saturday Evening Post*, 12 November 1936, p. 36

20 MILLION MILES
OF SAFE BUS TRAVEL

– the Record of these Greyhound Drivers

ALERT, responsible drivers in a hundred cities today swing into the control seats of the outbound Greyhound Buses. Before them stretch smooth highways to distant cities. In their competent charge is the good name of Greyhound Lines, largest motor transportation system in America.

Greyhound buses travel daily a distance equal to three times the mileage around the world. They carry millions of passengers in safety, in comfort, at the lowest cost ever offered for dependable overland travel.

Measures of Safety

Every Greyhound driver, schooled in the standards of safety and service which have built the Greyhound system, is a man of character, reliability. Physically and mentally he has stood the most rigorous of examinations.

He has come up through operating and mechanical departments that have taught him every nut and bolt in the coach he drives. Safety, courtesy and care he has learned in countless safety meetings and experience tests on the road. Not only is he courteous to his own passengers but to the thousands of other motorists he meets on the highways.

Responsible Ownership

In every terminal city great service garages check motors, chassis, tires and brakes, before each run. Every mechanism must be fit, every safety device operating at highest efficiency, always.

Winter and summer, day and night, millions of people depend on Greyhound bus travel. For a hundred miles or a trip across the continent you save money, enjoy new travel convenience and pleasure, on these Greyhounds of the highways.

Write for Greyhound bus fares and time tables from your city. An illuminating booklet "Motor Bus Transportation" will also be sent you. Address, Department of Travel Information, Motor Transit Management Company, Chicago.

Greyhound drivers operate under the strict supervision of a corps of traveling safety directors. They receive detailed information as to weather and road conditions. All changes in traffic codes and regulations must be thoroughly understood before a driver takes the road.

Frequent meetings of Greyhound drivers to promote safety are held at each division point of the system. Here safety commissioners, traffic officials and highway engineers gather to instruct and co-operate with the drivers of the Greyhound buses.

DEPENDABLE GREYHOUND Lines
MOTOR TRANSIT MANAGEMENT COMPANY

NEW YORK ᐧ LOS ANGELES ᐧ JACKSONVILLE ᐧ CHICAGO ᐧ PHILADELPHIA ᐧ CLEVELAND ᐧ DETROIT ᐧ CINCINNATI
BALTIMORE ᐧ WASHINGTON ᐧ PITTSBURGH ᐧ INDIANAPOLIS ᐧ ST. LOUIS ᐧ KANSAS CITY ᐧ DENVER ᐧ ATLANTA ᐧ NEW ORLEANS

Fig. 11 Greyhound Advertisement reprinted in *Saturday Evening Post*, 23 March 1929, p. 180

Fig. 12 Greyhound Advertisement reprinted in *Saturday Evening Post*, 25 October 1935, p. 97

"Maybe we can't carry rifles_*but we can help win the Battle of Transportation*"

Making available equipment meet the demands of wartime travel . . . that's the Battle of Transportation! And today this battle is critical—urgent. With present facilities already taxed to near-capacity, intercity bus lines must carry additional millions of essential travelers who will be in industry or uniform in 1943. This means that every loyal American has one more patriotic job to do—eliminate all unnecessary trips—make room for these millions of men and women who MUST travel by bus to get on with the war.

In this war of production and manpower, our highways must continue to "bring up the men"! And that's the job of the intercity bus lines—carrying war workers, soldiers, sailors and marines, selectees, farmers—an ever-growing number of all the people who must move back and forth to win the war.

Specializing in transporting manpower, intercity buses are carrying passengers at the incredible rate of 750 million per year. And millions of these can travel in no other way. For buses provide irreplaceable transportation to all of our factories, camps, farms and homes *along more than 330,000 miles of highway.* Thousands of communities, in all parts of America, have no other means of public travel!

And with private automobiles now traveling less, due to wartime restrictions, there are more and more essential travelers who must "take the bus."

This growing job for intercity buses cannot be shared by any other transportation. It's a job that must be done on the *highways*—a job that calls for flexibility of movement—the ability to go anywhere, anytime, over any route—*a job that only buses can do!*

And though carrying capacity has been greatly reduced by lower speed limits, by tire rationing, and by shortage of equipment, the bus lines are making every conceivable effort to keep their service to the job. Many changes have been made, but bus travel

still offers *all the comfort and convenience that possibly can be mustered under wartime regulations.*

The Battle of Transportation *must be won!* And your help is vitally important. Avoid holiday and week-end travel—eliminate all unnecessary trips . . . by doing so, you'll help *keep the highways at work for victory!*

★ ★ ★ ★

ADOPT THIS FOUR-POINT VICTORY PROGRAM NOW!
1. Buy War Bonds. 2. Take part in Civilian Defense. 3. Keep the scrap rolling in. 4. Don't waste transportation!

MOTOR BUS LINES OF AMERICA
NATIONAL ASSOCIATION OF MOTOR BUS OPERATORS, WASHINGTON, D.C.

Fig. 13 National Association of Motor Bus Operators (NAMBO) Advertisement, c. 1942

Fig. 14 Greyhound Advertisement reprinted in *Saturday Evening Post*, 20 December 1947, p. 11

Fig. 15 Greyhound Advertisement reprinted in *Saturday Evening Post*, 26 May 1934, p. 121

Fig. 16 Greyhound 'Mock-Up'

Part Three

Alternative Avenues

7   The Motor Carrier Act of 1935: The Origins and Establishment of Federal Regulation of the Interstate Bus Industry in the USA

In October 1935 Arthur M. Hill, president of the National Association of Motor Bus Operators (NAMBO), addressed the ninth annual meeting of the organization, held in New Orleans, with the following words: 'We are today standing upon the threshold of an important new era in the history of the motor bus industry – the era of federal regulation.[1] He was referring to the passage of the Motor Carrier Act of 9 August 1935.

This sector of the transport industry was neither the first nor the last to be subject to federal government control. In 1887 the Interstate Commerce Act had brought all railroads engaged in interstate commerce under federal supervision. In 1938 the Civil Aeronautics Act established rules for the conduct of airlines, while two years later water carriers came under the jurisdiction of the Interstate Commerce Commission (ICC). The motives for and the results of federal regulation in each sector were not the same, but the discussions on intervention in the bus and motor-carrier industries illustrate the arguments important to the changing concept of looking after the public interest in the early twentieth century.[2]

The background of government regulation of transport

Before the First World War Americans demanded and eventually received protection from discriminatory and excessive railroad rates. In this first surge of government regulation, shippers and consumers were concerned to prevent the railroads from charging high and unfair rates. But this protection of the public interest also came to include other groups. Both the railroads themselves and the regulatory agency, the ICC, became so involved in the legislative and judicial processes that the commission became partially captured by the railroads which it was established to control and regulation became, in part at least, 'self-regulation'.[3]

Yet even this approach to transport management did not remain static for long. With the advent and spread of the automobile, the motor coach, the truck (lorry) and the airplane, government regulation took on a broader canvas. On the one hand the railroads, increasingly threatened by these new modes of transport, sought to protect their declining business. Then within each of the new branches aggressive entrepreneurs claimed both government subsidies and protection. Regulation in the public interest became a means of advancing both their particular industry interests and the interest of the dominant firms within specific carrier branches. Government regulation of transport was becoming more complex as the twentieth century moved into its second quarter.

As the Depression struck and economic conditions deteriorated in the 1930s there were calls for economic harmony and coordination among transport industries in the public interest. There was even some discussion of national planning. But planning looked too much like authoritarianism. Only in the international crisis of the Second World War could the competitive ethos among public carriers be strangled politically. When peace and prosperity returned, Americans reconverted and adopted a flexible regulatory policy. Now not only did government agencies protect consumers, monitor monopoly, sanction cartels within industries and promote new activities, they also aimed to achieve an integrated transport system based on the inherent advantage of each mode, with competition being controlled. With such a wide mandate, government regulators could not and did not satisfy the greatest social needs and undoubtedly wasted resources, but they did reconcile the divergent transport groups within the country.

The early growth of the bus industry and state regulation

The long-distance bus industry in the USA originated in the second decade of the present century when numerous entrepreneurs throughout the country started local services between nearby towns or beyond the suburbs, using elongated saloon cars. Few were familiar with motor traffic management and operating practices, but many were willing to take on a new venture which had a low cost of entry. Starting up local services, frequently run on a customer-demand basis with cash fares paid to the driver, successful operators gradually built up steady routes and fixed schedules. Encouraged by their early success in both urban and rural areas, they welded together longer routes and by 1918 some companies ran vehicles a one-way distance of 45 miles. Subsequently, by connecting their routes with those of like-minded businessmen, bus men were able to offer a long-distance service of sorts. By 1920, hundreds of small bus companies were providing local transport while dozens were attempting a regional movement of passengers.[4]

Within a few years bus operations had multiplied and become more sophisticated. By 1925, 6,174 bus companies ran 31,975 vehicles over 218,601 route miles.[5] Most of these firms were still small and operated a handful of improvised and frequently second-hand vehicles over short distances. The demand for passenger transport was still growing, and men with little capital saw and took the opportunities to cater for this market. But alongside these numerous local venturers their more ambitious, more experienced or wealthier counterparts pushed the bus industry in new directions. Acquiring fleets of specially designed vehicles which were more reliable and more comfortable, and adopting systematic techniques of business operation and management, they pushed their routes further – even beyond state boundaries – and they offered facilities at terminals. These larger companies clearly envisaged long-distance travel as well as merely serving their communities.[6]

The growing popularity of road transport, which included the individualistic automobile and lorries and vans as well as buses, created problems for governments, ranging from the need to finance better roads to the desirability of ensuring public safety. At the state level pioneers attempted to resolve some of these problems in the years up to 1919 through general laws licensing vehicles and requiring driver insurance and competence. But, faced by the rapid expansion of motor vehicles after the First World War, many state governments passed more specific and stringent legislation and focused their attention on economic issues like competition and fares.[7]

Authorities became concerned to control entry into bus operation, usually through the granting of a certificate of public convenience and necessity. They also examined schedules of rates and charges to ensure that these were reasonable. Arguing that motor carriers were public utilities and that the public had to be protected, state regulatory agencies determined whether the applicant was financially secure enough to run a safe and adequate service throughout the year. Then, wishing to avoid unnecessary duplication of passenger services, they considered the impact of the proposed new service on existing transport agencies, both motorized and non-motorized.[8] By 1925 three-quarters of the states, including the most heavily populated ones, not only required that bus companies should conform to some minimum standards of conduct but adopted a policy of controlled monopoly, which attempted to balance the elimination of wasteful competition against protection from a potentially oppressive monopoly.[9] Long-distance bus transport was emerging from its pioneer phase of growth. Within the industry, improvement in operating practices and specifically designed vehicles promised better service, while within the economy at large, state regulations protecting companies from undue competition by new carrier entry, and establishing minimum codes of behaviour, promised stability.

Such stability, however, did not last long. Already bus transport was spilling beyond the confines of state boundaries. Those bus operators who were based near state lines, and ambitious firms looking to regional and even national trade, were engaged in interstate as well as intrastate transport. Up to 1925 this distinction was of minor significance, because states exercised some control over interstate motor carriers. Using the authority set out in Gibbons v. Ogden (1824) and reinforced by more recent decisions in the Minnesota rate cases (1913), Hendrick v. Maryland (1915) and Kane v. New Jersey (1916), states, in the absence of federal regulation, could prescribe reasonable provisions for local needs for those phases of interstate commerce not demanding general or uniform regulation. Thus, interstate bus operators were required to have a certificate of public convenience and necessity to operate in a given state, and failure to meet state requirements had led to denials of certification.[10] But this regulation of the interstate bus industry collapsed in 1925 when the Supreme Court handed down three decisions, Buck v. Kuykendall, Bush v. Maloy and Michigan Commission v. Duke, negating the doctrine of reasonable provisions.[11] In essence the court specified that state regulations could not restrict the operations of interstate carriers when they were intended to prevent competition. States had no authority over economic issues like the quality of service and fares: these were the responsibility of the federal government. Only in matters of safety and road maintenance could states restrict the operation of interstate motor carriers.

Following the Supreme Court decisions of 1925, many intrastate companies became interstate carriers not subject to regulation. Most instances of operators driving short distances to cross a state line merely to call their traffic 'interstate' took place in the heavily populated Atlantic coastal states. But the principle of freedom from restraint extended nationwide and paved the way for a surge of competition between uncertificated interstate motor carriers and regularly certificated intrastate carriers.[12] Deregulation did not bring either widespread or instant chaos in the long-distance bus industry, but it did revive some of the low standards and irregularity of service which was prevalent in the early 'jitney' days before and during the First World War and it did lead to rate-cutting, below the relevant costs of producing the service in certain regions.[13] Such a situation provided the impetus for federal regulation.

The path to federal regulation

Following the decision in the Buck and Bush cases Senator Cummins of Iowa introduced a bill in the 69th Congress in 1925, providing for the regulation of interstate commerce by motor vehicles operating on the public highways. The bill included common carriers of property as well as common carriers of persons, and state regulatory commissions were to administer the law. This was the first in a series of bills to come before succeeding Congresses for the next nine years. Variations in these forty bills called for regulation of carriers of persons only, and control by joint state boards and by the ICC.[14] In addition to the bills, hearings on the regulation of motor vehicles were conducted by both the Senate Committee on Interstate Commerce and the House Committee on Interstate and Foreign Commerce. The federal government regulatory agency, the ICC, also held two extensive investigations of the motor-transport industry, and the ensuing reports in 1928 and 1932 made suggestions for legislation. Then the Federal Coordinator of Transportation, Joseph Eastman, appointed in 1933, recommended regulation of interstate motor-vehicle operations in his first three reports, *Regulation of Transportation Agencies*. Furthermore, organized interest groups like the Chamber of Commerce of the USA, the National Transportation Committee, the National Association of Railroad and Utilities Commissioners and NAMBO discussed at length and frequently supported the principle of federal regulation. Among government legislators, officials and transport interests there was considerable concern over shaping the future of motor-carrier growth.[15]

None of these parties doubted that the federal government had the power to regulate interstate road transport to the full extent that such regulation was necessary in the public interest. That authority was clearly stated in the constitution, and precedents for regulating rail carriers had been established by the Interstate Commerce Act of 1887 and subsequent legislation in the early twentieth century. The lengthy debates on and the objections to specific motor-carrier bills stemmed primarily from the diversity of the interests involved, and these groups were further influenced by the changing economic environment in the USA. Only the railroads consistently supported regulation, in the hope that their motorized rivals would be subject to controls similar to those applied to themselves. The highly competitive and individualistic road-haulage, or trucking, industry opposed early regulatory bills as unnecessary, undesirable and impractical. Other motor interests like the NAMBO and the National Automobile Chamber of Commerce opposed specific bills which were not to their liking, while politicians, worried about the infringement of state rights by federal regulation or the possibility of railroad control over a regulated motor-carrier industry, blocked the progress of some legislation. The passing years and the maturing of the motor carrier trade altered some opinions, while the disastrous economic conditions of the 1930s provided another twist to the arguments as the feasibility and advisability of coordinating the transport sector were discussed. In the end an alliance of diverse bedfellows came together to back the Motor Carrier Act of 1935.[16]

The bus industry and its national organization, NAMBO, generally supported the federal regulation of interstate motor carriers. By 1925 most companies involved in long-distance passenger transport had experienced the impact of state regulation, and approved of the protection of carriers from excessive competition by the certification process as well as the enforcement of standards of operating practice. They realized that state regulation had brought financial stability to the early bus industry and felt both discouraged and threatened after the Buck and Bush decisions. As bus lines started to merge in 1926, climaxing in major consolidations in 1929 and 1930, so most larger firms continued to support regulation. They had already improved their internal operating practices and could conform to any safety, scheduling or accounting standards which the federal government might establish. Certification for new entrants and the publication of rates would indeed provide protection from irregular operators. As congressional debates lengthened and stalemate threatened, some dissenting bus spokesmen spoke more loudly in favour of the merits of free-market competition. Others worried that they would not be treated fairly if the railroad-dominated ICC was in charge of regulation.[17] Specific bus opposition to the 1934 bill stemmed primarily from the fact that the National Recovery Administration Bus Code, adopted in October 1933, had not been given adequate time in which to show its effectiveness. Increasing dissatisfaction with the code, and then, of more significance, the unconstitutional nature of the National Industrial Recovery Act in May 1935, once again rallied the bus industry to support federal regulation.[18]

Road hauliers were not as firmly committed to regulation as their bus counterparts, nor were government officials quite so anxious to regulate them. In the 1920s, when business was buoyant and the number of vehicles on the road was increasing rapidly, lorry owners argued that a new industry dominated by small firms with low fixed costs should be allowed to develop freely. Competition would stimulate the growth of cheap and efficient services. When the states did introduce regulatory laws they found that enforcement was problematic because most hauliers used few vehicles or frequently a single truck, and were troublesome to locate. Furthermore, it was often difficult to distinguish between common, contract and private carriers, thereby creating problems of enforcement.[19]

Not surprisingly, when the drive for regulation moved from the state to the federal level, hauliers continued to oppose those motor-carrier bills which included freight as well as passengers. But as small units consolidated into companies in the late 1920s some of the larger organizations began to see the benefits of regulation. They felt threatened by the 'chiselers' or fly-by-night operators who, aided by lorry dealers and manufacturers, managed to acquire a vehicle on credit and survived for a short time by undercutting rates, thereby creating a high degree of instability. And when the Depression reduced business, larger firms actively supported moves which would eliminate these irresponsible intra-industry rivals. They voiced such sentiments in the second ICC hearings on motor vehicles, and the 1932 report, unlike its predecessor, recommended the regulation of both buses and trucks. With the arrival of Franklin D. Roosevelt in the presidency and the advent of New Deal legislation in 1933, these hauliers responded positively to the establishment of a self-regulating National Recovery Administration Truck Code, which they preferred to congressional legislation. When the National Industrial Recovery Act was declared unconstitutional and when assurances were given that the ICC would be reorganized to include a special division for each kind of transport, the haulage lobby threw its weight behind the Wheeler Bill, which eventually became the Motor Carrier Act.[20]

The strongest and most active transport group favouring the federal regulation of motor carriers was ironically the railroads – not, however, on the grounds of maintaining order within the road sector, but as a means of ensuring their own survival in the face of increasing competition. Already, in the early 1920s, rail managers were voicing concern that buses were making inroads into their short- and medium-haul passenger traffic. They claimed that motor coaches offered cheaper services because they were inadequately taxed and were not subject to regulation. Yet, even when more states passed motor-carrier legislation, buses still offered a cheaper service because their demand for capital was lower and because they were a more flexible means of transport. Accordingly, in the mid-1920s several trunk rail lines decided to use buses and they organized their own motor subsidiaries rather than trying to curb competition through legislation. Expansion was rapid. In January 1925 three steam railroads operated buses: by the end of 1929 sixty-two ran 1,256 buses on 16,793 miles of route.[21]

But the growth of bus subsidiaries and the increasing willingness of state governments to protect existing rail operations through the certification of new motor-carrier entrants did not halt the flow of railroad complaints. Following the consolidation of bus lines and the emergence of transcontinental bus routes in the late 1920s, railroad leaders became more active in discussions of the federal regulation of interstate bus transport. Anxious to prevent further reductions in their passenger traffic, they flooded the hearings of congressional committees and the ICC with arguments similar to those propounded at the the state level a few years earlier.[22]

Then, in the generally depressed economic conditions of the early 1930s when freight and passenger revenues were declining, the railroads, facing severe financial difficulties, hardened their attitude to competition.[23] Anxious to preserve themselves at any cost, they decried all their competitors – trucks, buses, cars and ships – and called for financial assistance as well as government regulation of other carriers. Aid from the Railroad Credit Corporation and the Reconstruction Finance Corporation staved off a series of bankruptcies in 1932 but remedial legislation awaited the incoming administration of Franklin Roosevelt in 1933. The Emergency Railroad Transportation Act of 16 June

1933 offered help in the shape of a new agency – the Coordinator of Transportation. Appointed initially for one year, but serving in this office for three, Joseph Eastman conducted a series of extensive investigations into the operations of the railroads and into inter-carrier competition. He advised Congress that the USA had a wasteful and overdeveloped transport network, and that the most effective and cheapest system could be developed only by reliable and responsible managers subject to public authority. To achieve this objective he recommended economies and reorganization within the railroad industry, a comprehensive system of regulation for interstate motor and water carriers similar to that in force for the railroads, and the restructuring of the ICC to supervise the new regulation.[24]

The only proposal which was enacted promptly was the regulation of road transport, where much of the spadework for the Motor Carrier Act of 1935 had been done in the debates in and out of Congress during the previous nine years. With the major lobbies – bus, road haulage and railroad – all now in general agreement on the principle of regulation, it was possible to push a bill through Congress. Each interest group remained suspicious of the others and of the nature and degree of government control, but they recognized that some regulation was necessary and perhaps even desirable and that it ought not to be further delayed.

The Motor Carrier Act and its early implications

The Motor Carrier Act applied generally 'to the transportation of passengers or property by motor carriers engaged in interstate or foreign commerce and to the procurement of and the provision for such transportation'.[25] The main objectives of the legislation were to prevent wasteful and destructive competition within the bus and lorry industries in particular and in the transport sector in general, and to promote and protect the public interest. The ICC, as the federal government regulatory agency, would achieve these goals by exercising three main controls. In the first place, entry to the road transport industry would require a certificate of public convenience and necessity. Those carriers already in bona fide operation on 1 June 1935 were entitled, under 'grandfather' rights, to receive permits on filing the appropriate application.[26] Other firms could be certificated only after an investigation and/or hearing which established that any new business was in the public interest. Certificates could be suspended, changed or revoked. Mergers and issues of securities also had to receive official approval. Secondly, operators had to conform to regulations governing safety, insurance, finance, accounting and records. Aware of public concern about safety on the highway, Congress gave the ICC power to prescribe the qualifications and maximum working hours of employees and to establish standards of safe operation and vehicles of common and contract carriers. Surety bonds, insurance policies and securities were required to cover claims for injuries to persons and loss or damage to shipments and property. Thirdly, rates had to be reasonable and non-discriminatory. Carriers had to publish and adhere to rates and fares and they had to give thirty days' notice of any changes. If, after hearing complaints or on its own initiative, the ICC found that rates were unjust, then it could suspend any changes and prescribe maximum, minimum and actual rates to be charged.[27] Road transport had now entered a new regulatory era, and representatives of the bus and road haulage industries anxiously awaited the impact of the new legislation.

The new Act could not go into effect immediately, because an administrative bureau had to be set up and the industry needed time to become acquainted with the details of the legislation.[28] The Bureau of Motor Carriers was established as Division Five of the ICC to handle the motor-carrier work. Joseph B. Eastman was appointed chairman and John L. Rogers, previously an assistant examiner in the ICC and then executive assistant to the Federal Coordinator of Transportation, was appointed director. But time and money were needed to build up the unit. A filibuster in Congress delayed the initial appropriation, and recruitment of staff did not begin until 1 October 1935. Personnel were then selected carefully and slowly from the ICC's own experienced staff of examiners and attorneys, from state regulatory commissions, from industry and from the legal profession.

Before they could do any substantive work, however, they had to undertake an extensive educational campaign to inform carriers about their rights under the 'grandfather' clause and about the risks involved in not complying with the provisions of the Act. Then, proceeding patiently and cautiously, bureau staff found that most of their first two years were taken up with up with establishing the framework for administering the Act. Processing the 85,636 applications for certificates of convenience and necessity which had been received by November 1936 was a major task. Hearings rather than checking procedures were then required for some of the contested applications filed under the 'grandfather' clause as well as for those carriers who started operation after the passage of the Motor Carrier Act. Tariffs and schedules had to be submitted, examined and frequently reclassified before the bureau could make any decision on rates, while studies and extensive hearings were begun as preliminary measures for setting standards for safety, hours of work and insurance requirements. Such work was essential in breaking ground, but it had little immediate impact on the existing structure of the interstate bus industry.[29] When decisions were made in the late 1930s, the overall thrust of the motor-carrier cases then and during the 1940s was directed towards regulated competition.

Under the new regulations of the Motor Carrier Act competition between long-distance bus operators was limited. Existing companies who had filed for permits under the 'grandfather' clause protested against applications from new competitors on their routes, and after it had been established that services were adequate and traffic was light new applications were frequently turned down. An existing carrier could be authorized to provide an additional or a new service if that was in the public interest. The main exceptions to this principle were the establishment of 'bridge' or short-route extensions by non-Greyhound companies, usually members of the Trailways network, to build up a nation-wide system of comparable strength with that of the Greyhound Corporation, the largest national bus carrier. Bus subsidiaries of railroads initially could not acquire competing motor carriers if their sole purpose was to eliminate their rivals, but where traffic volume was insufficient to warrant two carriers a single carrier would be certificated over a given route. Motor subsidiaries could be extended into new territory, even though they might be unprofitable, provided that they contributed to the earning power of a system competing with Greyhound. The parent railroad company, on these occasions, could absorb the losses.[30]

The impact of these decisions on the structure of the long-distance bus industry was visible mainly in the encouragement of a new nationwide system in the shape of the National 'Trailways Bus System'. Greyhound had developed its network through the purchase of existing routes and operators in the later 1920s and the early 1930s, and by 1935 the corporation controlled some 14 per cent of the total route mileage in the USA. Trailways was formed in 1936 as an amalgamation of independent carriers who would coordinate their schedules, consolidate terminal operations, exchange passengers and jointly supervise equipment and personnel. The Motor Carrier Bureau officials clearly thought that it was in the 'public interest' to encourage this new venture to challenge the dominance of Greyhound. By 1937 Trailways operated over 12 per cent of total route miles. The large national systems were not equal, but they did provide some element of competition and some standards of comparison within the long-distance bus industry.[31]

The remaining sector of the interstate industry continued to be dominated by a large number of small operators, who carried huge numbers of passengers on short hauls, mainly in suburban areas. Though these companies had neither substantial route miles nor ran their vehicles long distances, they held on to a strong share of passenger traffic by dint of their location. Having qualified to run their operations under the 'grandfather' clause, most firms found that the main way in which the Motor Carrier Act affected their livelihood was through the imposition of standard business and accounting procedures and through the monitoring of adequate service. Public interest suggested that 'bunching' and duplication of service at periods of greatest demand should be avoided and that service should be offered at off-peak times. The establishment of minimum rates brought some downward movement, but the prior publication and filing of rates for state regulation had already checked much of the earlier financially destructive competition. There was some extension of regional carrier routes and motor subsidiary routes either to provide competition with the leading operator, Greyhound, or to ensure adequate service in sparsely populated regions. Within the bus industry, motor-carrier regulatory decisions both restricted and created competition to provide adequate service. Though officials did not follow a consistent policy in interpreting the 1935 Act, they seemed to favour the principles established for railroad regulation, namely restrictive entry and rate stabilization, in order to make carriers responsible and stable.[32]

But regulation by the mid-1930s was supposed to have regard to intermodal as well as intramodal competition. Monopoly, as defined during the early history of the railroads, was no longer the norm, and transport policy was still struggling to work out a fair and equitable solution to inter-industry competition. Pressure, mainly from carriers and regulators, to regulate the other two forms of common carrier, air and water, resulted in the Civil Aeronautics Act of 1938 and the Transportation Act of 1940. And in its preamble the latter piece of legislation attempted to set out a national transport policy. Safe, adequate, economical and efficient service was required and the inherent advantage of each mode was to be preserved without using unfair or destructive competitive practices. Given these guidelines, most regulatory efforts, while still locked into the old monopolistic rail patterns of restricted entry and minimum rates, recognized the problem of intermodal competition.[33]

Conclusion

Contemporaries and subsequent commentators have analysed the process of the federal government debate about motor-carrier regulation, the Motor Carrier Act itself and the tentative activity of the Motor Carrier Bureau in its formative years, hoping to ascertain the objectives of the parties concerned or some general principles underlying the legislation. As might be expected, opinions differ widely. Some observers saw in the hand of government a managerial supervision in which all forms of transport would be coordinated and integrated in the public interest.[34] Others saw motor-carrier regulation as a response primarily to the plight of the railroads and an attempt to equalize the terms of competition between the older and now declining transport medium and the new, dynamic and vigorous road services.[35] Yet others looked at the internal history and organization of motor carriers and regarded government regulation at both the state and federal levels as a twentieth-century attempt to obtain stability and security in a mature industrial economy.[36] The onset of depressed economic conditions after a period of prosperity complicated some of the arguments and seemingly strengthened the case for coordination, but government officials and transport leaders never ruled competition out of court. They might seek to alter the terms of competition, as they still do, and in altering those terms a judicious but unspecified mix of protecting and promoting the public interest – not merely in terms of injustice or dangerous conditions but also in terms of efficiency – was paramount. The interstate bus industry came under increasing federal scrutiny from the mid-1920s and it emerged in the 1930s as part of a larger regulated transport sector enjoying protection from open competition within the motor-carrier segment, yet offering competitive terms with its then major rival, the railroad. In a free-market oriented country, rather than establishing restrictive codes for each mode of transport or planning a coordinated transport network, Americans retained their options by writing general rules subject to varied official interpretations.

Notes

1. US Congress, Senate, Committee on Commerce, 89 Cong. 1 Sess. (1965), *An Evaluation of the Motor Carrier Act of 1935 on the Thirtieth Anniversary of its Enactment*, (Committee Print), 1 October, p. 47.
2. Regulation of transport activities by the federal and state governments has always been a controversial issue. Rules which were deemed necessary and desirable in the 1920s and 1930s have, since the late 1970s, been considered ineffective, stultifying and clumsy. Deregulation has become the conventional wisdom of the late twentieth century as technological, demographic and structural changes have encouraged competition. Operators, government officials and academics have differed widely in their pro-regulatory and deregulatory positions. Their discussions about the 'public interest' have been couched in terms of economic efficiency, social benefits and individual rights. For a useful explanation of 'public interest' see T.K. McCraw (1975), 'Regulation in America. A Review Article', *Business History Review*, **49**, pp. 159–83. For an overview of bus regulation, from the deregulatory stance, see E.A. Pinkston (1984), 'The Rise and Fall of Bus Regulation', *Regulation*, **8**, pp. 45–52. See also M. Walsh, 'In Whose Interest? Public Policy and Transport during Depression and War', in R.A. Garson and S.S. Kidd (eds) (1999), *The Roosevelt Years. New Essays on the United States, 1933–1945*, Edinburgh, pp. 11–29.
3. For divergent interpretations of the regulation of railroads see G. Kolko (1965), *Railroads and Regulation 1877–1916*, Princeton, NJ, and A. Martin (1971), *Enterprise Denied: Origins of the Decline of American Railroads, 1897–1917*, New York. Martin's later article, (1974), 'The Troubled Subject of Railroad Regulation in the Gilded Age – a Reappraisal', *Journal of American History*, **61**, pp. 339–71, restates his thesis with more impact. Textbooks in transport economics are more interested in the theory of regulation, though they tend to favour the marketplace approach. See, for example, D.F. Pegrum (1968), *Transportation Economics and Public Policy*, Homewood, IL, rev. edn, pp. 287–333.

4. M. Walsh, 'From Jitney to Giant', (chapter 2), pp. 17–19.
5. NAMBO, *Bus Facts for 1927*, Washington, DC, p. 3 (hereafter cited as *BF*). This is the first issue of an annual series of facts and figures on the bus industry compiled primarily from statistics given in the trade journal *Bus Transportation* (hereafter cited as *BT*). *BT* was the only effective source of national statistics on the intercity bus industry prior to 1937, when the ICC began publishing a more limited range of figures. See B.B. Crandall (1954), *The Growth of the Intercity Bus Industry*, Syracuse, NY, pp. 14, 280–82, and L.C. Sorrell and H.A. Wheeler (1944), *Passenger Transport in the United States 1920–1950*, Chicago, pp. 60–62. *BF* does not distinguish clearly between intercity, interstate and intrastate motor carriers.
6. Statistical information on these companies is not readily accessible. US Congress, Senate, 72 Cong. 1 Sess. (1932), *Coordination of Motor Transportation*, Doc. 43, p. 24 suggests that there were twenty-one companies operating fleets of 100 buses or more in 1925. These companies owned 4,771 buses which comprised 11.8 per cent of all revenue-producing buses. For further information about some outstanding companies like the California Transit Company, Pickwick Stages and Motor Transit Company see E. Bail (1976), 'California by Motor Stage', *California Historical Quarterly*, **55**, pp. 307–25; E. Bail (1984), *From Railway to Freeway: Pacific Electric and the Motor Coach*, Glendale CA; R.L. Tower, Jr (1972), 'The Road to Monopoly: the Development of the Bus Industry in California and Oregon, 1910–1930', unpublished paper, Berkeley, CA, pp. 1–42; G.L. Thompson (1993), *The Passenger Train in the Motor Age. California's Rail and Bus Industries, 1910–41*, Columbus, OH; M. Walsh, 'Tracing the Hound', (chapter 4), pp. 75–85.
7. The first state to regulate intercity buses was Pennsylvania in 1914. New York, Wisconsin and Colorado followed in 1915, Maryland in 1916, California and Utah in 1917, and Arizona, Massachusetts, New Hampshire and Vermont followed in 1919. A flurry of legislative activity took place in the early 1920s. In 1921 seven states regulated intercity buses; one in 1922; six in 1923; one in 1924; and ten in 1925, making 36 in all, including the most heavily populated states. See ICC (1932), *Coordination of Motor Transportation*, Docket 23400, Report **182**, Appendix F, pp. 410–13.
8. For state regulation see S. Szto (1934), *Federal and State Regulation of Motor Carrier Rates and Service*, Philadelphia, pp. 47–113; Crandall, *The Growth of the Intercity Bus Industry*, pp. 38–97; J.J. George (1929), *Motor Carrier Regulation in the United States*, Spartenburg, SC, pp. 1–213; E.R. Johnson (1938), *Government Regulation of Transportation*, New York, pp. 510–27. More detailed information is available either in trade journals like *BT*, **1–4** (1922–1925), and *Railway Age* **70–79** (1921–1925) (hereafter cited as RA), or in state publications and local newspaper reports of state commission hearings, as for example Minnesota State Warehouse and Railroad Comission, Auto Transportation Company Division *Biennial Reports* (1926), (1928), (1930) and *Minneapolis Journal*, (1925).
9. The main principles discussed in establishing motor-carrier regulation were those of public service and whether that service should be attained through competition or monopoly. There was little disagreement about most public-service requirements like safety regulations or even the licensing of vehicles, but the amount of competition which was either economically or socially desirable was a hotly contended issue. See George, *Motor Carrier Regulation* pp. 25–62; Johnson, *Government Regulation*, or the trade journals *BT* and *RA*.

10. George, *Motor Carrier Regulation*, pp. 214–17; Szto, *Federal and State Regulation*, pp. 193–9.

11. In Buck v. Kuykendall the Supreme Court held that the state of Washington could not deny a certificate of public convenience and necessity to an interstate carrier on the grounds that existing services were adequate. In Bush v. Maloy the state of Maryland was prevented from denying a certificate to an exclusively interstate carrier, while in Michigan Commission v. Duke the state could not deny a permit to a contract carrier engaged in interstate commerce. See ICC (1928), *Motor Bus and Motor Truck Operation*, Docket 18300 *Report*, **140**, Appendix A, pp. 750–53; George, *Motor Carrier Regulation*, pp. 214–37; Szto, *Federal and State Regulation*, pp. 193–226; Johnson, *Government Regulation*, pp. 527–31.

12. George, *Motor Carrier Regulation*, pp. 238–40, offers the best examples of the negative effects – namely obvious subterfuges and rate-cutting by interstate carriers – of the inability of the states to regulate interstate carriers. Like many contemporary commentators, he was dismayed at the prospects of an unregulated long-distance motor-carrier industry.

13. As many early bus men ran small firms for which no records have survived, it is impossible to provide evidence of running costs. But contemporaries noted the tendency to charge unremunerative rates when there was competition for traffic. The main reason for rate-cutting in the early 1920s seems to have been ignorance of the real costs of operation in a new industry. The low cost of entry which encouraged many persons with little experience and training to enter the business only aggravated the situation.

14. For a convenient listing of thirty-seven of these bills see Szto, *Federal and State Regulation*, pp. 240–43. This list does not include the Dill Bill, US Congress, 73 Cong. 2 Sess., (1934) S.3171; the Huddleston Bill, US Congress, 74 Cong. 1 Sess., (1935), HR.5262; or the Wheeler Bill, US Congress, 74 Cong. 1 Sess., (1935), S.1629. Nor does it consider the National Recovery Administration's Codes of Fair Competition for the transit, bus and road haulage industries. Another inventory of congressional events leading up to the Motor Carrier Act can be found in W.H. Wagner (1935), *A Legislative History of the Motor Carrier Act*, Denton, MD, pp. 93–9.

15. For a list of the congressional hearings see Wagner, *A Legislative History*, pp. 93–9; ICC (1928), *Motor Bus and Motor Truck Operations*, **140**; ICC (1932), *Coordination of Motor Transportation*, **182**; US Congress, Senate, 73 Cong. 2 Sess. (1934), *Regulation of Railroads*, Doc. 119; US Congress, Senate, 72 Cong. 2 Sess. (1934), *Regulation of Transportation*, Doc. 152; US Congress, House, 74 Cong. 1 Sess. (1935), *Report of the Federal Coordinator of Transportation*, Doc. 89; Johnson, *Government Regulation*, pp. 544–50; J.C. Nelson (1936), 'The Motor Carrier Act of 1935', *Journal of Political Economy*, **44**, pp. 464–71.

16. The issues are discussed at length in the hearings before the Senate Committee on Interstate Commerce, before the House Committee on Interstate and Foreign Commerce, and before the ICC. H.M. Muller (ed.) (1933), *Federal Regulation of Motor Transport*, New York, pp. 7–15, conveniently lists the briefs for and against the enactment of federal regulation of motor transport. Crandall, *The Growth of the Intercity Bus Industry*, pp. 141–6, examines the issues specifically relating to the regulation of the bus industry.

17. The discussions which took place within the industry are best followed in the trade journal, *BT*, **4–14** (1925–1935). The testimony of motor-bus officials at the congressional hearings on motor transport are also revealing.

18. The purpose of the National Industrial Recovery Act, adopted on 16 June 1933,

was to stimulate economic recovery by curtailing overproduction by raising prices and wages, by spreading out work through reducing hours and by preventing price cutting by competitors. Each industry was to develop its own code of fair practice, which was basically an agreement among its members to set minimum prices, limit output and establish minimum wages and maximum hours of work. Many of the larger interstate bus operators approved of the Motor Bus Code because it helped to stabilize the industry by eliminating the unfair competitive practices of 'wildcatters'. They much preferred the self-regulation of the codes, where they participated in arrangements, rather than congressional legislation, where they would be subject to decisions made by government officials, see L.V. Chandler (1970), *America's Greatest Depression, 1929–1941*, New York, pp. 223–39. For specific information on the Motor Bus Code and the Motor Bus Authority see *BT*, **12–14** (1933–1935).

19. Regulations frequently applied to hauliers with common carrier status or those operators who served the general public. In many instances, especially when truck owners had one vehicle or a small number of vehicles, the distinctions between common, contract and private carriers were blurred. Contract carriers served a limited class of shippers under special agreement while private carriers were engaged in transporting their own goods. For definitions of these carriers see D.P. Locklin (1935), *Economics of Transportation*, Chicago, pp. 75–64 and (1938), 2nd edn, p. 756; Johnson, *Government Regulation*, pp. 514–15.

20. For a summary of the attitudes of the road haulage industry to motor-carrier regulation see ICC (1928), *Motor Bus and Motor Truck Operations*; ICC (1932), *Coordination of Motor Transportation*; *Report of the Federal Coordinator of Transportation, 1934*; and US Congress, Senate, Committee on Interstate Commerce, 74 Cong, 1 Sess. (1935), *Hearings to Amend the Interstate Commerce Act*, 25 February – 6 March. Some lorry officials' reminiscences can be found in *An Evaluation of the Motor Carrier Act of 1935*, pp. 29–37. D.V. Harper (1959), *Economic Regulation of the Motor Trucking Industry by the States*, Urbana, IL, pp. 26–43, provides an overview of the road haulage industry in this period. W.R. Childs (1985), *Trucking and the Public Interest. The Emergence of Federal Regulation, 1914–40*, Knoxville, TN, offers a full analysis of regulation from the viewpoint of the motor-freight industry.

21. *BF*, (1927), p. 3; (1930), p. 5. The issues of *RA*, **72–85** (1921–1927), contain lengthy discussions of the attitudes of particular railroad companies to bus transport.

22. The continuing railroad arguments are stated in *RA*, **80–89** (1926–1935), and some bus officials' responses can be found in *BT*, **5–14** (1926–1935). As with the bus and truck industry, the reports of the hearings of the ICC, the reports of the Federal Coordinator of Transportation and the congressional hearings on regulating motor transport supply ample evidence of the sentiments of the railroad lobby.

23. Between 1928 and 1931 the total operating revenues of railroads declined by 33 per cent and in 1932 alone freight revenue fell by 25 per cent while passenger revenue fell by 30 per cent. L.S. Lyon and V. Abramson (1940), *Government and Economic Life*, **2**, Washington, DC, pp. 835–6.

24. See *Regulation of Railroads* (1934); *Regulation of Transportation* (1934); *Report of the Federal Coordinator of Transportation* (1934); US Congress, House, 7 Cong. 2 Sess. (1936), *Fourth Report of the Federal Coordinator of Transportation on Transportation Legislation*, Doc. 394. These reports are conveniently summarized in Lyon and Abramson, *Government and Economic*

Life, **2**, pp. 836–8. They are also discussed in Johnson, *Government Regulation*, pp. 163–72, 339–46, and C.M. Fuess (1952), *Joseph B. Eastman, Servant of the People*, New York, pp. 180–244.

25. Sec. 202(b) Motor Carrier Act, 1935, US Congress, 74 Cong. 1 and 2 Sess. (1935–6), Public Laws of the United States, *Statutes at Large*, **49**, Washington, DC, p. 543.

26. 'Grandfather' rights refer to the policy of issuing a certificate to any operator who was in bona fide operation at a specific date, without further proof that public convenience and necessity would be served by such operation. The date established in this instance was 1 June 1935. See sec. 206(a) of the Motor Carrier Act, *Statutes at Large*, **49**, p. 551; ICC, *Annual Report*, (hereafter cited as ICC, *AR*), **50**(November) (1936), pp. 69–70; Locklin (1947), *Economics of Transportation*, 3rd edn, pp. 717–22.

27. Motor Carrier Act, *Statutes at Large*, **49** (1935), pp. 543–69; I.L. Sharfman (1937), *The Interstate Commerce Commission: a Study in Adminstrative Law and Procedure*, New York, **4**, pp. 102–22; Wagner, *A Legislative History*; Nelson, 'The Motor Carrier Act of 1935', pp. 471–94; P. McCollester and F.J. Clark (1935), *Federal Motor Carrier Regulation*, New York, pp. 88ff; W.J. Hudson and J.A. Constantin (1958), *Motor Transportation, Principles and Practices*, New York, pp. 476–82.

28. The Motor Carrier Act was to he administered by the ICC. The Federal Coordinator of Transportation had recommended, in his third report, that the ICC should be reorganized to deal with the regulation of motor and water carriers, but Congress failed to act on the suggestion. Nevertheless, it was clearly understood that special divisions for handling each kind of transport were essential if regulation was to be effective. See Wagner, *A Legislative History*, pp.13–14, quoting Senator Wheeler, 79 Cong. Rec. 5650, 5656, 5657. On 1 October 1935 the ICC did reorganize, reducing the number of its divisions from seven to five and establishing Division Five as the Bureau of Motor Carriers. Time was needed to establish the bureau and also to establish a method for holding joint hearings with state authorities. State administrative machinery was to be utilized in certain proceedings where no more than three states were involved. When the issue concerned more than three states the decision to set up a joint board was optional. See Wagner, *A Legislative History*, pp. 19–20, 39–46; Sharfman, *The Interstate Commerce Commission*, **4**, pp. 121–6; Hudson, *Regulation of Motor Transportation*, pp. 478–81, and Johnson, *Government Regulation*, pp. 561–3.

29. *An Evaluation of the Motor Carrier Act of 1935*, pp. 2–3, 9–25; J.B. Eastman (1937), 'The Policy of the Motor Carrier Act', *American Transit Association Proceedings*, **55**, p. 294; Johnson, *Government Regulation*, pp. 561–4; Sharfman, *The Interstate Commerce Commission* **4**, pp. 126–41. ICC, *AR*, **49** (1935), pp. 73–5; **50** (1936), pp. 69–88; **51** (1937), pp. 66–84. *BT*, **14**(10) (1935), pp. 397–400.

30. Crandall, *The Growth of the Intercity Bus Industry*, pp. 166–200, provides the best summary of those early motor-carrier cases which affected buses. ICC, *AR*, from (1937), list the most important decisions made by the Bureau of Motor Carriers, but frequently these decisions are concerned with lorries. *BT*, **15–19** (1936–1940), summarizes the findings of the main motor-carrier cases as they occurred.

31. Crandall, *The Growth of the Intercity Bus Industry*, pp. 166–247. Detailed information on the regional divisions of Greyhound and the members of the

Trailways network can be found in the issues of *Motor Coach Age*, **1–28** (1954–1986),.

32. Crandall, *The Growth of the Intercity Bus Industry*, pp. 166–247; *BT*, **15–19** (1936–1940); Locklin (1947), *Economics of Transportation* 3rd edn, pp. 696–734.

33. Most textbooks on transport economics point out that the government and its regulatory bodies were still using the principles of monopoly regulation in a period in which competition flourished. Realization of the new market conditions emerged slowly and the process of adjustment was lengthy and painful. See, for example, R.J. Sampson and M.T. Farris (1979), *Domestic Transportation. Practice, Theory and Policy*, Boston, 4th edn, pp. 333–63. Other commentators have been very critical of the workings and thoughts of the regulatory bodies. See, for example, S.P. Huntington (1952), 'The Marasmus of the ICC: the Commission, the Railroads and the Public Interest', *Yale Law Review*, **61**, pp. 467–509; A. and O. Hoogenboom (1976), *A History of the ICC*, New York, pp. 119–44; M.H. Bernstein (1955), *Regulating Business by Independent Commission*, Princeton, NJ.

34. When motor- and water-carrier transport were regulated as Part II (1935) and Part III (1940) of the Interstate Commerce Act and air transport came under the aegis of a new board, the Civil Aeronautics Authority (1938), these moves seemed to give weight to a policy of coordination. The reports of the Federal Coordinator of Transportation present the clearest case for developing some national policy for transport, but they also point out that federal control could be achieved in various ways – for example, through a single commission, through a number of separate commissions or through self-regulation by code. Even in the major depression of the 1930s most Americans were reluctant to impose central planning and management.

35. The most accurate assessments of the position of the railroads in the nation's transportation are found in the four reports of the Federal Coordinator of Transportation. Arguments in trade journals like *RA* are highly-charged with emotion, while texts on the economics of transport frequently incorporate the political leanings of their authors.

36. Crandall, *The Growth of the Intercity Bus Industry*; Harper, *Economic Regulation of the Motor Trucking Industry*, pp. 10–43.

8 'See this Amazing America': The Long-Distance Bus Industry's Use of Advertising in its First Quarter Century

In the early years of the twentieth century new transport technologies brought both a huge increase in travel and competition between different types of passenger and freight carriers in the USA. With the advent of cars, buses, trucks and airlines alongside existing steam and electric railroads, pipelines and waterways, the different modes of transport attempted to gain, retain or increase their activities. This they did, not only through greater efficiency, better vehicles and modern business practices, but also through influencing consumer tastes by national advertising campaigns. The long-distance bus industry, though always a small contributor to intercity travel, quickly learnt how to market its facilities and soon came to rely on advertising for promoting both regular and special features. This chapter outlines the advertising efforts of the leading bus companies and the industry's trade association, the National Association of Motor Bus Operators (NAMBO), between 1925 and 1950 and relates them to the performance of the industry during these years.[1]

The bus industry and its advertising

By the late 1920s major changes in patterns of American transport were visible in the shift from railroads to roads. Cars were well established and had become so popular during the decade that they already accounted for over 80 per cent of intercity travel (see table 2.1 on page 27). Buses emerging from their experimental stage in the second decade of the century had gained 17.4 per cent of the public carrier passenger service by 1929 (see table 2.2 on page 28). In the freight sector trucks were entering the gaps left by the railroads and would soon challenge for the high-value, long-distance trade. The Depression of the 1930s curbed the buoyancy of the American economy but road transport withstood the pressures. Americans might not buy so many new cars, but they still drove their existing vehicles or acquired used cars. Buses increased their share of public carrier service to over a quarter of the total while trucking became a vibrant activity. The railroad, however, suffered severely, recovering only during the emergency of the Second World War, when gasoline and rubber shortages impeded private travel and cooperative efforts speeded rail freight flows. With the return of peace and an increased awareness of the need for better highways, road transport resumed its popularity, but new challenges in the passenger sector emerged with the airlines (see tables 2.1 and 2.2).[2]

The bus industry, which was providing local and regional services in the 1920s and offered a national service in the 1930s, was born into competition.[3] The car already offered short-distance mobility to many Americans while the train had a well-established short- and long-distance clientele. Bus operators who emerged from running local lines to provide routes which extended over 30 miles quickly adopted the systematic administrative structures and the business techniques of managerial capitalism to improve their efficiency, but they also recognized the importance of public relations and advertising in stimulating demand.[4] Initially in the 1920s bus operators relied on informational advertisements which listed towns and cities *en route* with departure and arrival times and fares. These schedules were frequently drafted by bus company employees. Then in the search for more passengers, entrepreneurs turned to the advertising industry, which, by the 1920s, had developed sophisticated sales techniques and was skilled in creating emotional copy which shaped tastes and moulded opinions in an age of rising consumption.[5]

Clearly, the basic commodity which the emerging long-distance bus industry and its advertising agents had to sell was travel.[6] Either those who already travelled must be enticed to use a bus rather than a car, train or plane, or more Americans must be encouraged to gain mobility by using a bus. For regular passengers, advertisements were designed to highlight the virtues of motor coaches, namely economy, convenience, comfort, safety and dependability. Whatever the condition of the economy, most of those who journeyed frequently for business or family reasons could be persuaded to take the bus by appealing to one of these themes which bus managers and their advertisers constantly reiterated in various guises and with catchy slogans. Only the emergency of the Second World War altered the messages with a patriotic appeal to travel selectively.

Tourism presented a different and highly promising market for bus operators. For those Americans who were interested in recreation, advertisements were designed not only to appeal to their good sense, but also to appeal to their desires to enjoy their leisure in different places.[7] By taking a bus they could become fashionable and relax in some exotic location at any time of the year. Indeed, this romantic or perhaps even therapeutic appeal of seeing new places came to dominate bus advertising. Bus promotional literature and imagery were clear, inventive and picturesque. The artistry and impact compared well with that produced by train and plane companies;[8] yet bus advertising captured the interest of only a small proportion of the travelling population. Most Americans preferred to drive their own cars. Some of those who used public services were persuaded to switch from trains to buses, but advertisers needed to be constantly alert to retain, let alone increase, the bus share of the travel market.

Advertising for regular clients

Among the practical advantages offered by bus travel, economy was a consistent selling point. Buses were cheaper than their main competitors, trains or cars.[9] In their first national advertising campaign in 1929 Greyhound informed the travelling public that they could now afford to go across the USA (figure 9). A decade later economy remained important, when Greyhound suggested that two bus passengers could travel as cheaply as one in a small car. Santa Fe Trailways supported this low-cost travel pitch by offering fares at less than 2 cents per mile. By the late 1940s Greyhound was still claiming to provide good value for money with bus fares one-half to two-thirds of the cost by private car. If Americans were interested in cheap travel then buses provided a sound answer.[10]

This appeal to economy could be made even more attractive when related to specific economic fluctuations. Facing a severe and lengthy depression in the early 1930s, Greyhound managers thought that they could make more inroads into middle- and upper-class markets. They thus appealed to those who normally travelled on Pullman trains, or who drove cars, by advertising their buses as '$20,000 autos' and as the 'Second car in a two car family' (figure 10). When prices rose in the two years before American entry into the Second World War, Santa Fe Trailways stressed that their fares stayed low, and in the 1940s, when average living costs increased by 64 per cent, Greyhound fares remained at their 1939 levels, making a bus trip an outstanding bargain. Economy was a theme which had a strong appeal to a variety of people.[11]

Cheap fares did not mean poor standards. Bus operators argued that buses offered low-cost luxury and thus their advertisements also featured comfort and safety. Comfort came in the shape of the modern motor coach, while safety depended both on the improved technology of vehicles and the skills and good sense of drivers. Comfort was rarely mentioned in the first days of bus travel, when vehicles were basic and road conditions appalling. In the 1920s, however, when manufacturers began to design motor coaches rather than build buses on wagon chassis, operators boasted of the merits of these new vehicles. Early national advertising in magazines featured all-steel buses with individual, deep-cushioned seats, cradle springs, balloon tyres and an effective heating and ventilation system. In the mid-1930s Greyhound's new Supercoach provided increased room for passengers and baggage, better visibility for driver and passengers, improved ventilation, new lighting systems and less vibration, all conducive to a more comfortable ride. The newly merged Trailways System offered the smooth-gliding luxury of the Nite-Coach Sleeper and was already experimenting with air-conditioning. In an effort to break into the car market, advertisements suggested that buses were more comfortable than cars in the late 1930s, and they also tried appealing to rail users by offering some of the attractive facilities of trains.[12]

The emergency of the Second World War had required many Americans to travel on overcrowded and uncomfortable buses. The advertisements of the leading companies in the late 1940s thus made strenuous efforts to make bus travel attractive again by asserting not only comfort but also luxury. In 1946 Greyhound's Silversides coach featured numerous advances for passengers, like wider seats, glare- and heat-resistant window glass, night reading lights and air conditioning, while safety features included superior brakes, better driver's mirrors and more room for the driver. The company's Scenicruiser, introduced in 1954, provided many more innovations for passenger comfort including excellent panoramic sightseeing, smoother riding and restful seating. Trailways' Aerocoach also offered high levels of comfort, and operators suggested that travelling could be a genuine pleasure for passengers.[13]

A refreshing, carefree journey was also important if more passengers were to be attracted from trains and cars, and this could be assured because drivers were well trained, skilled and courteous. Indeed, Greyhound prided itself on its driver training and safety, and encouraged high standards by a system of rewards and penalties. Early advertisements boasted that every Greyhound driver was a man of character and responsibility who had passed rigorous examinations, and they frequently pictured such a strong, reliable, uniformed man in support of their claim (figure 11). Announcements regularly pointed to the safety record of bus travel and by 1955 Greyhound boasted that their buses were eleven times as safe as travelling by car. Not only was safety important but driver courtesy was also a major ingredient in ensuring custom. Personnel managers stressed that politeness and passenger attention brought satisfaction and repeat business, and in the difficult post-war years, when Americans turned increasingly to cars, Greyhound made a concerted effort to identify their company name with courtesy. Bus operators wanted potential customers to know that they would be well looked after.[14]

Promotional literature and iconography also paid attention to the convenience and dependability of bus travel. Customers wanted frequent reliable service from easily accessible terminals, with good connections and stopover privileges, whether they were travelling regularly or taking occasional trips. Timetables were the simplest way of providing such information for frequent customers. At the same time, bus managers needed to reassure these clients that they were acting wisely, and they wanted to encourage more Americans to take to the buses. In 1940 Jefferson Lines frequently announced their convenient Iowa services in the local and daily newspapers of that state. The company thus hoped to increase their shorter-distance trade and bring bus travel into the daily lives of many people, like farmers' wives doing their shopping, teachers commuting home for the weekend and local business representatives.[15]

The ease of travelling longer distances needed to be advertised nationally as well as locally and not only in newspapers but also in popular magazines. As early as 1929, when Greyhound was a new entity, the corporation looked to an audience of millions when it informed readers of the *Saturday Evening Post* that the travel habits of a nation would change rapidly thanks to the convenience of frequent and time-saving bus services between 1,000 cities and towns.[16] As Greyhound's route network expanded to 50,000 miles, and more frequent and direct services were added, advertisements claimed that their buses reached more places than any other public transport system. Convenience meant swift, time-saving, prompt and dependable service. Further incentives of liberal stopovers, alternative return routes at no extra cost, one ticket only to any part of the country, and central city terminals aimed to maintain business in the depths of the Depression in the mid-1930s (figure 12). Greyhound was not alone in appealing to convenience. Trailways quickly put together a similar package in 1936. Within months of their formation as an integrated system, they operated a route network of 30,000 miles and glowingly reported good connections, frequent schedules, modern terminals and stopover facilities.[17] Indeed, bus passenger miles picked up in the second half of the 1930s (see table 1.1 on page 8).

In the post-war years the large companies once again emphasized the ease and speed of bus travel. Greyhound reported that improved scheduling brought express service on many runs under 200 miles and limited stops produced faster times on longer runs. Furthermore, additional services enabled the company to offer more frequent departures than any other form of transport. Indeed, Greyhound attempted to set a new pace with its smoothly running, highly integrated network of buses which were now supported by better amenities such as more and larger terminals, and the company's own chain of restaurants. Trailways also highlighted convenience with its new slogan 'Thru-Travel'. In a campaign started in 1951 the company's new advertising agency, J. Walter Thompson, told Americans that they would have no connection worries because they did not need to change buses when they chose Trailways. They could keep the same seat straight through to their destination.[18] Convenience was an essential ingredient in creating an attractive image of bus travel in a period when more Americans had access to cars and thus to greater individual flexibility.

Only in the war years when restrictions were placed on travelling did bus operators and their representatives modify their messages about economy, convenience, comfort, safety and efficiency. As it was very difficult to promote the consumption of bus travel in a period when this service was either scarce or unavailable, entrepreneurs decided to build up general good will and future patronage by putting their advertising efforts to the service of the nation with a hearty dose of patriotism. During the war it was still advantageous to take a bus, but only for some Americans and in some situations. Now the industry was making a major contribution to the war effort by carrying essential passengers like military personnel and war workers to their destinations promptly and efficiently; it also carried them economically by conserving necessary transport resources. Ease of travel and restful travel might no longer be available, but passengers were promised a return to comfort after the war.[19]

The major companies were joined in their advertising strategy by the trade association, NAMBO, who early in the war decided to use their long-delayed national campaign to work with the government. NAMBO would present the wartime story of bus service and would thereby promote national unity.[20] The trade association's advertisements followed two tracks. Some stressed the necessary conservation of vital materials like rubber and fuel, and thanked passengers for their cooperation in travelling midweek, taking small amounts of luggage and checking ahead about availability. Restrictions and inconveniences were only due to the emergency conditions (figure 13). Americans were reminded of these wartime conditions by the double imagery of the citizen worker or vacation-makers side-by-side with the military in all pictorial notices. Other advertisements cooperated with official government campaigns. The advertising industry's own voluntary war-planning group, the Advertising Council, subsequently renamed the War Advertising Council, undertook to promote the war messages free of charge. Bus propaganda thus sponsored drives not only for conservation and rationing, but also for war bonds, war manpower, civil defence and anti-inflationary measures. Such cooperation with the government judiciously mixed immediate official approval with long-term product consciousness by the public.[21] It was possible to press traditional messages in another guise. Whether these messages could counteract the legacy of overcrowded and shabby buses remained to be seen.

The necessity of advertising the main advantages of bus travel was ever-present in the second quarter of the twentieth century. Whether facing prosperity, depression, wartime restrictions or modest affluence, bus managers knew that they must keep telling Americans that scheduled service was economical, convenient, efficient, comfortable and safe if they were to hold, let alone increase, their business. Regular clients who travelled for work or family reasons needed to be assured that they were taking the right decision, especially in the post-war years.

Advertising in the leisure market

The vacation market was not a new phenomenon in the early twentieth century. The rich had regularly travelled to warmer, scenic or exotic parts of the USA, usually by train. The advent and mass production of the car, improved roads, the shorter working week and entitlement to vacations created much greater prospects for the tourist industry. A variety of businesses, including hotels, restaurants, construction firms and transport services, started to promote recreational travel in the 1920s. Progress was slow in the Depression and came to a virtual halt during the Second World War, but it surged in the more affluent and unrestricted mid-century years. The long-distance bus industry, well aware of the growing attractions of leisure travel to millions of Americans, rapidly promoted itself as an attractive tourist facility.[22]

While the merits of economy, comfort and convenience were useful assets in selling the vacation trade, as well as regular scheduled services, other features of recreational bus travel could be publicized. Seasonality or the viability of travel throughout the year was a feature which was attractive to consumers and producers alike. Bus operators early appreciated that their annual traffic flow was irregular. Following a steady build-up in the spring, peak demand came in the summer. Trade then declined in the fall to a low point in mid-winter. One way of stabilizing and even increasing this traffic was to persuade people to alter their existing travel habits or to acquire new ones. Such changes could be marketed creatively by suggesting new levels of social mobility. It would not only be adventurous and fulfilling, but also fashionable, to visit distant places at any time of the year.[23]

In the mid-1920s regional bus companies like Northland Transportation approached this type of advertising by extolling the newly discovered joys of vacationing in the wooded lakelands of northern Minnesota during the summer. Once they were part of the Greyhound system they quickly told Minnesotans that they could travel beyond the Midwest for pleasure at any time of the year. Early Greyhound advertisements, even in the depths of the Depression, offered exciting new kinds of vacations anywhere in the USA because regular bus routes reached such interesting places as national parks, mountain ranges, ocean beaches, major cities and historical sites.[24] Furthermore, each season could be promoted as a holiday venture. In the spring, when nature was at its best, there were many picturesque places to visit. In the summer, when most people took time off, the full variety of holidays was offered, with emphasis on better facilities and more scenic routes than other means of transport. Recreational travel usually declined in the autumn, but bus executives aimed to stimulate business by special campaigns stressing less crowding, pleasant weather and marvellous colours, in addition to bargain fares.[25] Winter, the low season for tourism, was marketed vigorously by suggesting that an escape to the southern sunbelt or even northern ski grounds was within everyone's reach (figure 14). In the more competitive and affluent post-war years travel agents increased the attraction and convenience of bus tours by selling individual packages, making hotel reservations and planning special sightseeing trips.[26] Bus advertisements sought to capture the public's imagination and to improve trade by portraying the positive features of each season for taking a break.

Other leisure trips could be marketed without reference to the weather. On national holidays like Thanksgiving and Christmas, Americans were urged to travel home to celebrate a traditional, family occasion in a new-fashioned way, on time, warm and relaxed in their motor coaches.[27] Special events, like sports matches, historic pageants or fairs, were excellent opportunities for day or weekend trips. A major breakthrough in this type of recreational travel came with the Chicago World's Fair in 1933 and 1934, when Greyhound successfully retailed package tours to the 'Century of Progress' (figure 15). For the rest of the 1930s Greyhound and Trailways offered cheap fares to all city and regional exhibitions. Even during the Depression, this type of advertising generated business by suggesting new areas of entertainment.[28]

Part of Greyhound's success in transporting Americans to and through the Chicago World's Fair in 1933 and 1934 was due to its novel offer of planned expense-paid tours. This product was very attractive to a variety of customers and both Greyhound and Trailways quickly organized a series of set itineraries taking tourists from one attraction to another, all with accommodation and meals pre-arranged and often with a tour guide. By 1937, Trailways offered seventy-five sightseeing tours. With greater demand for vacations and increased spending power in the post-war years, Greyhound extended its range of all-expense tours to over 200 and their selection grew in the 1950s. Bus firms were catering to the convenience of Americans by allowing tourists to purchase a package. Their promotional campaign further stressed the friendly and carefree nature of this travel adventure.[29]

Closely allied to planned and escorted trips was the charter business, which, thanks to the flexibility of buses in reaching places not served by trains, had potential for growth. By the early 1950s Greyhound offered a full range of chartered services not only for business trips and sports events but also as fun excursions for clubs, societies and groups. Furthermore, they attempted to evoke an air of luxury by suggesting that a chartered bus was akin to having a limousine and private chauffeur at one's beck and call.[30] Such advertising stimulated people to think about bus services as a private operation. At the same time it conveyed a new sense of well-being by offering a different type of social and geographical mobility. Charter operations became a bright spot for the long-distance bus industry in the growing post-war affluence.

How to get the message across

Bus managers and their advertising agents might well plan campaigns to sell bus travel, but unless their ideas were communicated to a wide audience, they were unlikely to be successful. From the variety of media outlets available in the second quarter of the twentieth century, they selected the press as the most effective.[31] The press consisted of two distinct parts. Newspapers were sold locally and regionally, while magazines circulated among a much larger and frequently nationwide audience. As most Americans travelled shorter distances, most advertising money went to newspapers. National bus companies spent their second-highest amounts in major periodicals in order to tap the growing leisure market. They then used newer means of communication – films, radio and television – judiciously, while a diverse range of auxiliary materials, including direct mail, pamphlets, billboards, calendars, window displays, printed cards and teaching aids, offered further backup.[32]

Newspapers were widely read and all bus operators were aware of the potential publicity of black and white newspaper space. Dailies were particularly good as a means of revenue promotion. Smaller companies often relied on informational copy which listed the 'nuts and bolts' aspects of travel like destinations, fares, company name, terminal location and telephone number. Such copy was sometimes illustrated by sketches of vehicles. Larger companies also used informational advertisements, but they tended to feature more graphic descriptions and scenic illustrations. Indeed, Greyhound and Trailways agencies were able to use a pool of national advertisements on which they 'piggybacked' local information.[33] They supplied dummy copy featuring tableaux, sketches, illustrations and suggested footage, and requested terminal managers or travel agents to insert specific destinations with appropriate fares and the location of terminals (figure 16). These local officials then selected the position, frequency and size of the advertisements so as to maximize their impact. The travel section was usually the best location for factual information, but the news section was more likely to attract the attention of people who used alternative means of transport. Midweek advertisements caught the attention of the weekend traveller and avoided the congestion of department-store promotions on Thursdays and Fridays. Special advertising like a chartered or a scheduled service to a football game obviously went on a sporting page. Newspapers had, and retained, the potential of attracting the attention of different types of audiences in numerous communities. Even after twenty years of experience as a national operator, Greyhound spent over 50 per cent of its mid-century advertising budget on advertising in local newspapers. Almost every daily – some 3,000 in number – and regularly over 2,000 weeklies carried Greyhound copy.[34]

While newspaper advertisements earned the bus companies their daily bread, the jam for the larger firms came from the full-page, brightly-coloured copy which they placed in 'national magazines. As soon as Greyhound became a national enterprise, in 1929, its executives followed the example of other corporations and undertook a nationwide promotional campaign. They broadcast the Greyhound idea by telling the middle-class readers of the *Saturday Evening Post* and the *American Magazine* about their new and exciting transcontinental service. The former magazine, with its large-page format suitable for dramatic pictures, had already been used by leading companies like Chrysler, General Electric and Fisher Body. The latter was a family periodical with the largest paid circulation of any magazine. Before the end of the year Greyhound also took to 'narrowcasting' and targeted special-interest groups reading *Liberty* and *College Humor*. Though sceptics questioned the uncertain payoff for such advertising expenditure, the bus managers thought that they had not only made readers more bus conscious but that they had also increased the number of bus users.[35]

Indeed, they were sufficiently persuaded to step up national promotions despite the onset of the Depression. By the mid-1930s Greyhound advertisements were carried in other general magazines, like *Colliers* and *Cosmopolitan*, as well as in review, women's, country homes, romance and movie periodicals, and also in educational publications. The backbone of the national campaign remained the full-colour pages in the *Saturday Evening Post*, but careful use of specialist publications meant that different groups of customers could be regularly targeted. This was of major importance at a time when long-distance buses did not yet have the image of low-status travel.[36] Bus companies continued to recognize the importance of reaching a middle-class audience through magazine advertising. In 1949 Greyhound spent 29 per cent of its promotional budget on magazines and in the following year it ran advertisements in forty-four such publications, with a possible audience of 250 million.[37] In a period when the mass media was deemed important in providing guidelines for patterns of personal behaviour, bus executives joined their business counterparts in using popular periodicals to make emotional appeals to a widespread and aspiring readership.

Success in the competitive travel market, however, was also dependent on having the enthusiastic support of producers as well as consumers. To encourage their employees to achieve high standards of public relations, Greyhound officials invested advertising dollars on in-house newspapers. As early as 1929 the monthly *Greyhound Limited* was distributed to employees, ticket agents and bus enthusiasts. This was soon replaced by regional house organs, like Pacific Greyhound's *Pace Maker*, Southeastern Lines' *Backfire* and Northland Greyhound's *Rear View Mirror*, which offered employees more personal contact. At the same time the *Highway Traveler* aimed to arouse the enthusiasm of tourists and travel agents through travel stories, humour, editorials and information on the latest developments in the bus industry. Initially free, this bimonthly publication with a circulation of between 75,000 and 100,000 generated sufficient interest among Americans enjoying recreational travel to reach a circulation of 410,000 in 1947, and to be available by subscription. For national companies it was important to have a high profile among as many groups of readers as possible and thus spending on employee and travel gazettes was worthwhile.[38]

While bus executives favoured newspapers and magazines for the bulk of their advertising, they did not neglect other means of communication in their promotional campaigns. Oral and visual media provided the advantages of speed and panoramic scenery. The radio, like the newspaper, was primarily a local instrument of news and entertainment, and could thus stimulate local business. In the late 1920s bus advertising was heard as spot announcements sandwiched in between programmes. These fifty-word messages had a direct sales appeal and induced enquiries about regular services and special attractions. Two other radio approaches became important in gaining attention and prestige. Fifteen-minute travelogues describing interesting places to visit, and sponsored programmes, gave bus companies exposure. More ambitious quiz programmes about places of historical and geographical importance in North America, backed up by listener contests, provided further information and entertainment. Yet, despite the ease with which radio found new audiences and stirred consumer interest, it did not become the leading promotional outlet. In 1940 no major intercity bus firm spent more than 15 per cent of its budget on radio, while the average was just over 7 per cent. Even in 1949, with radios playing in 39 million of the nation's 42 million homes, Greyhound devoted only 5.6 per cent of its expenditure to broadcasting. Certainly, the radio had a recognized function with spot announcements and this role was shared by television in the early 1950s, but bus executives preferred the written message.[39]

Films offered a more enticing means of attracting attention. Bus managers were interested in both the sponsored documentary and the popular motion picture featuring buses as romantic objects. Only major companies like Greyhound could afford to produce and distribute their own films, but these were reckoned to be a good investment in generating good will and prestige. By 1953 Greyhound had made four films – *They Discovered America*, *This Amazing America*, *Shortest Way Home* and *America for Me* – for showing to private groups and organizations and in movie theatres. Of more widespread impact were Hollywood films featuring buses, and these fortunately hit the screen when the bus industry was at a low point in the Depression. In 1934 MGM's *Fugitive Lovers* was the first motion picture to feature a bus as a source of drama. Universal Pictures soon followed with *Cross Country Cruise*, which used Greyhound buses as a background. The most famous movie of this genre, however, was Columbia Pictures' *It Happened One Night*, starring Clark Gable, Claudette Colbert and a Greyhound bus. The popularity of this film was such that some twenty years later Greyhound officials were delighted at the 1956 remake, *You Can't Run Away With It*, starring June Allyson. Greyhound saw the advantages of cooperating with films featuring their buses or even their terminals. As movie-going was a leading recreational activity in the second quarter of this century, this was virtually free advertising.[40]

Other subsidiary advertising methods varied widely among bus companies. In the early days of highway travel, promotional folders containing schedules, pictures and descriptions of scenic routes were available in terminals, hotels, restaurants, shops, bus agencies and chambers of commerce. Brochures promoting special services, like expense-paid tours, vacation packages and seasonal trips, continued to be popular and were available from agents, at terminals and by postal and phone requests. These materials were also distributed through direct mail. Posters were sufficiently attractive to be used not only in terminal window displays but also in department stores, hotels and travel bureaux. Wall exhibits in full-colour panels were available to teachers and schools, picturesque calendars were distributed to clients, and billboards, either near the terminal or on the bus routes, remained in regular use. Occasional novel schemes, like charms in the shape of the Greyhound dog, window streamers, lapel tags, stickers, souvenir booklets of trips and round-trip sales contests, added zest to particular campaigns.[41] Recognizing the function of advertising in providing information and arousing new consumer interest, bus companies used a range of secondary measures to reinforce their main campaigns.

Conclusion

Ironically, the impact of all the time, money and effort spent on advertising was immeasurable. The long-distance bus industry expanded rapidly in the 1920s, weathered the major Depression of the 1930s, grew during the emergency of the Second World War and retained a hold on intercity travel in the late 1940s (see tables 1.1 on page 8, 2.1 on page 27, 2.2 on page 28 and 3.1 on page 40). Throughout these years bus operators were committed to spending on promotional materials. They made regular expenditure on informational advertising in the form of schedules announcing changes in timetables, fares and routes. They also advertised each season, though with differing emphasis. In addition they allocated substantial 'one-off' amounts to underwrite specific campaigns, as, for example, in the depths of the Depression in the early 1930s, when trade was declining, or in the immediate aftermath of the Second World War, when they needed to re-establish peacetime travel flows.[42]

Executives and their advertising agencies were anxious to ascertain the effectiveness of their promotional efforts. They analyzed figures before a particular drive or for a similar time-period in a different year. They also obtained some feedback from telephone enquiries, letters and questionnaires completed by travellers. Nevertheless, they emerged with inexact answers. Their conclusions were generally positive but imprecise, as their review of the 1950 'Fall Round Up of Travel Bargains' suggests:

> We realize the overall income picture is not pleasing when compared with the previous periods – but who knows what our position would be had there been no campaign? Everyone who took an active part seems to agree, however, that [the campaign] was effective, and that it resulted in more sales than otherwise would have been made.[43]

Though such sentiments may seem unsatisfactory for enterprising business-men, the bus executives were not alone, either then or since. Other leading businessmen have faced similar situations and have publicly acknowledged that half of their advertising money was probably wasted – but they did not know which half.[44] Bus men joined their fellow entrepreneurs and accepted that advertising was part of a modern business enterprise even though its cost-effectiveness was problematic. They thus tended to spend as much as they could afford rather than asking how much was needed to do a specific job.[45]

Increasingly in the twentieth century advertising has come to be regarded as an integral part of any major enterprise and of a capitalistic economy. With the growing impersonality of national markets in the USA, producers needed some means of informing consumers about which goods and services were available. Advertising as a means of communication became a permanent force in business life. This fact was readily recognized by bus entrepreneurs who also quickly learned that advertising could create consumer demand by suggesting new patterns of social behaviour. Stimulated primarily by their desire to gain more passengers, but also by the established patterns of corporate behaviour and the presence of a dynamic advertising industry which could plan campaigns on a long-term basis, they offered their distinctive features – economy, convenience, safety, comfort and dependability – to any traveller and they promoted recreation as a new and fashionable activity for the middle classes. Consumer response to these messages, however, depended on the availability of alternative ways in which Americans might participate in geographical and social mobility. Increasing numbers wanted to drive their own cars to their chosen destinations, and public transport remained a low priority. Yet within the public sector, bus operators clearly demonstrated that they could win passengers and retain them in the face of competition. In this endeavour advertising played a necessary part.

Notes

1. This study is based primarily on the advertising material of the Greyhound Corporation and the National Trailways Bus System. The American intercity industry is composed of a large number of small operators who provided a local or regional service, and two large companies, Greyhound and Trailways. Greyhound emerged to national status in the late 1920s. Trailways was formed in 1936 as an amalgamation of independent carriers. In 1937 Greyhound operated 16 per cent of the bus miles in the USA while Trailways operated 12 per cent. By 1950 their shares were 20 per cent and 17 per cent respectively. Greyhound had 4 per cent of the passenger market in 1937 and Trailways had 1 per cent. The respective figures for 1950 were 15 per cent and 6 per cent. See B.B. Crandall (1954), *The Growth of the Intercity Bus Industry*, Syracuse, NY, p. 288.

2. Discussions of the growth of the main modes of transport in the USA in the early twentieth century can be found in J.B. Rae (1971), *The Road and the Car in American Life*, Cambridge, MA; W.R. Childs (1985), *Trucking and the Public Interest: The Emergence of Federal Regulation, 1914–1940*, Knoxville, TN; D.V. Harper (1959), *Economic Regulations of the Motor Trucking Industry by the States*, Urbana, IL; Crandall, *The Growth of the Intercity Bus Industry*; D.M. Itzkoff (1985), *Off the Track: the Decline of the Intercity Passenger Train in the United States*, Westport, CT; R.M. Kane and A.D. Vose (1982), *Air Transportation*, Dubuque, IO, 8th edn. For discussion of intermodal competition see M. Walsh, 'The Intercity Bus and Its Competitors in the United States in the Mid Twentieth Century' in C. Wrigley and J. Shepherd (eds) (1991), *On The Move: Essays in Labour and Transport History Presented to Philip Bagwell*, London, pp. 231–51; M. Walsh, 'Missing Connections', (chapter 3, pp. 32–64).

3. In addition to Crandall, *The Growth of the Intercity Bus Industry* and Walsh, *Making Connections*, chapters 2 and 3, pp. 17–64, there is one general history of buses and two studies of Greyhound; A.E. Meier and J.P. Hoscheck (1975), *Over the Road: a History of Intercity Bus Transportation in the United States*, Upper Montclair, NJ; C. Jackson (1984), *Hounds of the Road: a History of the Greyhound Bus Company*, Bowling Green, KY; and O. Schisgall (1985), *The Greyhound Story: from Hibbing to Everywhere*, Chicago.

4. The leading authority on the growth of managerial capitalism is Alfred D. Chandler, Jr (1977), *The Visible Hand: the Managerial Revolution in American Business*, Cambridge, MA. See also his (1962) *Strategy and Structure: Chapters in the History of American Industrial Enterprise*, Cambridge, MA.

5. For surveys on the growth of advertising see D. Pope (1983), *The Making of Modern Advertising*, New York; F.S. Presbrey (1929), *The History and Development of Advertising*, Garden City, NY; O.A. Pease (1958), *The Responsibilities of American Advertising*, New Haven, CT; D.M. Potter (1954), *People of Plenty*, Chicago, chapter 8. For contrasting discussions on the role of advertising and advertisers in American society see S. Ewen (1976), *Captains of Consciousness: Advertising and the Social Roots of the Consumer Culture*, New York; V. Packard (1957), *The Hidden Persuaders*, New York; S. Fox (1984), *The Mirror Makers: A History of American Advertising and its Creators*, New York; R. Marchand (1985), *Advertising the American Dream: Making Way for Modernity 1920–1940*, Berkeley, CA; M. Schudson (1984), *Advertising, the Uneasy Persuasion: its Dubious Impact on American Society*, New York. Advertising and cultural issues are examined in W.I. Susman (1984), *Culture*

as History: the Transformation of American Society in the Twentieth Century,
New York, and T.J. Jackson Lears (1984), 'Some Versions of Fantasy: Towards
a Cultural History of American Advertising, 1880–1930', Prospects, **9**, pp.
349–405.

6. Greyhound employed an advertising manager and an outside agency, Beaumont
& Hohman of Cleveland, OH. The company remained Greyhound's agency from
the late 1920s until 1956 when they were replaced by Grey Advertising.
Trailways employed Ferry Hanly Co. of Chicago in 1937 and Needham Louis &
Brorby of Chicago in 1939. With much stronger competition in the post-war years
they looked to a leading advertising agency, J. Walter Thompson. *Advertising
Age*, 20 February 1939, p. 1; 10 December 1956, pp. 3, 119 (hereafter cited as *AA*).
J. Walter Thompson, *Newsletter*, 28 May 1951, p. 5, (J. Walter Thompson
Archives, Manuscript Department, William R. Perkins Library, Duke University,
Durham, NC, hereafter cited as JWT).

7. W.R. Fowler, Jr, 'The Why of Greyhound Advertising', *Bus Journal*, **March**
(1929), pp. 26–7; W.R. Fowler, Jr, 'Advertising in the Motor Bus Business', file 3,
no. 5, c. 1929, 5pp; Greyhound Corporate Records, University of Wyoming
(hereafter cited as GCR). J.B. Walker (1931), 'How to sell bus rides', National
Association of Motor Bus Operators, *Proceedings*, **5**, pp. 86–91 (hereafter cited
as NAMBO, *Procs*); *Rear View Mirror*, **19**(2) (1952), p. 7; **20**(4) (1953), p. 9
(being the in-house news-sheet of Northland Greyhound Lines, hereafter cited as
RVM).

8. See, for example, advertisements for leading companies and for the trade
associations in the bus, railroad and airline industries published in the *Saturday
Evening Post* (hereafter abbreviated to *SEP*), and *Colliers*, during the Second
World War years 1940–1945.

9. Statistics on the comparative costs of travelling by different modes of transport
vary. The printed evidence in the major trade journals like *Railway Age* and *Bus
Transportation* (hereafter cited as *RA* and *BT*) point to lower running costs for
buses in the 1920s and 1930s as did Interstate Commerce Commission (ICC)
(1932), *Coordination of Motor Transportation*, Docket 23400, Report, **182**,
Washington, DC. However, the chief competitor of buses and trains was the
private car and here the evidence on comparative costs is much more difficult to
obtain. Both the bus and rail industries claimed that the true cost of driving a car
was higher than rail or bus fares, but motorists tended to measure costs of driving
in terms of individual mobility rather than dollar expenses only.

10. *SEP*, 14 September 1929, p. 244; 21 January 1939, 3rd cover; 24 September 1949,
p. 121. *Highway Traveler*, **1**(4) (1929), p. 3; **3**(5) (1931), p. 33; **22**(1) (1950),
4th cover (hereafter cited as *HT*). *Trailways*, **4**(11) (1938), p. 13 (hereafter cited
as *Tr.*). Many examples of Greyhound advertisements from popular magazines
can be conveniently found in the D'Arcy Collection of Clippings, Department of
Communications Library, University of Illinois Urbana-Champaign.

11. 'Report of the Committee on Advertising and Publicity', NAMBO, *Procs*, **5**
(1931), pp. 49–50; *RA*, **92**(22) (1932), pp. 913–14. *SEP*, 21 November 1936, p.
66; 22 January 1938, 3rd cover; 24 April 1948 n.p. *Tr.*, **7**(6) (1941), 3rd cover.

12. *SEP*, 22 February 1930, p. 151; 12 April 1930, p. 300; 27 March 1937, p. 131; 25
September 1937, p. 73. *HT*, **4**(2) (1932), p. 27; **8**(4) (1936), pp. 26, 46–7; *Tr.*, **1**(1)
(1935), 4th cover; **2**(1) (1936), 3rd cover; **2**(3) (1936), p. 19; **3**(4) (1937), pp. 10,
13. Northland Greyhound Lines Bus *Timetable*, 1 February 1937, p. 30 (hereafter
cited as *NGLBTT*).

13. *RVM*, **12**(8) (1946), p. 7; **15**(3) (1948), pp. 6–7; **16**(4) (1949), pp. 10–11. *HT*, **19**(4)

(1947), pp. 18–19; **20**(2) (1948), pp. 16–17, 46–7; **26**(3) (1954), 4th cover. *Tr.*, **12**(2) (1948), p. 31, 4th cover; **14**(3) (1950), 2nd cover. *NGLBTT*, 26 September 1954, 4th cover; 27 June, 1956, 4th cover. *Look*, 15 December 1954, p. 45; *Ladies Home Journal*, September 1955, p. 98; Meier and Hoschek, *Over the Road*, pp. 89–91, 98, 100, 103, 118, 121.

14. *SEP*, 23 March 1929, p. 180; 26 March 1955, p. 163. *HT*, **1**(2) (1929), p. 21; **1**(4) (1929), p. 3; **2**(2) (1930), p. 31; **4**(5) (1932), pp. 7–8; **9**(5) (1937), 3rd cover; **25**(3) (1953), 4th cover. *RVM*, **15**(1) (1948), pp. 1–2; **15**(2) (1948), p. 1; **15**(3) (1948), p. 2.

15. The Jefferson Company was a leading regional operator in the states of the Upper Mississippi Valley; *Indianola Record*, 15 February 1940; *Mason City Globe-Gazette*, 17 February, 30 September 1940; *Iowa Falls Citizen*, 24 September 1940; *Eldora Index*, 26 September 1940; *Hampton Chronicle*, 3 October 1940; *Sheffield Press*, 3 October 1940. (All clippings in the E.F. Zelle Records, the Jefferson Lines Inc., Minneapolis.)

16. *SEP*, 23 February 1929, p. 135; 'Advertising Budget and Revenue Quotas for 1929', n.p. File 1, no.1, GCR; Fowler, 'Advertising in the Motor Business' n.p. *The Greyhound Limited*, **1**(6) (1929), p. 2; **2**(2) (1929), p. 2. *Saturday Evening Post* had a circulation of 2,900,868 in 1928 and 3,028,408 in 1929; JWT, *Newsletter*, 1 October 1928, p. 2 and 'Advertising Budget and Revenue Quotas …', n.p. It was generally assumed that an average of three persons read each magazine, JWT, *Newsletter*, 6 September 1928, p. 1; 'Report of the National Advertising and Publicity Committee; NAMBO, *Procs*, **16** (1942), p. 134.

17. *SEP*, 12 September 1931, p. 120; 11 March 1933, p. 70; 15 July, 1933, p. 54; 14 September 1935, p. 73; 26 0ctober 1935, p. 97. *AA*, 2 September 1935, p. 15. *Tr.*, **1**(5) (1936), 2nd cover; **1**(6) (1936), p. 8; **2**(1) (1936), 4th cover; **2**(2) (1936), p. 8; **2**(4) (1937), p. 1, 4th cover; **2**(5–6) (1937), p. 21.

18. *RVM*, **12**(5) (1945), pp. 1, 7; *HT*, **20**(4) (1948), pp. 14–15, 40–41; *SEP*, 24 January 1948, p. 66. *NGLBTT*, 5 June 1946, p. 3, 4th cover; 12 November 1947, 4th cover. JWT, *Newsletter*, 28 May 1951, p. 5; Trailways Bus System, East Coast Group, 'Advertisements, 1951–59', Microfilm AD70 (JWT Records).

19. For more information on bus industry advertising during the Second World War see M. Walsh (1988), '"See/Serve America Now" – Advertising Bus Travel in the US during the Second World War', *Journal of Advertising History*, **11**(1) (published in association with the *European Journal of Marketing*, **22**(4), pp. 41–60.

20. NAMBO, *Procs*, (1942), **16**, pp. 133–6. The signature 'Motor Lines of America' was designed as a shorter, simpler and more descriptive name than NAMBO.

21. For general information on American advertising during the Second World War see F.W. Fox (1975), *Madison Avenue Goes to War. The Strange Military Career of American Advertising, 1941–45*, Provo, UT, and D.L. Jones (1976), 'The US Office of War Information and American Public Opinion during World War II, 1935–1945', PhD thesis, State University of New York at Binghamton.

22. For general information on tourism see E. Pomeroy (1957), *In Search of the Golden West*, New York, and J.A. Jakle (1985), *The Tourist: Travel in Twentieth Century North America*, Lincoln, NB. Some useful insights can also be found in W.J. Belasco (1979), *Americans on the Road: From Autocamp to Motel, 1910–45*, Cambridge, MA; J.B. Rae, *The Road and the Car in American Life*, especially chapter 7; J. Weinberger (1936–1937), 'Economic Aspects of Recreation', *Harvard Business Review*, **15**, pp. 448–63. For the bus industry see D. Short, 'What can Bus Lines do to Promote Year-Around Vacations?', an address to the

annual meeting of NAMBO in 1948. This address and the discussion which followed are in NAMBO, *Procs*, **19** (1948), pp. 170–85.

23. 'Advertising Budget and Revenue Quotas ...', n.p. *AA*, 3 October 1949, p. 18; 7 August 1950, p. 24. *RVM*, **17**(9) (1950), p. 10.

24. Minnesota Motor Bus Association, *Travel By Bus*, 25 June 1925, insert between pp. 16 and 17; *BT*, **6**(12) (1927), pp. 671–3. *SEP*, 23 May 1931, pp. 134–51; 10 June 1933, p. 52; 30 January 1934, p. 68. *Tr.*, **2**(1) (1936), 4th cover; **2**(5–6) (1937), p. 15. For the relationship of Northland Transportation to the Greyhound Corporation see M. Walsh, 'Tracing the Hound', (chapter 4), pp. 75–85.

25. *SEP*, 27 July 1935, p. 52; 27 March 1937, p. 121; 26 March 1949, p. 117; 28 March 1953, p. 191. *BT*, **16**(4) (1937), pp. 9–11. *Tr.*, **2**(2) (1936), 2nd cover, 4th cover; **4**(10) (1928), 3rd cover; **7**(5) (1941), p. 17; **11**(1) (1946), p. 31. *Ladies Home Journal*, October 1939, p. 107; May 1949, p. 244. *Colliers*, 6 September 1947, p. 58; 28 May 1949, p. 24. *RVM*, **14**(7) (1947), p. 3; **16**(4) (1949), p. 2; **17**(9) (1950), p. 10; **18**(10) (1951), p. 4; **20**(1) (1953), p. 17.

26. *SEP*, 9 November 1929, p. 208; 18 November 1933, p. 64; 17 November 1934, p. 71; 11 January 1936, 2nd cover; 21 December 1946, p. 88; 18 December 1948, p. 77. *HT*, (1932), **4**(1), p. 29. *Tr.*, **2**(7–8) (1937), 4th cover; **6**(1) (1940), 4th cover. *NGLBTT*, 1 February 1937, third cover; *BT*, **19**(2) (1940), pp. 79–80.

27. *SEP*, 21 December 1935, p. 48. *HT*, **6**(6) (1934–1935), 2nd cover; **11**(6) (1939–1940), pp. 4; **12**(6) (1940–1941), 4th cover. *Tr.*, **1**(3) (1935), 3rd cover; **2**(3) (1936), p. 17; **6**(4–5) (1940), 3rd cover.

28. *HT*, **5**(1) (1933), p. 4; **6**(3) (1934), pp. 7, 45; **12**(2) (1940), p. 2; **20**(2) (1948), 4th cover. *SEP*, 13 May 1933, p. 83; 26 May 1934, p. 121. *Ladies Home Journal*, May 1936, p. 104; June, 1939, p. 56. *AA*, 18 May 1936, p. 44; 27 February 1939, p. 1. *Tr.*, **6**(2) (1940), third cover. All Greyhound histories agree on the importance of the Chicago World's Fair in stimulating Greyhound's ailing business. Schisgall, *The Greyhound Story*, p. 41; Jackson, *Hounds of the Road*, pp. 45–8; Walsh, 'From Jitney to Giant' (chapter 2), p. 24.

29. *HT*, **5**(3) (1933), p. 3; **6**(2) (1934), pp. 34–5; **6**(3) (1934), p. 2; **6**(6) (1935), p. 8; **7**(5) (1935), 3rd cover; **19**(2) (1947), 3rd cover; **19**(3) (1947), 2nd cover; **23**(2) (1951), 4th cover. *Tr.*, **1**(5) (1936), 4th cover; **2**(5–6) (1937), 4th cover; **2**(7–8) (1937), p. 17; **4**(9) (1938), p. 6, 4th cover; **11**(4) (1947), pp. 1, 28–9; **13**(4) (1949), p. 23; **15**(1) (1950), 3rd cover. *AA*, 19 February 1940, p. 27. *BT*, **24**(9) (1945), p. 63; **25**(5) (1946), pp. 75–6; **34**(7) (1955), p. 44. *RVM*, **12**(12) (1945), p. 1; **13**(3) (1946), p. 8; **13**(8) (1946), p. 3; **17**(2) (1950), p. 6; **17**(8) (1950), p. 13. *NGLBTT*, 22 June 1952, fourth cover; 26 September 1954, p. 3; 27 June 1956, p. 3.

30. *HT*, **23**(3) (1951), pp. 21–3; **25**(3) (1953), pp. 40–41; **26**(3) (1954), pp. 36–7. *BT*, **29**(2) (1950), p. 60. *NGLBTT*, 28 October 1952, p. 3; 26 September 1954, 2nd cover; 27 June 1956, 2nd cover.

31. Newspapers and magazines have remained popular outlets for advertising. As late as 1982 newspapers in the USA received 27 per cent of the total advertising expenditure, with television coming second at 22 per cent and direct mail third with 15 per cent; Schudson, *Advertising, the Uneasy Persuasion*, p. 67.

32. 'How to Increase Bus Patronage?' Book 2, *Motorbus Transportation*, (1930), Scranton, PA, pp. 15–45. NAMBO, *Procs*, **4** (1930), pp. 70–75; **6** (1932), pp. 42, 45.

33. 'Piggybacking' describes the flexible way in which Greyhound could personalize and make every advertisement in the newspapers or on television a local advertisement. E.H. Holzer, 'Greyhound Bus Line', ms, n.d., p. 5 (Grey Advertising, Chicago).

34. *BT*, **3**(3) (1924), pp. 105–8; **6**(12) (1927), p. 673; **15**(3) (1936), pp. 118–20; **19**(5) (1940), pp. 208–9. *The Greyhound*, **1**(1) (1928), p. 4; *The Greyhound Limited*, **1**(5) (1929), p. 2; J.B. Walker, 'Advertising the Long Haul Operation', Report of the Committee on Advertising and Publicity, NAMBO, *Procs*, **3** (1929), pp. 31–3; 'Plan for Newspaper Advertising', Report of the Committee on Advertising and Publicity, NAMBO, *Procs* , **6** (1932), pp. 41–5; *RVM*, **17**(8) (1950), p. 6; L.A. Rossman to C.E. Wickman, O.S. Caesar and P. Tibbets, 'Advertising plans for the Northland Greyhound Lines' and 'Advertising problems of the Motor Transit Company and the Greyhound Lines', being part of discussion paper on subjects pertaining to the motor bus industry, 21 August 1929 (L.A. Rossman Records, Minnesota Historical Society, St Paul). Advertisements from the personal files of Walter B. Grosvenor, who worked for Beaumont & Hohman of Cleveland, OH and for Grey Advertising Incorporated, New York, and from Trailways Bus System, East Coast Group, 1951–1959, Microfilm AD 70 (JWT Records).

35. 'Advertising Budget and Revenue Quotas …', n.p.; untitled piece on advertising, 2pp., c. 1929, file 3 no. 3, GCR; Fowler, 'Advertising in the Motor Business', n.p. *The Greyhound Limited*, **1**(6) (1929), p. 2; **2**(2) (1929), p. 2. *BT*, **8**(3) (1929), p. 144. *SEP*, 23 February 1929, p. 135; 23 March 1929, p. 180; 20 April 1929, p. 200; 8 June 1929, p. 159; 14 September 1929, p. 244; 9 November 1929, p. 208. *American Magazine*, May 1929, p. 117; July 1929, p. 111; August 1929, p. 125; October 1929, p. 135. Marchand, *Advertising the American Dream*, pp. 5, 7; Presbrey, *The History and Development of Advertising*, pp. 590–97.

36. *AA*, 13 January 1936, p. 30; 10 January 1938, p. 20. The image of long-distance bus transport was not perceived as being suitable only for those on lower incomes. This post-war image tends to be projected backwards without any substantive evidence.

37. *AA*, 9 March 1936, pp. 1, 4; NAMBO, *Procs*, **16** (1942), pp. 135–8; *RVM*, **17**(8) (1950), pp. 6–7. Greyhound officials estimated that the forty-four periodicals had a total single issue circulation of 83.5 million, and that each copy of the magazine averaged at least two to three readers. No account was taken of how many of these people read more than one magazine and were thus included twice or several times.

38. Information on company newsletters is difficult to locate because until recently relatively few were deposited in libraries. Fowler, 'The Why of Greyhound advertising', pp. 26–7; *The Greyhound Limited*, **1**(8) (1921), p. 1; *HT*, **2**(2) (1930), p. 3; **3**(4) (1931), p. 31; **19**(6) (1947–1948), p. 48. *RVM*, **10**(1) (1943), p. 1; **19**(3) (1952), p. 2.

39. JWT, *Newsletter*, 15 September 1928, pp. 1–2; *Pickwick-Greyhound Highway Log*, **1**(8) (1930), p. 3; *BT*, **10**(11) (1931), pp. 578–80; **14**(9) (1935), pp. 347–8; **17**(4) (1938), p. 178; **19**(3) (1940), pp. 113; **19**(5) (1940), pp. 208–9. *RVM*, **17**(8) (1950), pp. 6–7; **18**(9) (1951), pp. 3, 10. *AA*, 1 October 1951, p. 70; E. Barnouw (1966), *A Tower in Babel*, **1**, to 1933, and (1968), *The Golden Web*, **2**, 1933–1952 of *A History of Broadcasting in the United States*, New York, and Marchand, *Advertising the American Dream*, pp. 88–110 offer some general insights on radio advertising.

40. *HT*, **6**(1) (1934), pp. 16–17, 38; *RVM*, **7**(3) (1940), p. 2; **8**(1) (1941), pp. 16–17; **13**(4) (1946), p. 7; **18**(1) (1951), p. 14; **18**(11) (1951), p. 13; **18**(12) (1951), p. 9; **19**(3) (1952), p. 3. *AA*, 28 May 1956, p. 77; Jackson, *Hounds of the Road*, pp. 48–9. For general information on the social impact of films, see R. Sklar (1975), *Movie-Made America: A Social History of American Movies*, New York.

41. Fowler, 'Advertising in the Motorbus Business', n.p.; W.C. Beaumont, 'Selling

Transportation to the Public', NAMBO, *Procs*, **4** (1930), pp. 90–91, 'Advertising as a Medium of Getting Additional Revenue', NAMBO, *Procs*, **20** (1949), pp. 171–5. *BT*, **4**(3) (1925), p. 129; **4**(7) (1925), p. 330; **5**(1) (1926), p. 18; **6**(11) (1927), pp. 613–16; **18**(3) (1939), pp. 122–6; **18**(6) (1939), pp. 294–6; **25**(11) (1946), pp. 66–9. *RVM*, **8**(11) (1941), p. 3; **8**(12) (1941), p. 7; **12**(2) (1945), p. 8; **13**(7) (1946), p. 6; **13**(12) (1946), p. 4; **14**(10) (1947), p. 3; **16**(5) (1949), p. 2; **17**(10) (1950), p. 4; **18**(12) (1951), p. 9.

42. 'Advertising Budget ...', n.p.; NAMBO, *Procs*, **5** (1931), pp. 49–50; NAMBO, 'Minutes of the Board of Directors', 26–27 October 1944, pp. 11–12 (American Heritage Center, University of Wyoming). *AA*, 12 April 1945, p. 22; 3 October 1949, p. 18; 18 August 1950, p. 24.

43. *RVM*, **17**(12) (1950), p. 4.

44. Schudson, *Advertising: the Uneasy Persuasion*, pp. 85–6.

45. The most frequently cited figures of advertising budgets in the 1920s and 1930s ranged between 2.5 and 5 per cent of gross revenue. Bus operators set aside a specific percentage and then added fixed amounts for particular campaigns. Fowler, 'The Why of Greyhound Advertising', pp. 26–7; Fowler, 'Advertising in the Motor Bus Business', n.p. *BT*, **10**(8) (1931), pp. 457–9; **17**(4) (1938), p. 178; **19**(5) (1940), p. 213. NAMBO, *Procs*, **4** (1930), pp. 74, 91.

9   Not Rosie the Riveter: Women's Diverse Roles in the Making of the American Long-Distance Bus Industry

Until relatively recently women were 'hidden from history'.[1] Women's role in transport history is no exception. Women were nearly invisible other than as emergency wartime workers. The image of 'Rosie the Riveter' is buried deep in American history as that of the heroic female worker meeting the nation's needs in time of peril. In the long-distance bus industry in the USA women played a substantial part in keeping the buses moving. Yet in saying this there is a need not to ignore, neglect or undervalue their contributions to the bus industry in peacetime. Women have been involved in bus transport from its onset and their involvement has increased in recent years. This chapter suggests new ways of considering a male-dominated business.

Starting at the top of the business pyramid with owners and managers, two biographical sketches suggest not only that female entrepreneurs existed in the American long-distance bus industry, but that they behaved like their male counterparts. Over half a century apart, their careers point to initiative, determination, organizational skill, the ability to command both capital and respect, and love of success. These are the characteristics which male historians have traditionally regarded as essential for business growth.

In April 1922 Helen Schultz, a 24-year-old single woman, founded Iowa's first intercity bus line. Inspired by the early motor-vehicle operations which she had seen while working in northern Minnesota and in California she decided to establish her own bus company in her home locale of northern Iowa. Adverse weather and dirt-top roads were the first obstacles in the path of the Red Ball Transportation Company. These were followed by rival bus companies and by city governments demanding high user fees. No sooner had Helen Schultz emerged successfully from these struggles than she faced the much stronger opposition of the steam and electric railroads. Armed with testimony from local residents about their need for a bus service, she argued her case before the Iowa Railroad Commission and won a licence to operate. Then, pushing further out of her base, Mason City, to Des Moines in the south and to Minneapolis in the north, she acquired not only more buses and drivers, but also the title of

'Iowa Bus Queen'. By now renowned as a determined fighter, she continued to expand in the mid-1920s. Financial problems surfaced following the imposition of high wheelage taxes on buses, failures among rural banks and more important the incursions of regional bus companies into Iowa. In 1930, realising the difficulties posed by the competition of major companies, she sold the Red Ball Transportation Company, at a profit, to the Jefferson Highway Transportation Company and retired from the bus industry.[2]

In 1978, 43-year-old Mrs Christiane Park joined Empire Trailways, Rochester, New York, as vice-president of finance. Empire Trailways was part of the nationwide association of independent bus companies which had coordinated their colour schemes and schedules in the 1930s to compete more effectively with the dominant bus corporation, Greyhound. The company had a regional business in upstate New York focusing on Rochester, Buffalo, Syracuse and Batavia, and had survived both the problems posed by widespread car ownership and the need to introduce more comfortable and safer buses in the post-Second World War years. More was needed if the company was going to flourish in the 1970s and 1980s, when the bus industry was suffering from poor investment, low revenue and a negative image among the travelling public. Chris Park had been headhunted by the company for her managerial, marketing and financial skills. Her career as homemaker, manager of non-appropriated funds at an air force base in Japan, management analyst with the Defense Department in Sacramento, manager of an amusement park, freelance securities dealer and controller of a small chain of restaurants suggested flexibility and knowledge of a broad range of service industries.

As a newcomer to the bus industry she had first to learn about the workings of the company and the industry before she could suggest improvements and innovations. Her early contributions to streamlining the company focused on the tour sector. From this base she became so confident of the business that in 1984 she bought 50 per cent of Empire Trailways with a partner, and long-serving company employee, William Hicks. Five years later, in 1989, she bought out Hicks and he retired. Then, the company owned thirty-four buses and revenues were fairly evenly split between regular route and charter service. By 1990, gross revenue exceeded $7 million and the fleet of buses was logging some 3 million miles per annum. By that time Chris Park had become well established in the bus industry at both state and national levels. She was the first woman to serve as president of the New York Bus Association, from 1987 to 1990, and from 1986 she sat on the board of the American Bus Association, serving as its marketplace chairperson in 1989. She was a woman bus executive who like Helen Schultz had won great respect and acclaim in what is considered to be a male-dominated industry.[3]

The biographical sketches suggest that both women had succeeded against the odds. It was, and still is, rare to find a woman at the head of a long-distance bus company in the USA. The industry has been run, owned and managed primarily by men. Men have manufactured the vehicles, invested the finance, made the rules of business conduct and operated the fleets of vehicles, whether as part of national corporations or as smaller regional firms. Women did not belong to the business culture of the bus industry. They were outsiders. As such they faced difficulties in knowing how to behave, let alone in being accepted. Their world was usually that of the domestic arena, as wives and mothers, or if they were gainfully employed then they were secretaries, or at best were in management positions that had routinized functions and had 'expert' roles rather than decision-making roles.[4]

As a female operator in the 1920s Helen Schultz built up a notable company and gained a reputation as a stalwart bus pioneer. In many respects she was like her male counterparts who had developed a new business by capitalizing on the desire of Americans to be mobile. All early bus entrepreneurs faced problems of securing finance, establishing routes, fighting competitors, both intra- and intermodal, and developing managerial and promotional skills. The conservative commercial ethos and the economically competitive climate of the 1920s was not one which encouraged women to start up in business, even in new industries which might not yet be sex-typed. Certainly, by this time women had gained the vote and were entering a wider range of professions. Yet they were still disadvantaged in several respects. They rarely had access to business or managerial training, and what they learned by experience was courtesy of male accountants, engineers, technicians and workers. Furthermore, they rarely had access to finance other than that which they had personally inherited.[5]

For Helen Schultz, the problems of obtaining loans for investment in capital equipment were overwhelming. Banks were not interested in supporting female enterprises, let alone unconventional female enterprises. She was especially hindered when facing competition from much larger companies who were better placed to tap into institutional financial networks. Like many small bus operators, she also lacked managerial training. The publicity which she faced at each stage of her unconventional career became intrusive and tiresome. Furthermore, following her marriage in 1925 and the birth of her children, domestic commitments needed attention, even though she had satisfactory child-care arrangements. It can be argued that rather than retiring with honour after running a bus company for eight years, she was marginalized into giving up her job. In a period when women were not welcome in business circles and when men systematically excluded them from the professions, it is not surprising that years of struggle should have taken their toll.[6]

Some fifty years later Chris Park found her working environment less crippling. A post-war generation which had witnessed female consciousness-raising and a legal enactment of equal opportunities at least suggested that women might be visible in a broader range of occupations, including those which were male-dominated. Educational opportunities in areas like law, accountancy, advertising and personnel brought training and skills which were increasingly required in bureaucratic organizations. It would not be very surprising to find women in a variety of middle-management positions, whether they entered these fields as trainees with qualifications or came in as mature women after raising their families. They might even be able to juggle child-care arrangements to stay in a bus-related career and work their way up the management ladder to an executive office. Yet though more doors were opening to women in the 1970s and 1980s the glass ceiling kept them out of top positions. The price for getting to the front, on the fast-track set up by males, was an ability to work long hours at anti-social times thereby neglecting or rearranging domestic commitments, and willingness, however hesitant, to be accepted into or to push oneself into a male networking culture.[7] Chris Park still encountered many problems as an ambitious female entrepreneur without a traditional bus culture. In 1994, facing financial difficulties, she sold the scheduled lines of Empire Trailways and later filed for bankruptcy.[8]

Chris Park and Helen Schultz were exceptional women and have a recoverable past. Yet even these women have been hidden from history. Traditional business historians, primarily male, still do not expect to find female entrepreneurs, let alone to look for them. When their consciousness is raised they are content to place such missing women into existing patriarchal frameworks. Some adjustments may be made to criticize the traditional male structure, which has sanctioned the absence of women, in both the historical and the business worlds. Such an approach, though worthy, will not suffice.[9] There are and have been many more women in transport endeavours and their contributions need to be recognized.

The recent upsurge of historical interest in small businesses and family firms may bring a fuller appreciation of the activities of both female entrepreneurs and of the wives, mothers, sisters and daughters of male entrepreneurs.[10] Chris Park has proudly remarked that when she first entered the bus industry, she was the only woman in the Trailways System, and possibly in the whole bus industry at that time, to hold an executive position and not to have any relative in the industry.[11] This is an achievement worth recording in its own right. What it further suggests is that there have been many women whose contributions have been neglected because they were unpaid or paid relatives.

Family firms and small organizations have always been important parts of the long-distance bus industry in the USA. Americans and foreign visitors alike may frequently have assumed that most buses belonged to the Greyhound Corporation or possibly to the Trailways companies, but in the mid 1930s Greyhound controlled only 14 per cent of the national bus route mileage while in the late 1960s it had only 50 per cent of the intercity bus traffic. In the early years of bus development most operations were small and were individually or family owned, or were partnerships. In the 1960s and 1970s regional and local intercity bus carriers still remained an active and viable part of transport services. Indeed, these businesses often proved to be more flexible in adapting to changing market demands.[12]

Historical information on family firms has been notoriously difficult to locate. Frequently, these firms have lasted for only a few years and have either failed to keep their records or have buried them in attics or basements.[13] Such 'Mom and Pop' enterprises in the bus industry have rarely featured in the local press, let alone academic writing. Even the regional bus companies, whether family owned or not, have been and still are small. Their records also are scarce and their activities rarely surface beyond short accounts or notices in provincial newspapers and in trade journals. Without considerable expenditure of time and an element of luck it is difficult to find material on small operators, let alone ascertain the contributions of their family members to the bus industry.

Yet, occasional glimpses suggest that women have not only been supportive in the ventures of their male kin; they have been essential to success. Peter Pan Bus Lines was established by Peter C. Picknelly in 1933 to offer a scheduled service between Springfield and Boston, Massachusetts. During the subsequent sixty years it became a regional business operating regular routes in Massachusetts, Connecticut and New York, with charter and special services developing in importance.[14] At first sight the information on this significant regional company suggests that it was run solely by men. In an account of the company written some twenty years after its founding, the only woman featured was Peter Picknelly's daughter, Janet. Initially mentioned because her father equated her to Wendy, whereas his son and the bus line were both Peter Pan, she subsequently was written up in a subordinate clause as the company bookkeeper. Clearly, she was deemed marginal to the progress of the company. Yet how many businesses can dismiss their financial manager in such a trivial manner? She was in an executive position until her marriage in the mid-1950s and subsequently she handled bookkeeping functions on a part-time basis from home.[15]

Janet Picknelly Collins was not the only female family member to be active in Peter Pan Bus Lines. Peter C. Picknelly's wife, Jennie, also performed bookkeeping functions in the 1950s and 1960s. When her husband died in 1964 she became chair of the board, taking a more active role in administrative functions as well as continuing to do accounting for the company. Yet this executive role would have been hidden had she not written a letter to introduce the fiftieth-anniversary story of the business and had not her granddaughter, Mary Jean Picknelly, and her son, Peter L. Picknelly, been willing to supply personal information.

The female contribution to the family firm continued into the third generation. As a teenager Mary Jean Picknelly worked for Peter Pan Bus Lines as a receptionist and ticket agent. While studying for a business degree she became involved with Travel Time Bus Lines, set up by her father to operate school bus transport and to develop charters and tours. As vice-president of this company she managed the office, marketing, planning and scheduling the routes. When Travel Time was sold in 1988 she became senior vice-president of Peter Pan Tours, being heavily involved in tour product development, pricing and office management, and being responsible for the general profitability of the section. With a third of the company's business coming from tours and charters, Mary Jean Picknelly holds a major executive position. Her sisters-in-law, Cynthia Picknelly and Melissa Beckstead Picknelly, work in the family business. In Peter Pan Bus Lines there was both female and male participation to ensure a smooth generational transmission of leadership.[16]

Female leadership was again crucial, albeit in different ways, to the survival of two other family firms, Adirondack Trailways in the 1970s and 1980s and Indian Trails from 1910 to the 1950s. Adirondack Trailways had originally been established in Kingston, New York, in 1926 by John J. Van Gonsic to serve the resort trade in the Adirondack and Catskill mountains. Expanding scheduled services, especially to New York city, he built up a sound regional business. When he was succeeded as president by his son, John J. Van Gonsic, Jr, in 1965 and then, after some temporary arrangements, by his son-in-law, Eugene Berardi, the company continued to flourish. The death of Eugene Berardi in 1976 created a managerial vacuum which was filled only when his wife, Cynthia Van Gonsic Berardi, assumed control of the company. Although she had grown up in a bus environment, she had not been involved in the business other than as a teenager holding down a summer job. When faced with leadership responsibilities she found that she had absorbed considerable knowledge through the mingling of work and domestic life. Not only was she able to keep the business going, she also demonstrated managerial skill in expanding the bus business and in serving in an executive capacity for the National Trailways Bus operations. In 1988 she was able to hand over the family business in good shape to her son Eugene.[17]

Indian Trails was established in 1910 as a taxi service by a wife and husband partnership, Cora and Wayne Taylor. From these small beginnings the bus company emerged firstly as a short-distance line operating between Flint and Owosso in the second decade of this century, and then as a flourishing intercity company which reached south as far as Chicago and northeast to the tip of the thumb of Michigan. Cora and Wayne Taylor always owned and controlled all the company stock, held the major offices and undertook most of the executive work themselves. Cora Taylor was not a sleeping partner. In the pioneer years she drove the taxi-cab; then she became involved in the office management and during the Second World War she was responsible for all branches of the business, even driving the buses when she was short of drivers. She was an integral part of a family firm.[18]

The fact that qualitative evidence exists to demonstrate female participation in these three family companies is either fortuitous or a result of increasing media consciousness of women's rights. Quantitative evidence is simply not available to demonstrate how representative the Picknelly, Van Gonsic–Berardi and Taylor families may be of successful small or regional bus firms. It can, however, be hypothesized that the mortality of some family-owned businesses resulted in part from a lack of commitment by all members, whatever their sex. Many firms went bankrupt as a result of poor management, others collapsed in the face of competition, but others needed the support of women in the family to remain in operation. Women were frequently essential to the well-being of small bus endeavours, although they have rarely been given credit by being officially recorded as entrepreneurs or management executives.[19]

If women owners and managers have received little attention, women workers have been even less regarded when the public profile of the American long-distance bus industry is under discussion. Yet in the twentieth century, most well-run businesses, whether small or large, have depended on a bureaucracy staffed in part by female personnel. The woman factor in the well-being of corporations and companies is thus not inconsiderable. Bus companies are no exception to the rule. They needed an office staff which included not only secretaries, stenographers and telephonists, but also ticket and freight agents, promotional officers, tour agents, bookkeepers and accountants. Bus depots needed cleaners, while their cafeterias needed cooks and waitresses. Buses have been crewed not only by hostesses, but also by female drivers. Women workers have always been a regular part of bus-line business. Yet only as 'Rosie the Riveter' stereotypes in the Second World War and more recently as a result of modern feminism and equal rights legislation have their contributions been recognized.

'Womanpower' was a commonly-used term during the emergency years of the Second World War. Then, federal government and top executives both acknowledged that the industry required the presence and ability of female workers. With increased use of public transport and a growing shortage of male workers by late 1942, bus managers started training women for jobs they thought more suitable. They knew that women were already familiar with the office routines of bus depots and offices. It was thus only a short step to placing women in the operating department, in charge of ticket counters and information systems. They could even be allowed in the stockrooms dispensing parts, in the baggage area, and in the garages cleaning and refuelling vehicles. Bus officials were more reluctant, however, to employ women as mechanics and drivers. Women were deemed not to have the necessary skill or inclination to repair or service buses, while driving was a task which required physical stamina and the authority to control passengers. Such characterizing of the weak, domesticated woman in need of protection gradually broke down, first in the local transit systems and then in the intercity bus network as pressure to find workers increased and as women demonstrated that they were capable of any job. There were problems in ensuring that state regulations on women's working hours and conditions were not breached, in establishing separate washroom facilities in traditional male work-spaces and in persuading the travelling public to accept women in non-traditional occupations; but they were not insurmountable. By 1944, women were visible in most sections of the intercity bus industry.[20]

They did not remain so noticeable at the end of the war. Plans for reversion to peacetime conditions assumed that the bus industry would be operated as before the war, with men returning to their old jobs. Women were expected to revert to or stay in their traditional sex-typed jobs of secretary, stenographer, local agent, tour adviser, bookkeeper, hostess or waitress. They should no longer be seen in the garage or the baggage room, driving the bus or in the manager's seat. When more vacancies opened up for women in the quarter-century after the war they were in information services and personnel relations. Here, as elsewhere, women's contributions were rarely deemed noteworthy other than in company magazines, where employees expected to find news about their colleagues, or in trade journals when photographs were needed to illustrate articles.[21] Nevertheless, the intercity bus industry could not have functioned without female labour.

By the 1970s women were becoming more visible as they and their traditional supportive posts were given greater recognition. An era in which equal opportunities legislation had opened doors to both jobs and training and in which women expected to be in the labour force for most of their adult life brought them nearer the centre of an industry which traditionally had a masculine face. Women served in decision-making and management positions at all levels and in all categories, not only in individual companies, but also in transport authorities and the American Bus Association (ABA). They were most visible in planning, marketing and finance, for example as accountants, tour brokers, retail travel agents, coach sales promotions managers and public information managers. Personnel relations both within companies and with the public took on a female face and in vehicle operation and maintenance women drivers became more frequent, while professional women started to see operations as a route to the position of general manager. No longer could the area of public transport be considered a single-sexed area. Women were entering the bus industry because they had the managerial and professional qualifications and because the industry offered a range of employment opportunities.[22]

The long-distance bus industry in the USA became a business in which women found careers and occupations. Yet organizing transport services may not be the most important way in which women have contributed to the industry. Women have always been significant consumers of bus travel and their decisions and preferences have not only had an effect on the quality and nature of the service; they have shaped the process of growth and decline. Had its male leaders been more aware of female needs, and attempted to construct a public bus service in which women felt more comfortable, the intercity bus industry might not have faced such a post-war struggle for survival.

Female passengers have accounted for at least half the revenue of the intercity bus industry. Though the National Association of Motor Bus Operators (NAMBO) and the ABA have not disaggregated their passenger statistics by sex or age, and individual company surveys of passengers are few, the direct and the indirect evidence available points to women as major consumers of bus services. In the 1920s and 1930s photographs of bus stops and terminals alike depict women queuing to board vehicles and waiting in bus depots, in the general waiting area or occasionally in a special women's waiting-room. Advertisements in popular magazines, such as the *Saturday Evening Post* or *Colliers*, or in specialist magazines such as *Ladies Home Journal* featuring women and families were designed to attract new customers and to retain existing ones by suggesting that bus travel was cheap, comfortable, reliable, safe, even fashionable and exotic. The iconography appealed to a female audience and the text was designed not only to be informative but also reassuring.[23] In a period when the growing popularity of the automobile was encouraging interest in road travel, and there was competition between railroads and buses for passengers, women were seen as important customers.

In those early years of bus transport women used buses for family visits and for shopping. These domestically-based journeys were expanded into a leisure activity as day trips and tours became more popular. By the 1930s women were travelling long distances in search of recreation, and they found that buses offered good value as well as geographical flexibility for both themselves and their families. Women welcomed buses as a means of mobility at a time when they were gaining more financial independence and a greater say in family decision-making. They were not passive consumers. They wanted bus services to be economical, reliable, comfortable and secure. Such concerns were acknowledged indirectly in the discussions of bus operators about hygiene, facilities and safety. Women did not want to wait in depots that were dirty, dark and lacked a washroom, and they wanted their luggage taken care of quickly. They were unhappy if the bus ran late or called at depots, restaurants or hotels which served poor or no refreshments. Whether because they were wearing high-heeled shoes or were carrying small children, women were also anxious about getting on and off buses, and they wanted wide aisles and adequate seating. Operators made concerted efforts to address these problems. New buses included washroom facilities, reducing the need for stops. Larger and better-equipped terminals replaced the old one-room depots, and agencies were inspected more frequently to improve standards.[24] The needs of female passengers were important to the bus industry's growth between the wars.

They remained important in the post-war years, but then they were not addressed satisfactorily. A generation of Americans had grown up with a range of bus services and frequently had first used buses as children. The familiar yellow school buses had not imbued a future clientele of either sex with enthusiasm about travelling long distances by bus. Certainly in youth, with low incomes, they might take Greyhound, Trailways or regional company buses to college as the cheapest way, but on graduating they quickly acquired a car, with its personal freedom and status. By the 1950s part of the problem of selling bus rides to Americans had become that of marketing public transport to a nation which loved and could increasingly afford personal transport. Americans would rather drive long distances in their autos, using ever-improved highways, than get on a bus.[25]

Female passengers or would-be passengers were more disenchanted with bus journeys than their male counterparts. By the 1950s rising incomes and widespread car ownership were giving long-distance bus travel a low status. 'Going by Greyhound' was no longer associated with flexibility and adventure; it was the poor person's option. Overcrowding and shabby vehicles during the war had helped to give the industry an image of inferior quality and unreliable service. Despite major campaigns advertising new vehicles, luxury service and courtesy, middle-class women were reluctant to travel by intercity bus. They remained worried about the location and facilities of the terminals. During the war, bus operators had been unable to improve bus stations and garages or build new ones. Their plans progressed slowly in the immediate post-war years because of high building costs, and when they did invest, the new terminals were often located downtown. Downtown was no longer so attractive or convenient to a population which was moving out to the suburbs. As the old central business districts became associated with poverty and danger, women felt less and less safe getting to the bus stations or comfortable waiting there. It was of no avail to claim that buses were the only means of public transport to and from 40,000 communities in the USA.[26] Only a minority of women, who had no alternatives, rode the buses in the 1960s and 1970s.

Many women had lost interest in taking a scheduled bus any distance because they had no control over the quality of their travelling space. Yet they could be persuaded to take a chartered or tour bus. When hired for a special occasion, motor coaches in effect became private vehicles and bus space became more appealing and agreeable. The expansion of the leisure market in planned vacations, sporting activities, cultural and historic visits, special events and group enterprises offered the intercity bus industry a lifeline. No longer an adjunct to main routes, the charter and tour divisions of intercity companies became a growth area with the right marketing. Women could once again be persuaded to travel by bus, now using a personalized service. Their interest could be maintained not just by better vehicles and depots, but by the presence of women offering transport services. With a growing number of them working in the industry at both managerial and semi-skilled level, more women reacted positively to entering bus space. They had more confidence that their demands for picking-up and dropping-off points, for sheltered and secure waiting areas, and for attention to child-care needs, would be treated seriously. Women were integral to the optimistic ethos which envisaged bus travel as a specialized niche service in the 1980s and 1990s.[27]

A closer look at the history of long-distance bus services in the USA reveals that women have played important and diverse roles in their development. As managers and workers they may have been invisible in most accounts, not only because they were few in number but because they were members of a family. Furthermore, the functions they undertook were frequently dismissed as auxiliary. The records of bus companies and trade associations preserved in archives have usually reinforced this marginality. Such records have been more concerned with vehicle design, engines, maintenance, operations, route networks, finance and regulation than with personnel, office routine, advertising, sales or passenger details. Yet even using traditional sources it is possible to show that women did play a significant role in running bus companies. They were also important as passengers demanding an economical, safe and comfortable service, and their reaction as consumers was often crucial to profitability. Thus women's role has been substantial and significant. It should not be dismissed as exceptional, the equivalent of the 'Rosie the Riveter' stereotype. Bus history needs to move forward from such myopic vision.

Notes

1. *Hidden from History*, London, the title of Sheila Rowbotham's (1973) book, about women in Britain from the Puritan revolution to the 1930s, became almost a slogan for the first generation of women's historians who insisted that women shaped the past, even though their contributions were traditionally ignored, marginalized and trivialized. Second-wave women's historians still talk about invisibility, but generally in the context of minority women and women of colour.
2. M. Walsh, 'Iowa's Bus Queen: Helen M. Schultz and the Red Ball Transportation Company', (chapter 5), pp. 89–101.
3. (1998), 'Doing It Her Way', *Destinations*, **10**(12) (1988), pp. 56, 117–18; *Business Journal*, **October** (1990), pp. 10–11; Mrs C.G. Park, 'Biographical Highlights', typescript; *Democrat & Chronicle*, (Rochester, NY), 10 August 1992.

4. For general surveys of the long-distance bus industry see M. Walsh, 'From Jitney to Giant', chapter 2, pp. 17–31 and M. Walsh, 'Missing Connections', chapter 3, pp. 32–64. For insights on the position of women in corporate management see R. Kanter (1977), *Men and Women of the Corporation*, New York, and C.F. Epstein (1971), *Woman's Place. Options and Limits in Professional Careers*, Berkeley, CA.
5. For suggestions about the position of women in the professions and in the business world in the 1920s see F. Stricker (1976), 'Cookbooks and Law Books: The Hidden History of Career Women in the Twentieth Century', *Journal of Social History*, **10**, pp. 1–19; M. Formanek-Brunell (1993), *Made to Play House. Dolls and the Commercialization of American Girlhood, 1830–1930*, New Haven, CT, pp. 135–60; A. Kwolek-Folland (1994), *Engendering Business: Men and Women in the Corporate Office, 1870–1930*, Baltimore; A. Kwolek-Folland (1998), *Incorporating Women. A History of Women and Business in the United States*, New York, pp. 85–129.
6. Walsh, 'Iowa's Bus Queen', chapter 5, pp. 89–101.
7. R. Goffee and R. Scase (1985), talk about the prospects of women in business in *Women in Charge. The Experiences of Female Entrepreneurs*, London. For discussion of the difficulties facing women in business see M. Hennig and A. Jardim (1978), *The Managerial Woman*, London, and F.N. Schwartz with J. Zimmerman (1992), *Breaking With Tradition. Women and Work, The New Facts of Life*, New York. The revival of feminism and its aftermath are examined in W.H. Chafe (1991), *The Paradox of Change: American Women in the Twentieth Century*, New York, pp. 194–229.
8. Adirondack Transit Lines acquired Empire Trailways in June 1994 when they formed a new company, New York Trailways. L. Friedmann, office manager, Adirondack Transit Lines, to M. Walsh, 23 August, 7 December 1994; New York Trailways *Bus Schedule*, effective 24 June 1994; *Democrat & Chronicle*, (Rochester, NY), 30 June 1994.
9. The traditional frameworks for putting women into history are examined in G. Lerner (1975), 'Placing Women in History: Definitions and Challenges', *Feminist Studies*, **3**, pp. 5–14 and in A.G. Gordon, M.J. Buhle and N.E. Schrom (1971), 'Women in American Society: An Historical Contribution', *Radical America*, **5**, pp. 1–71. More recent challenges to separate spheres and domesticity are considered in N.A. Hewitt (1985), 'Beyond the Search for Sisterhood: American Women's History in the 1980s', *Social History*, **10**, pp. 299–321 and S.M. Reverby and D.O. Helly, 'Introduction: Converging on History', in S.M. Reverby and D.O. Helly (eds) (1992), *Gendered Domains: Rethinking Public and Private in Women's History*, Ithaca, NY, pp. 1–24.
10. M.G. Blackford (1991), 'Small Business in America: A Historiographic Survey', *Business History Review*, **65**, pp. 1–26; *Business History*, **54** (1993), Special Issue on 'Family Capitalism'.
11. C. Park to M. Walsh, 27 June, 1991.
12. The percentage of the bus industry controlled by Greyhound and Trailways varies according to time and to the type of statistics used. In 1950 Greyhound operated 20 per cent of the route mileage in the USA while Trailways operated 17 per cent. In the same year Greyhound controlled 15 per cent of the passenger market while Trailways controlled 6 per cent. See B.B. Crandall (1954), *The Growth of the Intercity Bus Industry*, Syracuse, NY, p. 288. In 1979, together they carried 23 per cent of intercity bus passengers and had 60 per cent of intercity passenger revenue. Two years later in 1981 the respective figures were 21 per cent and

47 per cent. The two organizations have dominated Class I operations and regular scheduled services, but smaller companies have been very active in short-distance service and in charter and tour operations, which have a higher load factor than regular service. See Office of Transportation Analysis, Interstate Commerce Commission (hereafter cited as ICC), (1984), *The Intercity Bus Industry*, Washington, DC, pp. 11–13.

13. Blackford, pp. 10–21; M. Walsh (1991), 'Help Preserve the History of the Intercity Bus Industry', *Bus Ride*, **27**(6), pp. 60–61 (hereafter cited as *BR*).

14. *Bus Transportation*, **31**(2) (1952), pp. 53–5 (hereafter cited as *BT*). *BR*, **7**(5) (1971), pp. 17–9; **29**(8) (1993), pp. 36–8. *Motor Coach Age*, **35**(4) (1983), pp. 4–25 (hereafter cited as *MCA*).

15. *BT*, **31**(2) (1952), pp. 54, 55; telephone interview with M.J. Picknelly, by M. Walsh, 15 May 1991.

16. *MCA*, **35**(4) (1983), p. 4. *BR*, **25**(2) (1989), p. 52; **29**(8) (1993), p. 37. M.J. Picknelly phone interview; P. Picknelly, Snr, to M. Walsh, 20 March 1991.

17. L. Friedmann to M. Walsh, 23 August 1994; *Destinations*, **6**(8) (1984), pp. 25–7; *BR*, **19**(3) (1983), p. 48.

18. Newspaper clipping, 1950 (Greyhound Corporate Records, American Heritage Center Archives, University of Wyoming, Laramie); newspaper clipping, 1956 (Indian Trails, Inc., Owosso, MI).

19. *Bus Ride*, a trade magazine for the bus industry, has since the mid 1970s featured special reports on and from women in different parts of bus transportation. See *BR*, **10**(6) (1974/5), **16**(3) (1980), **23**(3) (1987), **25**(3) (1989), **27**(3) (1991) and **29**(4) (1993).

20. Several articles in the trade journal *BT* in the years 1942–1944, discuss the place of women in the bus industry's wartime business. See, for example, *BT*, **21**(5) (1942), pp. 222–3; **21**(11) (1942), pp. 511–13; **22**(1) (1943), pp. 28–31, 65–7; **22**(4) (1943), pp. 23–5; **22**(5) (1943), pp. 26–9, 35–7, 51; **22**(6) (1943), pp. 31–5; **22**(9) (1943), pp. 58, 59; **23**(1) (1944), pp. 50–52; **23**(3) (1944), pp. 42–3; **23**(5) (1944), pp. 28–30. For a general appreciation of women's economic role in wartime see Chafe, *Paradox*, pp. 121–53.

21. *BT*, **5**(4) (1926), p. 193; **7**(4) (1928), p. 188; **10**(11) (1931), p. 581; **12**(4) (1933), p. 159; **16**(4) (1937), pp. 152–4; **16**(12) (1937), p. 607; **17**(4) (1938), pp. 162, 163, 179; **17**(9) (1938), pp. 422–3; **17**(10) (1938), p. 521; **19**(2) (1940), pp. 77–8; **25**(7) (1946), p. 80; **26**(3) (1947), p. 59; **26**(4) (1947), p. 84; **27**(2) (1948), p. 88; **28**(3) (1949), p. 45; **30**(7) (1951), p. 36; **31**(8) (1952), p. 28; **33**(11) (1954), p. 46; **34**(1) (1955), pp. 32–3; **34**(2) (1955), pp. 48–9, 131, 133; **35**(7) (1956), p. 34; **35**(10) (1956), p. 59. *Rear View Mirror*, **13**(12) (1946), pp. 6, 7; **14**(2) (1947), p. 6; **16**(1) (1949), pp. 3; **17**(2) (1950), pp. 8, 9, 10. *Trails*, **1**(5) (1936), back cover; **2**(5–6) (1937), p. 4.

22. *BR*, **10**(6) (1974), pp. 21–23, 26; **12**(2) (1976), pp. 44–5; **16**(3) (1980), pp. 38, 40, 42, 44; **23**(3) (1987), pp. 52–3, 62, 68; **25**(3) (1989), pp. 50–53, 60; **27**(3) (1991), pp. 35, 37, 41, 42, 48–9, 50; **29**(4) (1993), pp. 29, 42, 43, 44, 46. C. Park to M. Walsh, 27 June 1991; M.J. Picknelly, phone interview; E.M. Hotard, General Manager Hotard Coaches Inc., to M. Walsh, 24 July 1991; interview with S. Perry, Senior Vice-President, Government Relations, American Business Association, by M. Walsh, 1 June 1991; L. Friedmann to M. Walsh, 11 August 1994.

23. Only recent surveys disaggregate bus statistics by sex. These show that women are a majority of intercity bus passengers. In 1972 59.5 per cent of such passengers were women, while in the late 1980s 60.9 per cent of Greyhound passengers were women. See ICC, (1978), *The Intercity Bus Industry*,

Washington, DC, p. 31 and F.D. Fravel (1990), *The Greyhound Story, 1979–1990. A Report*, Bethesda, MD, p. 10. An earlier article, 'Greyhound Still Growing', *Fortune*, **30**(3) (1944), p. 125, reported that women made up about 60 per cent of Greyhound's passengers. Photographs of buses in use or of terminals can be located in the trade journals like *BT*, *Trails*, *BR*, *Highway Traveler* and *Rear View Mirror*. Some of the best photographs of the intercity bus industry at work were taken by Esther Bubley in 1943 and 1947–1948 while working for the Office of War Information and Standard Oil (New Jersey). These photographs are available in Farm Security Administration Office – War Information Records, Library of Congress, Washington, DC and in Standard Oil (New Jersey) Records, Eckstrom Library, University of Louisville. Many examples of Greyhound advertisements from the popular magazines can be conveniently found in the D'Arcy Collection of Clippings, University of Illinois, Champaign-Urbana. Trailways advertisements can be found in *Trails* and in the J. Walter Thompson collection at Duke University, Durham, NC. For information on the style of bus company advertising see M. Walsh, ' "See This Amazing America" ', (see chapter 8), pp. 154–72.

24. Surveys of what women long-haul riders wanted are rare. Some material can be found in *BT*, **11**(7) (1932), pp. 301–2; **11**(9) (1932), pp. 384–6; **28**(4) (1949), pp. 51–3. Occasional references to women's needs can be found buried in detailed examinations of technical improvements to motor coaches and in advertisements.

25. M. Walsh, 'Missing Connections', chapter 3, pp. 40–44.

26. M. Walsh, 'Missing Connections', chapter 3, pp. 40–54; ICC (1978), *The Intercity Bus Industry*.

27. C. Park to M. Walsh, 27 June 1991; M.J. Picknelly telephone interview.

10 On and Off the Buses: 1940s Images from New York[1]

The years following the Second World War were transitional in the development of the long-distance bus industry in the USA. Prior to the war, the industry was growing despite the severe economic conditions of the Depression and Americans then regarded motor coaches as viable, economic, safe and comfortable. Furthermore, visual and written evidence suggests that a variety of people travelled by this mode of transport. During the war, bus business boomed thanks to shortages of petrol, parts for private vehicles and new vehicles. This form of public transport then had potential. However, increasingly in the 1950s, the bus industry failed to meet the challenge of the private motor car and the development of the plane as a regular passenger carrier. Those Americans with sufficient income to purchase one or more family automobiles abandoned public surface transport other than for commuting into large cities to work. Buses became a minor segment of the transport network, used mainly by those with low incomes and those unable to drive. The immediate post-war years were a period in which opportunities for growth may have been lost: a transitional time when evidence of popularity remained, yet signs of consumer discontent were visible.

Visual records can offer additional insights into historical developments above and beyond written and spoken evidence. Visual texts are not merely illustrations chosen to substantiate what has been argued through words. Nor are they unmediated copies of the real world. They are expressions of the real world and can be used as gateways and as starting points for discussion.[2] Photographs of the bus industry in operation suggest fascinating and diverse points of view, portraying perspectives that are not immediately visible in documents created by and for the industry. They also raise new questions, though of course their views are as subjective as most other sources. Photographers select the moments and places to take images, presenting these individually or juxtaposed in a series. Their pictures are representations of life. The pictorial record of the bus industry in the late 1940s provided by photographs suggests themes which are worth exploring in ascertaining its contemporary and future well-being.

The written text of the bus industry in the late 1940s

Written evidence about the intercity bus industry in the late 1940s has offered many suggestions about its operations and about its travelling and working conditions, few of which are flattering. It is commonly characterized as a system which was in need of modernizing; crowding, old coaches, poorly-equipped terminals and inadequate public relations all remained primarily as a wartime legacy. Though management had accumulated funds for investment during the war, rising construction and labour costs due to high inflation delayed rapid and significant improvements. Operators were also very concerned to ensure uniformity of state legislation on size, length and weight of vehicles before substantially re-equipping their fleets.

Yet many Americans were still travelling by bus. Ideally, they might prefer to travel in their own vehicles but there was still a shortage of both new automobiles coming off the production lines and spare parts to repair existing vehicles. Moreover, most bus passengers knew that the service was competent and practical and many still enjoyed travelling across the country, with frequent stops for rest and refreshment and opportunities to talk to their companions. During 1947 some 421 million passengers were carried by intercity bus carriers. The average journey for most travellers was 47.1 miles, a third shorter than that of the average train traveller, but more people travelled by bus than train.[3] These bus passengers rarely booked their seats in advance as service was frequent and in busy periods a second or a third extra vehicle would be brought into service. The bus was an informal but sensible mode of getting to one's destination.

Bus passengers came from a wide variety of economic and ethnic or racial backgrounds. In their choice of transport they suggested not only post-war shortages of automobiles but also the popularity of buses which had been visible in both the 1920s and the 1930s. Then all groups took to the buses, not only because they were economical, but because they were varied in their routes and destinations. They were also safe and convenient. Automobiles might well provide individual choice and freedom, but they also had limitations. Road surfaces remained poor and the distances that could be travelled were short and often restricted to good weather. Maintenance and repairs could be both time-consuming and expensive. Prior to the war, buses were a rational choice of transport.

This ethos of rationality, normality and popularity was lost in the 1950s as automobile ownership expanded rapidly and as the plane started to offer another alternative mode of long-distance travel. In 1947 auto manufacturers produced 3,558,100 new vehicles and 30,849,300 automobiles were registered. In 1950 6,665,800 new cars were available for purchase and the auto registrations had increased to 40,339,000. Soon the government would sponsor major improvements in highways which would enable individuals and families to drive longer distances in comfort and with a greater sense of motoring security. In an era of relatively full employment and increasing affluence for many groups in the nation, car ownership became widespread and travelling longer distances became more common. Commercial aviation was still in its infancy, but flight was becoming more popular for long distances for middle- and upper-income citizens and businessmen.[4] Increasingly, the intercity bus became associated primarily with lower-income groups and, despite all the marketing schemes of bus companies, it would remain tagged with that label for the remainder of the century. The late 1940s were years of transition in marketing bus travel.

Some commentators would argue that the decline in the relative standing of the bus industry as an intercity passenger carrier in the post-war years was inevitable. The high degree of individualism which had always flourished in the USA, the mass production of automobiles and their financial accessibility, whether on account of good wages or of credit schemes, were conducive to the creation of an automobile culture.[5] Individual preference for private ownership of vehicles had not been influenced by the federal government despite debates about the desirability of a national transport policy in which mixed systems would operate. There had been much talk of coordination of transport modes and cooperation between modes in the 1930s, and the emergencies of wartime had forced some degree of interaction. But considerations of government policy after the war demonstrated a lack of interest in positively encouraging Americans to take public transport. There was no specific legislation to deter car ownership.[6] Freedom of choice was paramount and if the bus industry could not persuade its existing and potential customers to remain on the buses, then the industry would naturally find a new and lower level of operation as an intercity carrier.

The photographic text of the bus industry in the late 1940s

Pictorial evidence of the bus industry in the late 1940s has suggested contrasting viewpoints. Some photographs positively demonstrated a well-organized business operation and suggested a buoyant technology fully geared up for future growth. Customers should be impressed by the systematic and rational arrangements and by the advertising both of which offered better regular service and much expanded recreational opportunities. Other photographs revealed inadequacies which were not being addressed quickly enough to satisfy a clientele no longer constrained by economic distress or wartime shortages, and desirous of greater geographical and upward mobility. The visual evidence could be read in diverse ways.

But which photographic records should be used for historical analysis of the conditions of the bus industry? Bus pictures fall into three categories: those produced by the industry and by bus enthusiasts; those designed to illustrate articles in popular media outlets; and those which are documents of economic and social commentary. The pictorial account provided by the bus industry's managers, by the manufacturers of motor coaches and by bus enthusiasts are affirmative, functional and optimistic. All bus operators were concerned to portray the industry in the best possible light and to persuade potential passengers about the advantages of bus travel. Their photographs in trade magazines, travel journals, company archives and advertising media like timetables and brochures demonstrated state-of-the-art vehicles, modern, clean and well-operating terminals and a labour force which was smart, efficient, courteous and reliable. Coach manufacturers directed their attention to persuading large organizations like Greyhound and Trailways, regional companies like Jefferson and Peter Pan, or numerous small firms to buy their vehicles. They thus illustrated the construction and engineering of their buses, paying attention to technological advances in such basics as engines, chassis, seat arrangements and wheels.[7] Photographs were often of vehicles in a pristine condition and without passengers. If passengers or drivers were portrayed, they were frequently posed for persuasive value. Bus enthusiasts tended to follow in the footsteps of the coach manufacturers and have displayed much more interest in the design, mechanics and operating capacity of vehicles than in their routine business of carrying passengers. For some, the chassis and the engine number are the key features.[8] Such photographs are technologically informative, but offer little interpretative scope in examining the running of bus operations.

Photojournalists were in the business of selling stories. Mass-circulation magazines wanted illustrations for their texts and independent photographers or employees hired for their camera-work had to produce pictures which were versatile, flexible and appealed to audiences. Those photojournalists involved with bus journeys often narrated and illustrated their own trips as travelogues, emphasizing the scenery and collecting the human-interest anecdotes of passengers to create a more marketable piece for publication. The adventure, conviviality and the problems of the trip were present for all readers to follow, but the text informed more than the pictures, which were designed to please and to tantalize a mass audience by portraying faraway places and romance rather than the function of a bus service.[9] Nevertheless, the existence of such illustrated accounts suggests that there was both a constituency to be persuaded and an industry with potential.

The documentary photograph was noted for its technical precision, discernment and originality of perception, but it was also a social commentary. Early exponents in the late nineteenth and early twentieth centuries included the reformers Jacob Riis and Lewis Hine, and in the 1930s the photographers of the historical division of the New Deal government agency, the Farm Security Administration (FSA), created numerous powerful images of rural life.[10] The bus industry was the subject matter of two specific, but linked, series of documentary photographs taken by Esther Bubley in 1943 and 1947. As a trained photographer who worked first for the federal government and then for Standard Oil (New Jersey) (SONJ), she re-presented the industry through the eyes of a female outsider interested in the systematic performance of an organization, the daily routines of bus workers and the attitudes of passengers. Engines, chassis and selling magazines were not her prime concern; people and systems were.[11] Her photographs offer additional insights and raise different questions about the condition of the bus industry in the 1940s.

Esther Bubley's connections with the bus industry

Esther Bubley, born in 1921 and the daughter of an automobile supply store manager in Superior, Wisconsin, started using a camera as a teenager. She left home in the late 1930s to take a course in photography at the Minneapolis School of Design and then moved east in search of work. Finding only a temporary job in New York, she moved to Washington in 1941 to become a microfilmer at the National Archives.[12] Here Vernon Tate, the director of the archives, introduced her to Roy Stryker who was in charge of the photography unit of the FSA which was about to be merged into the Office of War Information (OWI).[13] He hired her as a laboratory technician in the FSA-OWI darkroom. As well as developing official pictures she took her own photographs of the Washington area and developed them in the darkroom. Roy Stryker was encouraging, but as she did not drive, her work was geographically limited. He thus decided to send her on a bus trip in 1943 to demonstrate the contribution of public transport to the war effort. This assignment was one of Stryker's last for the government and Esther Bubley submitted her work to the caretaker manager.[14]

The young photographer's first intercity bus assignment to the Midwest and Upper South took place in September 1943. She travelled from Washington, DC to Columbus, Ohio, stopping off in Pittsburgh where she took pictures of the Greyhound garage. She then moved on to Cincinnati where she paid attention to the Greyhound terminal and to the life of bus driver Bernard Cochran. Next she travelled further west to Chicago before heading back to Washington via Indianapolis, Louisville and Memphis. Lacking a precise shooting script, Esther Bubley recorded a variety of experiences on this journey. Her approach was mixed, viewing crowded vehicles and empty roads from the inside of a bus, often framed by its windows and its closed space.

Some terminal and garage pictures reveal the organization and system within the industry; others demonstrate the confusion of emergency conditions. Some images are clearly posed with passengers and workers fully aware of the camera; many are taken anonymously and without permission. All 445 pictures offer a variety of profiles interpreting the condition of the bus industry, the work of bus employees and the behaviour of bus passengers at a time of considerable disruption.[15]

Crowded buses and bus terminals were a feature of these pictures, bringing to life what in the annual bus company reports and government's wartime documents is the subject of bland statistics. Indeed, the brief textual notes which accompanied the photographs suggested that passengers at times were packed on board, a feature which contributed to a negative image of the industry.[16] A wide variety of Americans used the buses during the war, ranging from armed services personnel, to relatives visiting family, salesmen, women with children, war-industry workers going home for a holiday, women looking for war jobs, schoolchildren, workers and commuters on short trips. There was, as yet, no class distinction between bus patrons. Though buses undertook long journeys, stops were frequent, not only to pick up and drop off passengers at flag stops and in small towns, but to unload newspapers and parcels and for rest stops. Coaches were a convenient means of transport. The roads might be relatively unoccupied because of the fuel and rubber shortages, but the buses were busy.

Their drivers were also busy, given the maximum speed limits which increased journey times and the leakage of personnel into the armed services and to war industries. They were nevertheless expected to be competent and versatile and to promote the company image. Flexibility in shift work, extra work and staying away from home were part of the drivers' expected role alongside adequate mechanical skills to make safety checks on their vehicles and to deal with minor problems. Yet despite difficult conditions, the drivers had to exhibit good customer relations, showing courtesy and fairness to all passengers, tolerance of wide-ranging patterns of behaviour, but firmness in dealing with rowdy passengers. Working conditions were never easy driving buses, but wartime conditions added considerably to the usual stress. Their colleagues in the Greyhound garages and terminals also worked under pressure of shortages with only some relief as women joined the garage staff as well as the terminal staff.[17]

Esther Bubley continued to take documentary photographs when she followed Roy Stryker and joined the photographic unit of SONJ in the summer of 1944. Here Roy Stryker's mandate was to create a portfolio of pictures which would display the significance of oil in the daily lives of the nation.[18] It was not certain that Esther Bubley would portray more buses at work even though there was a logical connection between motor coaches and oil. Certainly, transport was a popular subject for SONJ photographers and, indeed, there were series of images about highways, trucks, harbours, rivers and canals as well as buses.[19] Esther Bubley first travelled to Texas. She now drove a car to undertake several rural and small-town assignments before picking up the bus theme again in the spring, summer and autumn of 1947 and the spring of 1948.

When she rode the coaches in the post-war years she travelled fewer miles and on shorter trips, mainly as a short-haul intercity passenger from New York City.[20] She also visited garages and terminals. As in 1943, the range of Esther Bubley's images was varied in subject matter and photographic technique. The 250 prints and slightly larger number of negatives retained in the SONJ collection form what is collectively titled 'Bus Story'. They include views of Greyhound bus terminals, with details of the dispatchers' and reservations offices, waiting-rooms, ticket windows and information desks, and the baggage checking. They portray passengers waiting to board buses, aboard buses and eating in restaurants and Post Houses. They also display buses on the road and at rest stops, views through bus windows, bus drivers and garage mechanics and cleaners.[21]

Esther Bubley's 1947 and 1948 bus photographs, unlike their 1943 counterparts, were not neglected. Two SONJ publications of 1949 reproduced a selection of her pictures. In January, *Photo Memo*, a specialized picture catalogue in magazine format for circulation to newspapers, magazines, book editors and publishers, schools, university libraries and museums, published a four-page photo-essay, 'By Bus', displaying ten Bubley images. As part of its general pictorial survey of the oil industry *Photo Memo* captioned these images of bus travel and included a paragraph of text, but the pictures told their own story of life on the buses. The editors expressed their willingness to supply copies of the bus pictures free provided that the corporation was credited. In September, *The Lamp*, which circulated among middle-class professionals and such opinion-shapers as politicians, publishers and stockbrokers, produced an article, 'Via Bus', describing the bus industry and a bus journey and featuring twelve Bubley photographs. In a sequenced arrangement illustrating bus workers and passengers, the text and pictures suggested an adequate, flexible, somewhat boring, but economic mode of transport and one which neither aspired to, nor attained, the style of the train or the plane. Esther Bubley's bus images gained more publicity when she won first prize in the picture sequence category in a photography competition jointly sponsored by the University of Missouri and *Encyclopedia Britannica*.[22]

Though popular at the time and helping Bubley to start her career as a freelance photographer working for such publications as *Life*, *Ladies Home Journal*, *Look*, *Harper's Bazaar*, *Time*, *Fortune* and *The New York Times Magazine*, the pictures subsequently were overlooked. Only in the 1980s when cultural historians became interested in examining the multiple meanings of

photography and the interactive process between image and viewer did the
Bubley photographs surface again, to be subject now to critical examination.
Though not as popular a portfolio for interpretative treatment as the main
body of FSA-OWI pictures, Esther Bubley's output has been recovered and
displayed to exemplify a forgotten photographer, a photographer who was
educated in the documentary tradition and was subsequently employed as a
photojournalist, and a female artist using her gender an integral part of her
work.[23]

Her specific focus on buses has been portrayed within the context of both
the FSA-OWI and the SONJ photographic collections and within her own
productive life. It has not previously been considered as a tool for viewing the
bus industry, and especially the industry in transition between a period when
public surface transport was viable and respected and a period dominated by an
emerging automotive culture when individual and private transport became
dominant. Esther Bubley's images of the bus industry and bus travel in New
York in the post-war years are used here as entry points to the framing of
questions and hypotheses about the workings and well-being of a major mode
of public transport.[24] Trained in camera skills and social observation, and
versed in being part of a team with a message, Bubley nevertheless retained her
own values. She used her initiative as well as directions when taking pictures,
and as a woman was interested in capturing the nuances of daily life – in
this instance the human face of the bus industry as well as its systematic
organization.[25]

Esther Bubley's images of the post-war bus industry

As director of photography at SONJ, Roy Stryker did not give Esther Bubley
specific instructions for investigating buses and contributing to what was later
to be called the 'bus story.' He knew she was based in the New York city area,
had time to 'poke around' the local terminals and garages and to undertake
short-distance bus journeys. Her incomplete shooting script for the FSA-OWI
photographs and her experiences in 1943 may have served as a guide.
Alternatively, she may have been influenced by her colleagues at SONJ who
frequently worked on highway and transport themes. Sol Libsohn, in particular,
had shot a trucking story in the spring of 1945 and had also taken pictures of
buses. Most likely she went to her local Greyhound terminals and garages
knowing what to expect, and took her pictures to show an industry at work
carrying a range of passengers over both short and long distances within and
from the Northeast.[26]

When Esther Bubley recorded her pictures of buses for SONJ in 1947 and
1948 she visited two Greyhound bus terminals in midtown New York City, one

at 245 West 50th Street and the other at 34th Street between 7th and 8th Avenue. The history of these terminals is pertinent to their functioning in the post-war years. An early version of the 50th Street terminal had, in the 1920s, used the ground floor of the Capitol Hotel, with the back lobby as the loading area. Its replacement was opened in 1937 on the grounds of the Capitol Theatre and the back of the hotel was sealed off from the new terminal driveway. The 34th Street terminal, formerly known as the Pennsylvania Motor Coach Terminal, was opened in 1929 and was rebuilt and extended in 1935. Located next to the Pennsylvania Railroad Station it was directly connected by an escalator at the side.[27]

The Greyhound Corporation modernized both terminals as part of their expansion drive in the 1930s. Both new buildings were Art Deco in architectural style, thereby offering a smart and attractive appearance, and both were two storeys high. In addition, the Capitol Terminal had more facilities in the basement. The interiors of both midtown terminals were designed for increased capacity, comfort, convenience and effective throughput. There were large waiting-rooms, ticket and information desks, either a restaurant or lunch counter, news stands, rest rooms, baggage rooms and office space. Both terminals had vastly improved loading bays for boarding buses. This 1930s development formed part of Greyhound's plans for increasing both intercity and commuting trade to and from the Manhattan business district, and at the time was deemed to be very progressive and state-of-the-art. The Greyhound Corporation was also well aware of the importance of the pleasant appeal of the terminals for public relations. Terminals set the tone of the industry as a whole for passengers or prospective passengers.[28]

Ten years later, however, the terminals were badly in need of refurbishing. Heavy usage during the war and the inability of Greyhound to make any major building improvements due to shortages of construction materials and manpower had led to a deterioration of facilities. Government regulations concerning housing shortages and inflation in the immediate post-war years further halted any plans which the corporation had for rapid development. But even had Greyhound not been constrained by construction priorities and financial circumstances it would have been constrained by city planning permission. Even before the war New York City officials had been concerned about midtown traffic congestion and had recommended bus-free zones. Soon the Port of New York Authority discussed plans for a large union bus terminal near the Manhattan end of the Lincoln Tunnel which had been opened in 1937. Greyhound refused to be involved in the joint venture, fearing competition for its passengers and considering that it could run its own terminals more economically than paying user fees for shared facilities. This refusal to cooperate impeded modernizing schemes for the corporation's terminals. Permission to enlarge midtown terminals was refused in 1947 and permission to consolidate Greyhound's Manhattan operations at the 34th Street terminal in 1950 was turned down.[29] So when Esther Bubley took her New York City terminal pictures they were of buildings much in need of remodelling or replacing. This Manhattan situation, though locationally specific in respect to city planning, was not atypical of bus terminals in the USA in the late 1940s. Management was conscious of the need for more modern terminals, but conditions beyond their control impeded many plans for new buildings and for upgrading older buildings in the late 1940s.[30]

The Greyhound bus terminal at 245 West 50th Street might no longer be state-of-the-art in 1947, but it had been planned to function systematically and was still so doing when Esther Bubley visited with her camera in the spring of 1947. In May she shot the outside of the terminal looking down on to 51st Street, showing one side of the terminal's saw-toothed loading bays (see figure 17). The image is almost abstract and modernistic in its angles with people barely visible. Street-level photographs of the building reflect a more consumer-attractive appearance displaying glazed-faced brick for both exterior fronts on 50th and 51st Streets, entrance canopies and windows, the Greyhound name in large letters and the logo, the Greyhound dog. This Bubley image, however, shows the terminal at work with the buses awaiting passengers. Of the four coaches in view only the top one was a Greyhound vehicle. The others belonged to suburban and intercity lines who paid user fees to Greyhound to use this busy and convenient midtown terminal. Though the loading-bay view suggests a drab, perhaps even negative, appearance, it is a practical scene rather than one which is visibly appealing. Outside facilities backing on to main streets were neither spacious nor spotless. Passengers were, however, sheltered from the weather and were reminded by the posters on the side wall that they were travelling by a smart, smooth and economical means. They were also informed that they could travel for leisure and see 'This Amazing America'. Greyhound had used this particular advertising slogan before and during the war and now needed to update its billboard.[31]

Esther Bubley returned to the Capitol Terminal in July and September 1947 when she took more photographs of the indoor activity of bus transport. A busy morning in September with brisk trade from commuters and long-distance passengers was one of her choices. Here the camera lens, with its distance vision, clearly displays the order and purpose of a building designed for passenger throughput (see figure 18). Bubley was conveying the idea of a rational and modern form of travel. Yet the image is also cluttered with people on the move. The bus industry was still thriving, whether as a result of the legacy of scarcity of private automobiles or through the sheer convenience of being conveyed into the heart of the city's business district by public transport. Customers needing assistance might first consult the traveller's aide stand, located under the clock. Those who knew their way around or had ascertained their travel details by telephone from the travel bureau or through a timetable, moved quickly to the ticket windows where they queued for service. Clearly the hot weather had encouraged most passengers to dress lightly or to carry their jackets. Nevertheless, most still gave the impression of belonging to either the working or middle classes. A closer view of a ticket queue in July (see figure 19) confirmed the respectability and diversity of bus patrons and pointed out their relationship to the orderly planning of bus transport. There was no general distaste of bus transport.[32]

Having bought their ticket and found the number of their loading platform, passengers then waited for their bus to be called over the loudspeaker. Most waited in the main hall which had a seating capacity of 134. Some, perhaps influenced by crowded wartime conditions, preferred to stand near the relevant loading bay to ensure either that they could get on the first scheduled bus or that they could choose their seats. Others took the opportunity to buy a drink or a snack at the restaurant or a magazine or newspaper from the news-stand.[33] Such waiting travellers have subsequently been perceived by cultural historians and art critics as either bored or trance-like, as though they were in a state of lethargic suspension. More likely, they were 'killing time' as a normal function of being in transit.[34] Bus passengers in the late 1940s, like most consumers of public transport then and now, allowed ample time to catch their scheduled coach. At times they were also held up by the late arrival of their coach. In either situation they simply waited or found ways to pass the time. Some, like the couple reading the Edwards Lakes to Sea Stages Timetable – a route from New York to Cleveland via Williamsport, Pennsylvania, but one not serviced by Greyhound – contemplated the route and timing of their journey (see figure 20). Conversation was popular for those with travelling companions. Reading appealed to many more while those sufficiently confident about waking up at the announcement of their bus, or who had long waits between connections, dozed. Sleep, however, was more frequently a diversion for the bus journey itself.[35]

The visual and written testimonies of buses in operation in the late 1940s offers interrelated if somewhat divergent stories. Statistical evidence points to a drop in the numbers of passengers since the wartime peak year of 1945, but the figures for both 1947 and 1948 were still buoyant when compared to those of the pre-war years. In 1949 more than a third of all intercity travel by public carrier was by bus.[36] But bus operators knew that the threat to their business came more from the automobile than from the train or the plane. They were well aware that they urgently needed to improve vehicles, service and terminals and that they must convince passengers and potential passengers of the quality and convenience of buses if they were to hold onto a significant share of the travel market. Yet in a period prior to the building of interstate highways designed for fast travel, and when rest stops and stops to pick up and discharge passengers were frequent, bus journeys were slow and were interrupted frequently. They could also be slow and interrupted because some of the buses in service were beyond their 'sell-by' date. Normal bus life was between eight and ten years, leaving any pre-1940 vehicle as obsolete in design, carrying capacity, efficiency and operating cost. Until 1947 the intercity bus industry was starved for new buses. An all-time record production of these vehicles in 1947 and a high production in 1948 enabled many to be retired, but some old coaches were still in service.[37]

Passengers in 1947 were not as aware of the limitations of travelling by bus as were the bus operators and subsequent generations of observers and car drivers. Short-haul intercity journeys like the one that Esther Bubley took from Scranton, Pennsylvania to Buffalo, New York in September 1947, were still popular with a range of consumers (see figure 21). Pleasure-riders and business riders alike chose to go by bus because it was convenient, economical, safe and comfortable and because the age of mass automobility had not yet arrived. On this particular journey, passengers travelled in a Silversides bus, a Supercoach which Greyhound had introduced prior to the war and which the corporation continued to buy in large quantities in 1947 and 1948.[38] Whether this coach was a pre-war model or one of the new 1947 versions, the air-conditioning, so often advertised as a feature of modern bus travel, was not working because some of the windows were open. Other style features which Esther Bubley picked up in her wide angle shot of the interior of the bus were the reclining seats with their head-rest covers, the baggage rack, sufficiently large enough to carry light or overnight bags and cases, and the translucent pull-down blinds. The adjustable rubber footrests, the directed beam lights for reading, the omission of the step-down aisle and the retractable steps for easy street-level boarding were not visible, though were features welcomed by passengers in the 1940s.[39]

The passengers on the Scranton–Buffalo bus appeared to accept, if not to enjoy, their informal journey in close proximity to each other. As passengers they were in a confined space and were engaged in a cooperative undertaking of getting to their destinations on time. The atmosphere on their bus, with its close personal proximity, was more relaxed and casual than that of the contemporary train with its several carriages, its distance from the driver, its more spacious seating and its own dining and toilet facilities. Like many journeys this bus trip was often silent as people looked out of the windows at the ever-changing landscape, slept, read or let their minds wander aimlessly. Some passengers were alert and talking, but there were no general passing of comments or jokes along the length of the vehicle as could happen occasionally. African American passengers, as was the custom in the pre civil-rights era, sat at the rear of the vehicle.[40] Though subsequent car-culture generations have perceived the bus interior as a disconcerting space because of the enforced intermingling of public and private lives, and have interpreted the bus journey as a penance to be endured by disenchanted individuals who could not afford alternative means of travel, such distaste was not revealed on the faces or in the demeanour of Esther Bubley's travelling companions in 1947. Like modern airline travellers they were passing their time in transit either resting, daydreaming or enjoying the view. For them, the bus journey offered an accessible and reasonable mode of public transport rather than a disturbing experience. Public surface transport was still a viable option and the culture of American mobility was still fluid.[41]

As buses were compact and flexible modes of transport they had to make regular rest stops both for refreshments and for toilet facilities. In the 1940s some 10 to 15 minutes were allowed for a rest stop and between 20 to 30 minutes for a meal stop. One of the nominated rest stops on bus routes to Buffalo was the Greyhound Post House at Kanona near Bath in upstate New York (see figure 22). Post Houses had been introduced by Greyhound in 1937 as a means of improving and standardizing meal and comfort stops at intermediate points on journeys. Previously, buses had stopped at private lunchrooms where the condition of the toilets was often poor and the quality of the food and the speed of the service was unsatisfactory. Complaints about such facilities, especially from women, who were the majority of Greyhound passengers, had been loud and vigorous, so even during the war Greyhound continued to expand their Post Houses and to supervise other concessions. By the end of 1947 there were ninety-eight such hostelries. Esther Bubley's co-passengers, other bus passengers en route to and from Buffalo, and some auto passengers, were thus fortunate to be among the millions of travellers annually breaking their journey at a quality-controlled rest stop rather than an independent alternative. Whether using the facilities or not, travellers seemed happy to take the opportunity to stand around outside, gossiping or merely stretching their legs before restarting their journey.[42]

Part of the merit of bus transport in the late 1940s lay in the expectation that the journey would not only be reasonably comfortable, but would also be efficient and safe. Such anticipation depended in large part on the labour force of drivers, mechanics and a variety of terminal workers, ranging from cleaners through waitresses and information clerks to ticket agents. These Greyhound employees were reputed to be competent at their jobs, but at the time of Esther Bubley's photographs they were not necessarily satisfied with their terms of employment, as recently demonstrated in strike action. In the northeastern region, both Central Greyhound Lines and Pennsylvania Greyhound Lines were paralysed by a strike which lasted from 1 November 1945 to 3 January 1946 and was only halted by the appointment of a government fact-finding panel. In February 1946 management reluctantly accepted the majority recommendations of the panel and awarded a pay rise of 14 per cent for drivers and a flat increase of 13 cents an hour for maintenance and terminal workers. The union had asked for higher increases for both groups of workers and for improvements in other conditions of labour, but the panel only commented on pay scales. By 1947, inflation had cancelled out the wage rises and workers still wanted to improve other conditions of labour. Strike action, however, might not be the way forward in a period of readjustment to peacetime travel patterns. Aware of national discussions about labour relations, both management and labour looked to resolving difficulties through collective bargaining.[43]

Although there was discontent and negotiations, generally workers cooperated with management to produce an efficient bus service. At the centre of this service and in direct contact with passengers was the driver. In the late 1940s Greyhound drivers were highly trained, skilled workers, monitored by regular appraisals. Before being hired, men had to undergo a battery of aptitude tests and an interview. These were followed by psycho-physical examinations checking reaction time, acuteness of vision, health and intelligence. Once employed, men received classroom education in safe driving and the management of passengers, schedules and luggage, followed by instruction in the maintenance and operation of buses at the garage and finally training on the road with a veteran driver.[44] They would then be eligible for the drivers' board, usually starting as extra men who were on twenty-four-hour call to fill any additional sections needed for particular routes. Here the shifts were irregular. On gaining some seniority drivers could progress to a regular route of no more than eight hours driving daily and then to a regular route of their preference. Even with years of service, drivers were regularly supervised, both through testing clinics and checking their road procedures. A system of merit awards helped to ensure continuing safety. Greyhound drivers were in a highly-demanding occupation and were in the public view.[45]

During her photographic assignments Esther Bubley made a deliberate point of tracking specific drivers as well as observing the general running of bus operations. Part of her informal training as a member of the OWI team of photographers was getting to know individuals. In 1943 she followed both bus driver Bernard Cochran, who had driven for Greyhound for fourteen years, and Clem Carson who worked as an 'extra'. In March 1948 she shadowed J.J. Murphy on his short-distance trip from New York City to Wilkes Barre in eastern Pennsylvania. Murphy, trained in Greyhound protocol, reported in at the Greyhound Bus Garage, Long Island City, Brooklyn, some two hours before his bus was due to depart. Here he went to the drivers' quarters to report for duty to the dispatcher, check his assignment for that day and complete any necessary paperwork. He could then talk, read or perhaps even play games with other drivers until it was time to collect his bus.[46]

On this particular day in March 1948, J.J. Murphy was taking out a Silversides coach. As part of the drivers' routine he examined the vehicle's roadworthiness. Still in the back yard of the Long Island City Garage he started with the outside of the bus, testing the tyres. Here in figure 23 Driver Murphy uses a door crank-handle to strike the tyre, expecting the handle to bounce off the tyre, thereby indicating the right amount of air pressure. The angle of the Bubley image suggests that he is about to be in control of a very large vehicle. Driver Murphy then moved to the inside of the bus to inspect the various driving mechanisms. In figure 24 he is either checking play in the steering wheel or checking the brake pressure. This time Esther Bubley has chosen to view him through the front window of the bus, thereby emphasizing his commanding position in a confined space. On completion of his coach scrutiny he posted his name in the name-plate slot above his head at the front of the bus and drove it from the Long Island City Garage across the Queensboro Bridge to the terminal in midtown Manhattan. Here, when the announcement for the bus's departure had been called and he was ready for loading, he checked passengers' tickets, stored any heavy baggage or large parcels in the luggage compartment and departed on time. Several stops were made en route through New Jersey to Wilkes Barre on what was a busy run. With a crowded bus and a journey through built-up areas he had to be both decisive in managing a variety of short-haul passengers and watchful of heavy traffic. The return journey to the terminal completed safely, J.J. Murphy had not yet finished his shift. He still had the thirty-minute journey to return the bus to the garage. Then he would complete his report on the day's work and check his tickets. It was unlikely that he would remain overnight in the drivers' sleeping quarters at the garage as he was on a short-haul route.[47]

For the travelling public a driver like J.J. Murphy was fully in command of his bus; yet he was part of an organized team. He was the public face of the Greyhound maintenance crew, representing many other workers who facilitated his smooth, safe and satisfactory journey. Buses required regular overhauling if they were to perform reliably, as was demanded in the post-war years. Servicing was especially important in the late 1940s because Greyhound was still running some buses which should have been retired after their normal lifespan of eight to ten years. Maintenance at the Long Island City Garage, as elsewhere in the Greyhound system, was of two main varieties: daily following each trip, and regular, after a specific mileage, when a full servicing was undertaken. Periodically, buses were completely overhauled. But the Long Island City Garage was small, having a capacity for maintaining some twelve vehicles, with parking for about thirty others. Additional storage for buses was available in sheds on an adjacent plot. Service was slow when compared to Pacific Greyhound Lines' streamlined repair shop in San Francisco or the new Great Lakes Greyhound Maintenance Center in Detroit. Like the Capitol Terminal in Manhattan, the garage in Brooklyn had been a state-of-the-art investment for Greyhound in the mid-1930s, but it had undergone considerable wear and tear during the war without substantial improvements.[48]

At the Long Island City Garage the routine maintenance process involved cleaning a coach both outside on a double wash rack and inside by attendants, then greasing, lubricating, refuelling and checking the tyre pressures before the vehicle was parked ready for next use. Esther Bubley was given special permission to go into the pit area, an area normally reserved only for mechanics, to take close-up photographs of Greyhound employees at work. In figure 25 she has caught Charles Wright, a gas man at the garage, as he checked off the list of detailed items to be inspected on incoming buses. She has positioned him in the foreground of her image, concentrating on the routine involved in servicing vehicles. As in viewing the Capitol Terminal she has emphasized a rational and organized throughput, only now of vehicles rather than people. The bus being serviced and occupying attention was then an ageing vehicle as it was a pre-war 1939 Yellow Coach model. Originally belonging to Champlain Coach Company it was bought by Central Greyhound Lines of New York around 1942. At the side of this bus stood, possibly, the interior coach cleaner, pausing to look at the vehicle. The bucket might belong to him or possibly has been left there by a female cleaner as women were employed by Greyhound in this capacity.[49]

In another part of the garage Esther Bubley has captured two other mechanics at work. Again, in figure 26, she has portrayed working men as part of a systematic organization. The close shot, angled and tilted upwards, demonstrates how mechanic Benjamin Green and his helper are removing the outer rear wheel from a bus in order to change a spring. They are working with a 'wheel dolly', a fork-like tool designed to facilitate easier wheel removal. The air wrench lying in the foreground of the view has been used to loosen the wheel nuts. Concentration and strength were needed to undertake this heavy but skilled manual work. This study of men at work was one of a series of photographs portraying the routine but complex mechanical labour involved in servicing buses.[50] Whether seen singly or in sequence these images suggest the careful upkeep of the corporation's buses. Coaches required high capital investment and whether they were old or recently purchased they were treated with care both in and out of the public view.

Esther Bubley pictured the leading bus company in the USA in 1947 and 1948, years in which the intercity bus industry was attempting to come to terms with post-war adjustment and the advent of automobility. Although some passengers were leaving public transport as soon as they could acquire cars, others remained, and the industry as a whole hoped that it could persuade Americans that it was capable of providing a useful and effective service. The hope was misplaced. The well-being of the bus industry would decline in the affluent years of the 1950s. Though the Greyhound Corporation, as the leading operator, made considerable headway in re-equipping its fleet of vehicles, improving and rebuilding its terminals and garages and refurbishing its public image, custom fell nationwide. In the New York metropolitan area the corporation's plans for modernization were particularly limited because the city refused permission to rebuild or expand the midtown terminals, hoping to persuade Greyhound to move to the New York Port Authority union bus terminal.[51] But Americans everywhere more and more preferred to use their cars for short and medium journeys and started to look to the plane for long-distance connections. Only those who could not afford to drive or had no car used the long-distance buses and only the foreign visitors saw the Greyhound bus as a romantic, as well as a practical way of travelling through America. Esther Bubley thus captured and left a vivid pictorial record of the social history of the bus industry at a time of transition between being a going concern and a struggling enterprise.

Notes

1. I wish to thank B. Carner, D.M. Coffin, S.S. Kidd and D.G. Tallack for their constructive comments on an earlier version of this chapter.
2. J.F. Kasson (1998), 'Seeing Coney Island, Seeing Culture: Joseph Stella's Battle of Lights', *The Yale Journal of Criticism*, 11(1), p. 95; A. Sekula, 'On the Invention of Photographic Meaning' in V. Burgin (ed.) (1982), *Thinking Photography*, Basingstoke, pp. 84–8.
3. *Bus Facts*, (1949), pp. 12, 13. These passenger statistics are for Class I bus carriers, whose annual revenues then amounted to $100,000 or more.
4. B.J. Wattenburg (1976), Introduction, *The Statistical History of the United States: From Colonial Times to the Present*, New York, p. 716; B.E. Seely (1987), *Building the American Highway System: Engineers as Policy Makers*, Philadelphia, *passim*; C.A. Taff (1980), *Commercial Motor Transportation*, Centerville, MD: 6th edn, pp. 15–55; R.E. Bilstein (1984), *Flight in America. From the Wrights to the Astronauts*, Baltimore, pp. 169–78, 227–39, 257–66.
5. For information on the American love affair with the car see J.B. Rae (1971), *The Road and the Car in American Life*, Cambridge, MA. J.J. Flink (1965), *The Car Culture*, Cambridge, MA, has more reservations about the impact of the car. See also A. Offer, 'The American Automobile Frenzy of the 1950s', in K. Bruland and P. O'Brien (eds) (1999), *From Family Firms to Corporate Capitalism. Essays in Business and Industrial History in Honour of Peter Mathias*, Oxford, pp. 315–53.
6. M. Walsh, 'In Whose Interests? Public Policy and Transport in Depression and War' in R.A. Garson and S.S. Kidd (eds) (1999), *The Roosevelt Years: New Essays on the United States, 1933–1945*, Edinburgh, pp. 11–29 ; C.L. Dearing and W. Owen (1949), *National Transportation Policy*, Washington, DC; US Congress, Senate, Committee on Interstate and Foreign Commerce, 78 Cong. 1 Sess., (1961), *National Transportation Policy*, Committee Print, pp. 155–63.
7. Such photographs are located in early editions of *Bus Transportation* (hereafter cited as *BT*) when manufacturers had special sections displaying their vehicles. They are also in the photographic collections in the Greyhound Corporate Records, American Heritage Center, University of Wyoming (hereafter cited as GCR) and in William A. Luke Records, Spokane, WA (hereafter cited as WALR).
8. Examples of these photographs can be found in *Motor Coach Age*, produced by the Motor Bus Society. These images are drawn either from the collection in the

John P. Hoschek Memorial Bus Transportation Library, Hopewell Township, NJ or from the private collections of individual members of the Motor Bus Society.

9. Examples of this genre are R.D. Altick (1935), 'Adventure by Bus', *The Highway Traveler*, (hereafter cited as *HT*), **7**(1), pp. 23, 54; L. Harper (1944), 'Cross Country by Bus', *Trailways*, **8**(Spring), pp. 6–8; and H. Walker (1950), 'You Can't Miss America by Bus', *The National Geographic Magazine*, **98**(1), pp. 1–16, 33–42.

10. R.E. Stryker and N. Wood (1973), *In this Proud Land. America, 1935–1943. As Seen in the FSA Photographs*, New York; F.J. Hurley (1972), *Portrait of a Decade. Roy Stryker and the Development of Documentary Photography in the Thirties*, Baton Rouge, LA. For a more general discussion on the documentary movement of the 1930s and early 1940s see W. Stott (1973), *Documentary Expression and Thirties America*, New York.

11. E. Bubley interview with M.Walsh, 20 August, 1992, New York City. I am grateful to Bill Carner, Photographic Archives, Eckstrom Library, University of Kentucky (hereafter cited as Photo Archives) for pointing out the correct citation of Standard Oil (New Jersey).

12. E. Bubley interview with M. Walsh; E. Bubley Clippings File, Photo Archives; Esther Bubley Website, http://www.estherbubley.com/.

13. The Historical Division of the FSA which was transferred to the OWI in 1942, produced a unique collection of some 270,000 photographs, of which some 170,000 survived to be stored in the Library of Congress. Many of the photographs taken for the FSA portray life in the rural South and Midwest. Those taken for the OWI increasingly recorded the activities of a nation preparing for and being involved in war. Hurley, *Portrait of a Decade*; Stryker and Wood, *In this Proud Land*, pp. 7–9; A. Melville (1985), *Farm Security Administration, Historical Section. A Guide to the Textual Records in the Library of Congress*, Washington, DC; P. Dixon (1983), *Photographers of the Farm Security Administration. An Annotated Bibliography, 1930–1980*, New York. Cultural historians contest the meaning and interpretation of the FSA photographs in particular. Their debates range widely and include discussions on the social conscience of the photographers who wanted to expose the disaster of rural poverty in a period of major depression, the role of Roy Stryker as manager of the unit, the method of using photographs to illustrate ideas and the ability of photographers and darkroom technicians to alter meanings by positioning the camera or by cropping and framing pictures. See, for example, J. Guimond (1991), *American Photography and the American Dream*, Chapel Hill, NC, pp. 109–40 and M. Stange (1989), *Symbols of Ideal Life. Social Documentary Photography in America, 1890–1950*, New York, pp. 105–31.

14. E. Bubley interview with M. Walsh; C. Fleischhauer and B.W. Brannan (eds), (1988), *Documenting America, 1935–1943*, Berkeley, CA, pp. 312–14; J.R. Whiting (1951), 'Esther Bubley' *Modern Photography*, **15**(December), pp. 50, 52, 118; K. Dieckmann (1989), 'A Nation of Zombies. Government files contain the extraordinary, unpublished photographs that Esther Bubley took on one long bus trip across wartime America', *Art in America*, **November**, pp. 55, 56.

15. Information on the 1943 bus journey is based on the Bubley photographs, lots 882–5, the textual Supplementary Reference files for lots 882–5, FSA-OWI photographic files, Prints and Photographic Division, Library of Congress, and on the Bubley interview with Walsh. A published sample of these pictures can be found in the photographic essay, 'Cross-Country Bus Trip' in Fleischhauer and Brannan (eds), *Documenting America*, pp. 315–39. Other samples can be seen in

Katherine Dieckmann's revisionist interpretation, 'A Nation of Zombies', pp. 55–61. Jacqueline Ellis offers a contentious view of Bubley's wartime pictures in (1998) *Silent Witnesses: Representations of Working-Class Women in the United States*, Bowling Green, OH, pp. 91–127. She suggests that a broader range of photographs than the bus images both departed from the traditional themes of government agency photography and highlighted a new identity for American working-class women.

16. 'Supplementary reference files for lots 882–5, FSA-OWI, written records.

17. Bubley photographs, lots 882–5 and Supplementary Reference files for lots 882–5, FSA-OWI files, written records.

18. SONJ had decided to create a documentary photographic record of the oil industry modelled on the FSA to improve its public relations. The corporation had received bad publicity following a 1942 government investigation which revealed its pre-war agreement to halt research into the development of synthetic rubber. As middle-class Americans in particular had been positively influenced by the visual media and art of the New Deal, SONJ decided to rehabilitate its image through a photo archive keyed into the national importance of oil. Roy Stryker was persuaded to head up the unit where, between 1943 and 1950, he helped build the largest non-governmental photographic documentary project undertaken in the USA. He retained many of the methods and concepts which he had evolved at the FSA, hiring some of the same photographers and insisting that the pictures depict not only oil, but also diverse patterns of American life. See S.W. Plattner (1983), *Roy Stryker: USA, 1943–1950. The Standard Oil (New Jersey) Photography Project*, Austin, TX, pp. 7–13 and R.J. Doherty, 'The Elusive Roy Stryker' in J.C. Anderson (ed.) (1977), *Roy Stryker: The Humane Propagandist*, Louisville, KY, pp. 8–9.

19. SONJ volume listing and story titles, US and Canada, Photo Archives.

20. Short-haul intercity carriers were the only category of motor-bus operations where revenue and passengers increased in 1947, *BT*, **27**(4) (1948), pp. 43–4.

21. Bubley interview with Walsh; Bubley, selection of 82 SONJ photographs taken in 1947 and 1948, Photo Archives; SONJ volume listing of photographers and story titles, Photo Archives; J. Anderson, Head, Photo Archives, to M. Walsh, 3 December 1991; Plattner, *Roy Stryker*, p. 55.

22. 'By Bus', *Photo Memo*, January (1949), pp. 12–15; 'Via Bus', *The Lamp*, 31(3) (1949), pp. 19–23; Keller, *The Highway as Habitat*, pp. 46–9; Plattner, *Roy Stryker*, p. 55; Whiting, 'Esther Bubley', p. 120.

23. A selection of photographs from Esther Bubley's 1943 bus trip is available in Fleishhauer and Brannan (eds), *Documenting America*, pp. 315–29, a volume which accompanied the exhibition held at the Library of Congress in 1989. A collection of pictures from her SONJ bus photography is available in U. Keller (1986), *The Highway As Habitat. A Roy Stryker Documentation, 1943–1955*, Santa Barbara, CA, pp. 82–95. This is an interpretive text accompanying the catalogue of an exhibition of Stryker materials held at the Art Museum, University of California, Santa Barbara in 1986. Dieckmann, 'A Nation of Zombies', uses images from the 1943 bus trip to question the human dignity which Stryker claimed for FSA-era photographs while J. Ellis, *Silent Witnesses*, pp. 91–127, uses a variety of Bubley pictures from the FSA-OWI files to envisage a new portrait of working-class women. Some of Bubley's Washington, DC boarding-house scenes are reprinted in A. Fisher (1987), *Let Us Now Praise Famous Women. Women Photographers for the US Government 1935–1944*, London and New York, a volume which accompanied an exhibition at the

National Museum of Photography, Film and Television in Bradford, UK, in April 1987. Fisher's text acknowledges partial truths and the myriad historical and contemporary meanings which can be recreated from past images. The Kathleen Ewing Gallery, Washington, DC held an exhibition of Bubley photographs in 1989–1990. A smaller selection was showed at the Phillips collection, Washington, DC in 1995 and Bubley's work was also celebrated in an exhibition, 'Women Come to the Front: Journalists, Photographers and Broadcasters During World War II' held in the Madison Gallery of the Madison Building, Library of Congress, Washington, DC in 1995. This exhibition was subsequently taken on tour in 1996 and 1997. Bubley Clippings File; Esther Bubley Web Site.

24.   The photographs used for analysis here have been chosen to depict aspects of the operation of the bus industry. They include differing photographic techniques, including distance shots and close-ups and posed and random views.

25.   Bubley interview with Walsh.

26.   For a discussion of highway themes visible in the work of SONJ photographers see Keller, *The Highway as Habitat*; Bubley interview with Walsh. The SONJ volume listing of photographers and story titles notes three photographers' names against the 'Bus Story', (Esther) Bubley, (Sol) Libsohn and (Richard) Saunders.

27.   C.W. Stocks (1950), 'Bus Terminals – How They Began', *The Westsider*, **15**(2), pp. 25–7, 91–4 in GCR, Box 14; M. Burleigh and C.M. Adams (ed.) (1941), *Modern Bus Terminals and Post Houses*, Ypsilanti, MI, p. 80; D.M. Coffin, former long-serving officer of the Motor Bus Society and former curator of Greyhound memorabilia, to M. Walsh, 1 June 1999.

28.   Stocks, 'Bus Terminals', pp. 25–7, 91–4; Burleigh and Adams, *Modern Bus Terminals*, pp. 78–85; D. Coffin to M. Walsh, 1 June 1999; *Making Bus Operations Pay*, (1932), New York, pp. 71–2; A.N. Brion (1938), 'The Intercity Bus Terminal', National Association of Motor Bus Operators, *Proceedings*, (herafter cited as NAMBO, *Procs*), **12**, pp. 82–96. *BT*, **13**(9) (1934), pp. 308–9; **14**(5) (1935), p. 168; **14**(7) (1935), pp. 255–6.

29.   Stocks (1950), 'Bus Terminals', pp. 91–6; Greyhound Corporation, *Annual Report* (1950), (hereafter cited as GC, *AR*), p. 14; *Business Week*, 10 February, 1951, pp. 100–101. *BT*, **19**(1) (1940), pp. 55–6; **23**(6) (1944), p. 75; **25**(5) (1946), p. 40; **26**(3) (1947), pp. 72–4. *New York Times*, 13 March, 25:2; 6 June, 23:1; 7 June, 21:2; 11 June, 30:7; 14 June, 18:2; 18 August, 13:5; 19 October, 40:5; 21 November, 23:6; 29 November, 25:8; 20 December, 25:8; 21 December, 22:3, all 1945; 31 January, 22:3; 8 November, 19:5, both 1947; 13 January, 25:1; 14 January, 14:2; 1 February, 28:6; 7 February, 1:6; 20 April, 27:5; 25 April, 54:1; 28 July, 23:1, all 1950.

30.   M. Walsh, 'Passenger Connections: Views of the Intercity Bus Terminal in the United States' in W. Bond and C. Divall (eds) (forthcoming), *Suburbanising the Masses: Public Transport and Urban Development in Historical Perspective*, Aldershot; GC, *AR* (1946–54).

31.   Burleigh and Adams, *Modern Bus Terminals*, pp. 81–5; D. Coffin to M. Walsh, 1 June 1999; SONJ photograph, negative 47294 (all SONJ negative numbers refer to Esther Bubley's bus photographs and hereafter will be called SONJ with their negative number). The more recent advertising slogan used by Greyhound in 1946 was 'Only By Highway'. *HT*, **18**(2), **18**(3), **18**(4), **18**(5), **18**(6), all 1946 and all back covers.

32.   SONJ negatives, 47278, 47299 M–12, 49532 M–15, 52711 M–17; D. Coffin to M. Walsh, 1 June 1999.

33. SONJ negatives 47299 M–12, 49532 M–15, 52711 M–17; Burleigh and Adams, *Modern Bus Terminals*, p. 82.
34. Dieckmann, 'A Nation of Zombies', pp. 55–7, envisages Esther Bubley's subjects as remote, disaffected, dazed and often asleep. Such images are claimed to display the anonymity and disembodiment of American people in contrast to the noble dignity of much of the FSA work or the buoyant industriousness of many of the OWI photographs. SONJ editorial interpretation of the 1947 bus pictures in 'Via Bus', *The Lamp*, pp. 19–23, hints that the boredom of waiting is a function of using public transport.
35. SONJ negatives 47283, 47298 M–14, 49548 M–19; 'Via Bus', *The Lamp*, pp. 20–21; 'By Bus', *Photo Memo*, p. 13; Keller, *The Habitat As Highway*, p. 84; D. Coffin to M. Walsh, 7 April 1999.
36. *Bus Facts* (1949), pp. 4, 6, 7.
37. *BT*, **27**(2) (1948), pp. 44, 56, 57–8; **28**(2) (1949), pp. 60–61. *Business Week*, 6 March 1948, p. 42.
38. The prototype Silversides was exhibited at the New York World's Fair of 1939–1940. Some 600 of these buses were manufactured with either gasoline or diesel engines before war ended production in 1942. For the post-war years Greyhound proposed a double-decker fifty passenger coach, the Highway Traveler, but design and engineering problems prevented development beyond the prototype stage. Greyhound thus ordered some 1,500 diesel-powered Silversides, mainly of the thirty-seven rather than the forty-one passenger version, for delivery in 1947 and 1948. GC, *AR*, (1946), p. 9, (1947), p. 10, (1948), p. 10 . *HT*, **12**(1) (1940), pp. 25, 32–3; **18**(4) (1946), pp. 16–17, 45. *BT*, **19**(7) (1940), p. 305; **26**(5) (1947), pp. 92–3. A.E. Meier and J.P. Hoschek (1975), *Over the Road. A History of Bus Transportation in the United States*, Upper Montclair, NJ, pp. 89, 90–91, 99–100.
39. *HT*, **12**(1) (1940), pp. 25, 32–3; **12**(5) (1940), p. 4; **18**(4) (1946), pp. 16–17, 45. I am assuming that this bus was manufactured before war halted production in 1942. New models were often used on prestige routes like the Boston–Washington corridor and the routes from the east to Chicago, St Louis and Detroit, and insufficient Silversides had been produced for wide distribution by September 1947 when this photograph was taken.
40. 'Via Bus', *The Lamp*, pp. 19–23; 'By Bus', *Photo Memo*, pp. 12–15; Walker, 'You Can't Miss America by Bus', pp. 1–16, 33–42. Esther Bubley's written report of her 1943 bus trip suggests that passengers were tolerant of bus travel. Supplementary reference files for lots 882–5, written text.
41. Dieckmann, 'A Nation of Zombies', pp. 55–61. Modern technology has allowed air travellers to be amused by films or audio recordings in lieu of looking out of windows at the scenery.
42. SONJ negatives 52703–M12, 52704 M–18, 52707 M–18, 52708 M–22, 59858, 59882 M–37, 59885 M–16. GC, *AR*, (1939), p. 6; (1947), p. 14; (1948), p. 14. *HT*, **11**(4) (1939), p. 32; 'Greyhound Still Growing', *Fortune*, 30 September 1944, pp. 125–6; A.S. Genet (1958), ' "Profile of Greyhound!" The Greyhound Corporation', Newcomen Society Address, New York, p. 19; D.M. Coffin to M. Walsh, 29 March 1999.
43. The drivers' awards were based on both mileage and hourly rates which varied between Eastern and Western divisions and between classes of drivers. US Department of Labor, 'Report and Recommendations of the Fact Finding Panel in the Greyhound Bus Dispute', 21 February 1946, typescript, Washington, DC, (Interstate Commerce Commission Library). *New York Times*, 1 November, 1:6, 14:3; 2 November, 1:6, 6:4, both 1945; 3 January, 14:1; 4 January, 23:3; 7 January,

11:6; 19 January, 3:8; 24 February, 1:7, 4:2,3; 13 March, 21:2, all 1946. GC, *AR*, (1945), pp. 9–10; (1946), p. 10; (1947), pp. 14–15; (1948), p. 14. Management was resistant to wage rises because labour costs had risen by 76 per cent between 1939 and 1947 without a comparable increase in productivity. They were even more outraged by requests for fringe benefits which they called 'featherbed rules', and were anxious to improve their negotiating position. They generally welcomed tougher labour legislation which would become effective with the Taft-Hartley Act of 1947. NAMBO *Procs*, 18 (1947), pp. 93–107.

44. *BT*, **27**(8) (1948), p. 67.

45. *BT*, **27**(8) (1948), p. 67; (1939), Greyhound Publicity Brochure, n.p., pp. 14, 15, (Collection of late W.B. Grosvenor); Bubley, Supplementary reference files for lots 882–5, written text.

46. Bubley, Supplementary reference files for lots 882–5, written text; SONJ negative 49519; *BT*, **14**(7) (1935), p. 259; D.M. Coffin to M. Walsh, 1 June 1999.

47. SONJ negatives, 59831, 59833, 59839, 59842, 59845, 59846; D.M. Coffin to M. Walsh, 1 March, 29 March, 7 April, 1999; *BT*, **14**(7) (1935), pp. 257, 259.

48. *BT*, **14**(7) (1935), pp. 256–9; **25**(4) (1946), pp. 58–60; **25**(6) (1946), pp. 80–85; **25**(8) (1946), p. 52; **27**(8) (1948), pp. 46–8; **27**(12) (1948), pp. 47–8. D.M. Coffin to M. Walsh, 1 March 1999.

49. SONJ Negatives, 48633, 48634, 48659. *BT*, **14**(7) (1935), p. 257; **25**(4) (1946), pp. 58–60, **25**(6) (1946), pp. 80–85. D.M. Coffin to M. Walsh, 7 April 1999.

50. SONJ Negatives, 47234, 47239, 48629, 49524; D.M. Coffin to M.Walsh, 7 April 1999.

51. *New York Times*, 13 January, 25:1; 20 April, 27:5; 28 July, 23:1, all 1950; 19 February, 33:8; 19 March, 35:1; 16 July, 29:1, all 1959.

Fig. 17 Exterior View of the Greyhound Capital Terminal, 245 West 50th Street, New York City, May 1947

Fig. 18 View of waiting-room in busy morning hours at the Greyhound Bus Terminal, 245 West 50th Street, New York City, September 1947

Fig. 19 Passengers line up at the ticket window at the Greyhound Bus Terminal, 245 West 50th Street, New York City, July 1947

Fig. 20 Passengers checking a timetable at the Greyhound Bus Terminal, 245 West 50th Street, New York City, July 1947

Fig. 21 Inside a Greyhound Bus leaving Scranton, Pennsylvania bound for Buffalo, New York, September 1947

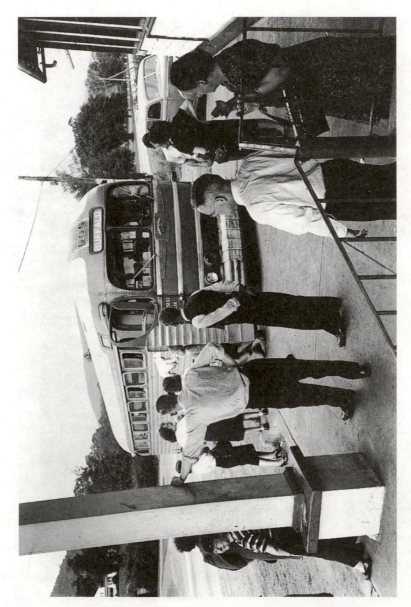

Fig. 22 Passengers from a Buffalo-bound bus at the Kanona rest stop, near Bath, New York, September 1947

Fig. 23 Driver J.J. Murphy checking tyres on a Silverside bus, March 1948

Fig. 24   Driver J.J. Murphy checking driving mechanisms on a Silverside bus, March 1948

Fig 25 Charles Wright, gas man, checking off the list of servicing requirements on an incoming bus at the Central Greyhound Lines Garage, Long Island City, New York, April 1947

Fig 26 Benjamin Green, mechanic, and his helper, removing the outer rear wheel of a bus in preparation for changing a spring at the Central Greyhound Lines Garage, Long Island City, New York, July 1947

Bibliographical Essay and
Bibliography

The history of the long-distance or intercity bus industry in the USA has been neglected by academics, whether as historians or as transport analysts. A few notable exceptions, like Burton B. Crandall's published dissertation, *The Growth of the Intercity Bus Industry* (1954); Charles Taff's text, *Commercial Motor Transportation*, published originally in 1951 and revised many times, and more recently Gregory L. Thompson's *The Passenger Train in the Motor Age. California's Rail and Bus Industries, 1910–1941* (1993) confirm this point by their character and scope. Most students or researchers who want to find out information about motor-carrier passenger transport are more likely to have gained their knowledge from Albert E. Meier and John P. Hoschek's *Over the Road. A History of Intercity Bus Transportation in the United States*, published by the Motor Bus Society in 1975, Carlton Jackson's critical, but partial social and cultural history of the Greyhound Bus Company, *Hounds of the Road* (1984), and Oscar Schisgall's officially-sponsored *The Greyhound Story. From Hibbing to Everywhere* (1985).

Most academics have either dismissed motor coaches as being of minor importance in transport history or have resorted to generalizations about government transport policy or to images and myths in popular culture concerning Greyhound dogs and unsafe bus terminals. Part of the explanation for this neglect lies in the unpopularity of buses as a mode of distance transport in the USA. Only for urban transit and school journeys are buses deemed to be satisfactory. Trains, cars and planes are or have been preferred by the majority of Americans, and so these modes of passenger transport offer more scope for historical attention and discussion. A larger part of academic neglect, however, stems from the paucity of business archives and the intermittent availability and scattered location of published records dealing with buses. Many company and trade association materials have been destroyed, while valuable information remains hidden or unavailable in private collections. The published data is diverse, ranging from trade journals, through bus timetables, annual reports of companies and associations, newspapers and advertising copy to legal hearings and government statistics.

The sources used in *Making Connections* reflect the inconsistency and

219

variability of archival materials and the unpredictable scope of extant published data. Several essays suggest alternative ways of working with piecemeal evidence generated at local, regional and national levels. This bibliographical inventory comments on and brings together materials which have been used during a long and interrupted period of research and presents them in a systematic way which has previously not been possible in the endnotes of individual articles. Specific references to each archival collection are cited in individual essays.

Archival materials

Neither of the two major bus carriers, Greyhound and Trailways, have an accessible corporate archive. Both have changed ownership and moved headquarters during the course of their existence and these alterations, rather than fire damage, have resulted in the loss of data. One can speculate as to whether the lack of storage space for bulky paper records or the lack of sentiment about historical knowledge is more at fault for the loss. It is more understandable that records are not available for the National Trailways Bus System. As an association of independently-owned local and regional companies formed in 1936, Trailways has always experienced considerable decentralised record-keeping. It is still, nevertheless, unfortunate that little of the executive board and jointly-published material remains. Greyhound, which has been a holding company with a group of subsidiaries for much of its eighty-five year history, holds some historic records. These include vehicles, artefacts and unspecified photographic, printed and manuscript materials. As these materials have been made available only to persons working in the bus industry and with the official sanction of the company, their historical value remains largely unknown.

Fortunately, documentary and photographic evidence on Greyhound is available elsewhere – in two major archival collections. Materials relating to the early growth of the Greyhound company in Minnesota and the Midwest can be found in the records of the Great Northern Railway Company housed at the Minnesota Historical Society Library, in St Paul. Full inventories to the Great Northern Archives, which contain much useful information on bus companies and bus-related companies, offer useful guides. Specific histories and corporate records are available for Northland Greyhound Lines Incorporated, of Delaware and of Illinois, for Northland Transportation Company of Delaware and Minnesota, for Norgrey, for the Pacific Greyhound Corporation and for the Greyhound Corporation. A more detailed search through the voluminous President's Office Subject Files revealed much more bus-related information. These files contain correspondence with company officials, bus operators and persons involved with bus financing and publicity, newspaper clippings, information about government hearings and investigations, memoranda on bus and train operations, balance sheets and bulletins. The Subject Files of the Vice President-Operating proved less rewarding. Other bus-related archival records available at the Minnesota Historical Society Library include those of the Northern Pacific Railway Company, the Minnesota State Railroad and Warehouse Commission and the Minnesota State Public Services Department. All these records are catalogued. Furthermore, a useful subject guide to archival collections – in this instance to buses and bus operations – acts as an important cross-referencing system.

A second valuable cache of Greyhound materials is held at the American Heritage Center at the University of Wyoming, Laramie. The Greyhound Corporation Collection, Accession Number 3191, consists of twenty-three boxes of assorted data. These include correspondence to and from Greyhound officials dating from the 1920s to the 1950s, financial statements, stock reports, biographical sketches of major personnel, manuscript histories of the company and its subsidiaries, fare schedules, printed annual reports, in-house news-letters, legal papers, motor-carrier hearings, government hearings, advertising and public relations materials, photographs, maps, newspaper clippings and artefacts. This diverse collection offers the most lucid body of information on the nation's major motor carrier. Other archival holdings relating to buses held at the American Heritage Center are the John S. Brunelle collection, Accession Number 4292, and the National Association of Motor Bus Owners Collection, Accession Number 7275. In the latter, the minute books of the association dating from 1927 to 1968 provide helpful insights into the management of the bus industry's major trade association and the ways in which it dealt with problems.

Further details on Greyhound and the early growth of the bus industry are located in the papers of one of their most ardent supporters, Laurence A. Rossman. Rossman, who edited the *Grand Rapids Herald-Review* (Minnesota), witnessed the beginnings of the Greyhound Company in the Iron Range country of northern Minnesota. He remained friends with some of the bus industry's major entrepreneurs for forty years and was a special consultant to Northland Greyhound, the Greyhound Corporation and the bus industry, undertaking research and writing pamphlets, addresses and memoranda. The Rossman papers consist primarily of public relations materials and correspondence with bus operators, bus advisors and highway officials concerning national issues which affected the bus industry, especially in the years following the Second World War. Originally a private collection housed in the offices of the *Grand Rapids Herald* in Grand Rapids, the papers have been deposited by Rossman's son George in the Minnesota Historical Society Library, St Paul, and are now available there as the Laurence A. Rossman Papers.

Other accessible bus-company archives remain few in number. A small set of bus records relating to Edgar F. Zelle and the Jefferson Company offers information on bus entrepreneurship and the growth of a Midwestern regional company from the second decade of the twentieth century to the 1950s. These miscellaneous materials include minute books, letters to and from Edgar Zelle from the 1920s to the 1940s, Jefferson Transportation Company Annual Reports, timetables, photographs, newspaper clippings and scrapbooks. The collection remains in private ownership and was consulted at the company offices in Minneapolis. A fragmentary and very small package of personal and business records concerning Helen M. Schultz and the Red Ball Transportation Company in the 1920s is held privately by the family and in photocopy format at the Mason City Public Library, Mason City, Iowa.

Some other bus companies own records of historical value, but little, if any, of this material can be accessed without executive authority and company inconvenience. Many individuals also hold considerable historical material on motor coaches, and some of this has been donated to the Motor Bus Society which was formed in 1948 to collect and publish information about the history and progress of the bus industry in North America. The society's holdings, now in the John P. Hoscheck Memorial Bus Transportation Library, Hopewell Township, NJ, consists of thousands of photographs and a large quantity of information and printed matter concerned with the history of many bus companies, but especially with Greyhound. When the Museum of Bus Transportation in Lemoyne, Pennsylvania opens and the Greyhound Bus Origin Museum in Hibbing, Minnesota, opened in 1999, grows in reputation, bus companies and individuals may feel more disposed to deposit artefacts and records in public holdings.

Further bus records are held in government institutions and in historical libraries. Of these, the manuscript materials held by the federal government are the most significant. Substantial documentation emerged from three major inquiries into the status of the intercity bus industry, in 1926, between 1930 and 1931, and between 1946 and 1949. Printed reports were subsequently published in 1928, 1932 and 1950, but the typescript materials have offered more detailed information on patterns of business behaviour at both the local and national level.

The Interstate Commerce Commission (ICC) hearings on 'Motorbus and Motor Truck Operations', Docket Number 18300, held at thirteen locations in the USA between July and October 1926, consisted of twenty volumes of testimony and exhibits provided by bus and truck operators, state officials, trade associations, railway companies, transit companies, automobile chambers of commerce and legal advisors. The ICC hearings on 'The Coordination of Motor Transportation', Docket Number 23400, held at seventeen locations in the USA between November 1930 and March 1931, consisted of eighty-three volumes of testimony and exhibits provided by persons involved in the business, together with questionnaires completed by all carriers reporting the operation of motor vehicles. The typescripts for both hearings were in the custody of the ICC, and later the Surface Transportation Board, before they were recently destroyed. They were used in the Docket File Room of the then ICC in 1985.

The ICC, 'Investigation of Bus Fares', Docket Number MC–C–550, provided the first extensive inquiry into the fares and charges of motor-bus operators, and the rules, regulations and practices governing them. Pre-hearings were held in Washington, DC in 1946 and 1947 and hearings were held in eight locations between 1947 and 1949. Briefs were filed early in 1950. Further testimony was subsequently held in 1950. There were twenty-five volumes of testimony and exhibits submitted for the 225 respondents. These were held at the Washington National Records Center in Suitland Maryland and were used in 1990. They were destroyed in 1999.

Other archival collections which have yielded scattered information include those of the Office of Defense Transportation (RG219) and the Office of War Information (RG208), both held at the National Archives in College Park, Maryland; the Atchison, Topeka and Santa Fe Railway Company Records at Topeka, Kansas; the Santa Fe Collection at the State Historical Society of Kansas, Topeka, Kansas; the Union Pacific Railroad materials at Omaha, Nebraska and at the State Historical Society of Nebraska, Lincoln, Nebraska; the Pennsylvania Railroad records (Accession Number 1807) at the Hagley Museum and Library, Wilmington, Delaware; the Richard L. Griggs papers at the Northeast Minnesota Historical Center, Duluth, Minnesota; the J. Walter Thompson Company Archives now held at Duke University, Durham North Carolina; Greyhound advertising materials at Grey-Chicago; Greyhound advertising materials from the collection of the late Walter B. Grosvenor of Cleveland, Ohio and New York; Greyhound bus materials now held at the Greyhound Bus Origin Museum in Hibbing Minnesota; the Motor Bus Society records, now housed at the John P. Hoschek Memorial Bus Transportation Library in Hopewell Township, New Jersey; the Ralph and Muriel Hidy Papers, James J. Hill Library, St Paul, Minnesota; miscellaneous materials at the American Bus Association, Washington, DC; the private collections of miscellaneous materials held by William A. Luke, former owner and editor of *Bus Ride* in Spokane, Washington and by Donald M. Coffin, former secretary-treasurer of the Motor Bus Society and consultant to the Greyhound Corporation, in Hemlock Farms, Pennsylvania. Several of these collections include photographs which have provided useful information on both bus companies and motor-coach building. Other photographic material is available in the Standard Oil (New Jersey) Collection in the Ekstrom Library of the University of Kentucky and in the US Farm Security Administration/Office of War Information (FSA-OWI) Collection held in the Library of Congress, Prints and Photographs Division, Washington, DC. The D'Arcy Collection of Clippings located at the Department of Communications Library of the University of Illinois at Urbana-Champaign provided advertising information.

Periodicals and annual publications and reports

Trade periodicals have been an invaluable guide to the development of the bus industry. These periodicals fall into three categories which are sometimes indistinguishable: those which have been published by the industry itself, those which have been published commercially for sale to the industry and to interested persons, and those which have been produced by bus enthusiasts primarily for bus enthusiasts.

The second variety has been the most helpful in my research. *Bus Transportation*, published by McGraw Hill for thirty-five years, reported statistics on the industry as a whole, by region, by type of carrier and by operating revenue, and it recounted company developments, legislation, both state and federal, technical and design details of motor coaches, operating, maintenance and public-relations guides, articles by bus entrepreneurs and biographical information. On its demise bus operators and other readers were advised to take another McGraw Hill publication, *Fleet Owner*, which broadened its scope to include the interests of all who operated fleets of automotive vehicles. Buses, however, constituted only a small proportion of the revamped journal. *Bus Ride* originated in 1965 as a newsletter published by the Bus History Association and aimed at the bus hobbyist. Under the management and editorship of William A. Luke, 1965–1996, it developed into a glossy publication with wide circulation in the bus industry, and it continues to have wide circulation. It contains articles on specific companies, both national and international, technical developments in motor coaches, news of current bus-related events and legislation, biographical information, news about maintenance forums, and advice and opinions from bus entrepreneurs and transport consultants. Other early trade periodicals in the 1920s like *Bus Age*, or *The Truck and Bus Owner*, had short runs or shared coverage with trucks, while the railroad journal, *Railway Age*, offered insights on buses in the years in which railroads operated bus subsidiaries.

Motor Coach Age, published by the Motor Bus Society, is a bus enthusiasts' journal. An historical magazine, published quarterly, its articles are and have been written mainly by Motor Bus Society members both on commission and by independent submission. Drawing on authors' personal archives, some of which are substantial, and on their sub-specialities as well as on the extensive written and photographic records and artefacts of the society's library and archives, these articles clearly demonstrate the in-depth knowledge of individuals and historians with an avid interest in buses. Academics may, however, be disappointed in the articles because they lack some of the professional tools of the historian, most notably endnote citations and bibliographies.

The major companies in the bus industry have periodically published in-house organs and journals designed to stimulate bus travel. Both Greyhound's *Highway Traveler* and National Trailways' *Trailways* contained interesting and well-illustrated articles about scenic and historic attractions. The publications also carried advertising, both by the national bus companies and their subsidiaries or associated members and by tourist and resort associations, chambers of commerce and hotels. As public-relations media, the magazines were distributed free at bus depots or in travel agencies or could be obtained regularly through membership subscription in the companies' travel clubs. Though they did not reach the national audiences which other bus advertisements in such popular magazines as the *Saturday Evening Post*, *Colliers* and *Ladies Home Journal* could ensure, they were sufficiently successful to be maintained until the bus industry faced economic difficulties in the 1950s.

The Greyhound Corporation and its operating companies also published gazettes for the amusement, instruction and general benefit of their employees. Northland Greyhound Lines' *Rear View Mirror*, Pacific Greyhound Lines' *Pace Maker*, Southwestern Greyhound Lines' *Backfire* and Pickwick-Greyhound's *Pickwick-Greyhound Highway Log* were a mixture of news of employees and their families, developments within their division of Greyhound and in the national corporation, advice on stimulating good public relations, items of local interest, letters and advertising. At different times the Greyhound Corporation published one magazine for all its employees, like *The Greyhound Limited* or *Go Greyhound*. These journals offer information on bus companies which is not otherwise available. The most complete run of in-house magazines is located in the library of the Motor Bus Society, Hopewell Township, New Jersey. *The Motor Carrier*, the official organ of the Motor Carriers Association of California, was also designed to print news items and human-interest stories for its members.

The annual publication of *Bus Facts* by the National Association of Motor Bus Owners (formerly Operators) (NAMBO) provided the bus industry with a statistical profile generated by its trade association and associated research agencies from 1927 into the 1980s. These booklets primarily contain figures, but there is also some useful descriptive commentary. The information comprises general statistics for city, intercity and school bus operations, for electric and steam railroad bus operations, trends in bus production, bus taxes, state regulations and information on NAMBO. Unfortunately, the figures reported here, those given in *Bus Transportation* and those on motor carriers generated by the Bureau of Transport, Economics and Statistics at the ICC, do not agree. Discussion in the minutes and correspondence of NAMBO in the mid-1940s expressed concern that there were no dependable statistics for the industry at a time when authoritative data was required for legislative, other government research and public-relations purposes. Despite this concern, the problem of conflicting estimates from various sources continued. The historical statistics of the bus industry thus remain less than precise.

The annual reports and publications of the industry's trade association and its main companies offer guides to both national trends and particular developments within firms. The proceedings of the annual meeting of NAMBO contain both the reports of the executive officers on the state of the association and the industry, and the papers presented at specialized sessions together with the ensuing discussions. The annual conference and the proceedings kept executives and managers of the intercity bus industry abreast of current trends and activities in such areas as traffic management, operation and maintenance, public relations, safety, labour relations, legislation, business promotion, and special events. The annual reports of the Greyhound Corporation, Continental Trailways and the Jefferson Transportation Company provided financial statements, operating statistics, news of acquisitions, improvements, other new developments, employee relations and publicity primarily for stockholders. These details were useful as examples to illustrate general trends. Less practical were the timetables, though some early issues included advertising, artwork and promotional material. Annual reports of federal government agencies like the ICC provided general information on the work of the Motor Carrier Bureau.

[ ] = incomplete series

American Bus Association, *Annual Report*, 1977–1984.
Backfire, [1922–1927].
Bus Age, [1922–1927].
Bus Facts, 1927–1982.
Bus Ride, 1965–1998.
Bus Transportation, 1922–1956.
Commercial West,[1922–1936].
Continental Trailways, *Annual Report*, 1950–1967.
Fleet Owner, 1957–1965.
Greyhound Corporation, *Annual Report*, 1930–1972.
Highway Traveller, 1929–1955/6.
Interstate Commerce Commission, *Annual Report*, 1926–1959.
Iowa State Highway Commission, *Annual Report*, 1923–1933.
Jefferson Transportation Company, *Annual Report*, 1931–1960.
Jefferson Transportation Company, *Bus Timetables*, [1926–1947].

Moody's Manual of Investments, *Public Utilities*, 1940–1951 and *Transportation*, 1954–1963.
Motor Coach Age, 1954–1992.
National Association of Motor Bus Operators, *Proceedings*, 1927–1966.
Northland Greyhound Lines, *Bus Timetables*, [1924–1934].
Railway Age, 1922–1939.
Rear View Mirror, [1940–1955].
The Grapevine, [1939–1956].
The Motor Carrier, [1924–1934].
Trailways, [1936–1951].
Union Pacific Magazine, [1922–1934].

Other intermittent periodical literature and reports found in archival holdings included *Go Greyhound*, *Greyhound News*, *Greyhound Reporter*, *Overland Life*, *Pace Maker*, *Pickway-Greyhound Highway Log*, *The Greyhound Limited*, *The Greyhound Lines* and *The Truck and Bus Owner*. Newspapers offer considerable information on both small companies and state and national developments, but unless these have been indexed or are weekly and local, they are best consulted through clippings files. Individual bus companies, conscious of the value of publicity, hired clipping agencies to keep track of any reports of their activities.

Government documents

Printed government documents been a very useful source of information on the general development of the bus industry and on the official perception of how the industry should be monitored in the public interest. The summaries of lengthy debates by elected representatives and senators, and of hearings in which bus representatives were asked to testify, point to the changing economic and social environment in which the bus industry had to conduct its business, to official concern for transport systems and to public opinion regarding the industry.

Federal

In chronological order. All published in Washington, DC.

US Congress, Senate, (1926), *To Regulate Interstate Commerce By Motor Vehicles Operating As Common Carriers on the Public Highways*, 69 Cong. 1 Sess., Hearings.
US Congress, House, (1928), *Regulation of Interstate Motor Buses On Public Highways*, 70 Cong. 1 Sess., Hearing.

US ICC, (1928), 'Motor Bus and Motor Truck Operation', *Report*, vol. 140.

US Congress, House, (1930), *Regulation of Interstate Motor Buses on Public Highways*, 71 Cong. 2 Sess., Hearing.

US Congress, Senate, (1931), *Transportation of Persons in Interstate and Foreign Commerce by Motor Carriers*, 71 Cong. 3 Sess., Hearing.

US Congress, Senate, (1932), *Coordination of Motor Transportation*, A Report, 72 Cong. 1 Sess., Doc. 43.

US Congress, Senate, (1932), *Regulation of Motor Carrier Transportation*, Hearings, 72 Cong. 1 Sess.

US ICC, (1932), 'Coordination of Motor Transportation', *Report*, vol. 182.

US Congress, House, (1934), *Regulation of Interstate Motor Busses and Trucks on Public Highways*, Hearing, 73 Cong. 2 Sess.

US National Recovery Administration, (1934), *Codes of Fair Competition*, vol. II.

US Congress, Senate, (1934), *Regulation of Transportation Agencies*, 73 Cong. 2 Sess., Doc. 152.

US Congress, Senate, (1934), *First Report of the Federal Coordinator of Transportation*, 73 Cong. 2 Sess., Doc. 119.

US Congress, Senate, (1934), *Second Report of the Federal Coordinator of Transportation*, 73 Cong. 2 Sess., Doc. 152.

US Congress, House, (1935), *Third Report of the Federal Coordinator of Transportation, 1934*, 74 Cong. 1 Sess., Doc. 89.

US Congress, House, (1935), *Regulation of Interstate Motor Carriers*, Hearing, 74 Cong. 1 Sess., HR 5262 and H.R. 6016.

US Congress, Senate, (1935), *To Amend the Interstate Commerce Act, 1935*, Hearings, 74 Cong. 1 Sess.

US Department of Commerce, Bureau of the Census, (1935), *Census of Business, Motor Bus Transportation*.

US Congress, (1936), *Public Laws of the United States of America, Passed by 74 Congress, 1935–36*, vol. 49, *Statutes at Large*.

US Congress, House, (1936), *Fourth Report of the Federal Coordinator of Transportation*, 74 Cong. 2 Sess., Doc. 394.

US Federal Coordinator of Transportation, (1936), *Hours, Wages and Working Conditions in the Intercity Motor Transport Industries*, part 1, *Motor-Bus Transportation*.

US Congress, House, (1938), *Amending Motor Carrier Act*, Hearings, 75 Cong. 3 Sess.

US Congress, (1941), *Public Laws of the United States of America, Passed by 76 Congress, 2 and 3 Sessions, 1939–41*, vol. 54, part. 1, *Statutes as Large*.

US Congress, House, (1946) *National Transportation Inquiry*, 79 Cong. 2 Sess., Report 2735.

US Department of Labor, (1946) 'Report and Recommendations of the Fact Finding Panel in the Greyhound Bus Dispute'.

US ICC, (1950), 'Investigation of Bus Fares' *Briefs of Respondents*, 3 vols.

In the US Court of Appeals for the Seventh Circuit, (1951), US v. National City Lines, et al.

US Congress, Senate, (1951), *Domestic Land and Water Transportation*, 82 Cong. 1 Sess.

US Congress, Senate, (1961), *National Transportation Policy*, 87 Cong. 1 Sess., Committee Print.

US Congress, Senate, (1965), *An Evaluation of the Motor Carrier Act of 1935 on the Thirtieth Anniversary of its Enactment*, 89 Cong. 1 Sess., Committee Print.

US Congress, Senate, (1974), *The Industrial Reorganization Act*, part 4A, 'American Ground Transport' and 'The Truth About "American Ground Transport" – A Reply by General Motors', Hearings, 93 Cong. 2 Sess.

US Department of Transportation, (1975), *1974 National Transportation Report. Current Performance and Future Prospects*.

US Congress, Senate, (1977), *Financial Condition of the Intercity Bus Industry*, 95 Cong. 1 Sess., Serial No. 95–29.

US Congress, Senate, (1977), *Intercity Domestic Transportation System for Passengers and Freight*, 95 Cong. 1 Sess., Committee Print.

US Congress, Senate, (1978), *Intercity Bus Service in Small Communities*, 95 Cong. 2 Sess., Committee Print.

US ICC, (1978), *The Intercity Bus Industry. A Preliminary Study*.

US ICC, (1979), *Report of the Bus Industry Study Group*.

US Congress, Senate, (1982), *Deregulation of the Intercity Bus Industry*, Hearing, 97 Cong. 2 Sess., Serial No. 97–100.

US ICC, (1984), *The Intercity Bus Industry*.

US Department of Transportation, (1984), *The Intercity Bus Terminal*.

Federal government serials

US, ICC, *Motor Carrier Cases*, [1936–1958].

State

In chronological order.

Iowa Board of Railroad Commissioners, *Annual Report*, 1923–1940.

Iowa State Highway Commission, *Annual Report*, 1923–1933.

Minnesota Railroad and Warehouse Commission, Auto Transportation Company Division, *Biennial Reports*, 1925/6–1942/4.

Iowa Department of Transportation, '1983 Intercity Bus Plan', (Draft) (Ames, IO, 1983).

Other agency reports

In chronological order.

NAMBO, (1943), *The Intercity Bus Industry at War*, Washington, DC.
NAMBO, (1944), *Intercity Buses at War*, Washington, DC.
NAMBO, (1978), *1926–1976. One-Half Century of Service to America*, Washington, DC.
Greyhound Lines, Inc., (1979), *A Proposal for Federal Legislative Deregulation of the Intercity Bus Industry*, Phoenix, AZ.
Transportation Research Board, (1980), *Proceedings: Conference on Intercity Bus Transportation*, Washington, DC.
National Transportation Policy Study Commission, (1979/80), *Intercity Bus Transportation*, (Special Report No. 7, 1979) (Iowa City, IO, Revised edition, 1980).
F.D. Fravel, H. Tauchen and G. Gilbert, (1980), 'Economies of Scale in the US Intercity Bus Industry', (prepared for US Department of Transportation).
Management Analysis Center, Inc., (1981), *Deregulation of the Intercity Bus Industry*, Washington, DC.
American Association of State Highway and Transportation Officials (AASHTO), (1983), *Deregulation of the Transportation Industry. Task Force Report*, Denver, CO.
F.D. Fravel, (1990), *The Greyhound Story, 1979–1990. Final Report*, Bethesda, MD.

Interviews

Alphabetical Order: All with Margaret Walsh unless otherwise stated

Robert M. Bowen, Minneapolis, 3 July 1985.
Esther Bubley, New York, 20 August 1992.
Donald M. Coffin, Hemlock Farms, PA, 30 November 1999.
William A. Luke, Spokane, WN, 22 October 1990.
Mary Martin, Mason City, IO, 20 May 1991 (with Art Fischbeck).
Mary Martin, (telephone), 15 October 1993.
Susan Perry, Washington, DC, 1 June 1991.
Mary Jean Picknelly, (telephone), 15 May 1991.
Robert Slater, St Paul, MN, 2 January 1985.

Robert Tracy, Mason City, IO, 20 May 1991 (with Mary Martin and Art Fischbeck).

Louis N. Zelle, Minneapolis, 8 October 1990.

Selected secondary sources

The secondary sources used were varied in quality and diverse in type. The most valuable were texts in transport economics which were published as contemporary or recent commentaries on trends and legislation. A few historical volumes offered useful observations on business behaviour, regulation and transport modes other than buses. Other sources on specific themes such as photography, advertising, gender and local history were consulted for particular chapters.

Books

American Association of State Highway Officials (AASHO) (1964), *A Story of the Beginning, Purposes, Growth Activities and Achievements of the American Association of State Highway Officials*, Washington, DC.

Anderson, J.C. (ed.) (1977), *Roy Stryker: The Humane Propagandist*, Louisville, KY.

Association of American Railroads (1945), *Highway Motor Transportation*, Washington, DC.

Bail, E. (1984), *From Railway to Freeway: Pacific Electric and the Motor Coach*, Glendale, CA.

Barger, H. (1951), *The Transportation Industries, 1899–1946. A Study of Output, Employment and Productivity*, New York.

Belasco, W.J. (1979), *Americans on the Road: from Autocamp to Motel, 1910–1945*, Cambridge, MA.

Bilstein, R.E. (1984), *Flight in America. From the Wrights to the Astronauts*, Baltimore.

Breyer, S.G. (1982), *Regulation and Its Reform*, Cambridge, MA.

Bryant, K.L., Jr (ed.) (1988), *Railroads in the Age of Regulation, 1900–1980*, New York.

Burnstein, M. (1955), *Regulating Business by Independent Commission*, Princeton, NJ.

Bus Transportation (1932), *Making Bus Operations Pay*, New York.

Bus Transportation (1934), *Handbook A Guide to New, Successful Ideas and Methods in Bus Maintenance, Operating and Management*, New York.

Byrd, R.A. (1945), *Russ's Bus. Adventures of an American Bus Driver*, repr. edn West Trenton, NJ, 1987.

Caves, R.E. (1962), *Air Transport and Its Regulation*, Cambridge, MA.

Chandler, A.D., Jr (1977), *The Visible Hand: The Managerial Revolution in American Business*, Cambridge, MA.

Childs, W.R. (1985), *Trucking and the Public Interest: The Emergence of Federal Regulation, 1914–1940*, Knoxville, TN.

Crandall, B.B. (1954), *The Growth of the Intercity Bus Industry*, Syracuse, NY.

Cushman, R.E. (1941), *The Independent Regulatory Commissions*, New York.

Daggett, S. (1934), *Principles of Inland Transportation*, rev. edn, New York.

Davies, R.E.G. (1972), *Airlines of the United States Since 1914*, London.

Dearing, C.L. (1941), *American Highway Policy*, Washington, DC.

Dearing, C.L. and Owen, W. (1949), *National Transportation Policy*, Washington, DC.

Derthick, M. and Quirk, P.J. (1985), *The Politics of Deregulation*, Washington, DC.

Edwards, F.K. (1933), *Principles of Motor Transportation*, New York.

Ellis, J. (1988), *Silent Witnesses: Representations of Working-Class Women in the United States*, Bowling Green, OH.

Felton, J.R. and Anderson, D.G. (1989), *Regulation and Deregulation of the Motor Carrier Industry*, Ames, IO.

Fleischauer, C. and Brannon, B. (1988), *Documenting America, 1935–1943*, Berkeley, CA.

Flink, J.J. (1975), *The Car Culture*, Cambridge, MA.

Flink, J.J. (1988), *The Automobile Age*, Cambridge, MA.

Fuess, C.M. (1952), *Joseph B. Eastman, Servant of the People*, New York.

George, J.J. (1929), *Motor Carrier Regulation in the United States*, Spartansburg, SC.

Guimond, J. (1991), *American Photography and the American Dream*, Chapel Hill, NC.

Harper, D.V. (1959), *Economic Regulation of the Motor Trucking Industry by the States*, Urbana, IL.

Harper, D.V. (1978), *Transportation in America: Users, Carriers, Government*, Englewood Cliffs, NJ.

Hidy, R.W. et al. (1988), *The Great Northern Railway*, Boston.

High, J. (ed.) (1991), *Regulation. Economic Theory and History*, Ann Arbor, MI.

Hilton, G.W. (1969), *The Transportation Act of 1958: A Decade of Experience*, Bloomington, IN.

Hilton, G.W. and Due, J.F. (1960), *The Electric Railways in America*, Stanford, CA.

Hudson, W.J. and Constantin, J.A. (1958), *Motor Transportation, Principles and Practice*, New York.

Hurley, F.J. (1972), *Portrait of a Decade. Roy Stryker and the Development of Documentary Photography in the Thirties*, Baton Rouge, LA.

Itzkoff, D.M. (1985), *Off the Track: The Decline of the Intercity Passenger Train in the United States*, Westport, CN.

Jackson, C. (1984), *Hounds of the Road: a History of the Greyhound Bus Company*, Bowling Green, OH.

Johnston, E.R. (1938), *Government Regulation of Transportation*, New York.

Kane, R.M. and Vose, A.D. (1982), *Air Transportation*, 8th edn, Dubuque, IO.

Keeler, T.E. (1983), *Railroads, Freight and Public Policy*, Washington, DC.

Keller, U. (1986), *The Highway as Habitat. A Roy Stryker Documentation, 1943–1955*, Santa Barbara, CA.

Klein, M. (1994), *Unfinished Business. The Railroad in American Life*, Hanover, NH.

Kolko, G. (1965), *Railroads and Regulation, 1877–1916*, Princeton, NJ.

Kwolek-Folland, A. (1998), *Incorporating Women. A History of Women and Business in the United States*, New York.

Lemann, N. (1981), *Out of the Forties*, Austin, TX.

Lieb, R.C. (1978), *Transportation: The Domestic System*, Reeston, VA.

Locklin, P.D. (1935), *Economics of Transportation*, Chicago, 1st edn, 1935, 3rd edn, 1947, Homewood, IL, 5th edn, 1960, 7th edn, 1972.

MacAvoy, P.W. (1979), *The Regulated Industries and the Economy*, New York.

McCollester, P. and Clark, F.J. (1935), *Federal Motor Carrier Regulation*, New York.

McCraw, T.K. (1984), *Prophets of Regulation*, Cambridge, MA.

Marchand, R. (1985), *Advertising the American Dream: Making Way for Modernity, 1920–1940*, Berkeley, CA.

Martin, A. (1971), *Enterprise Denied: Origins of the Decline of American Railroads, 1897–1917*, New York.

Martin, A. (1992), *Railroads Triumphant. The Growth, Regulation and Rebirth of a Vital American Force*, New York.

Meier, A.E. and Hoschek, J.P. (1975), *Over the Road: A History of Intercity Bus Transportation in the United States*, Upper Montclair, NJ.

Meyer, J.R. and Oster, C.V., Jr, et al. (1987), *Deregulation and the Future of Intercity Passenger Travel*, Cambridge, MA.

Muller, H.M. (ed.) (1933), *Federal Regulation of Motor Transport*, New York.

Nelson, J.C. (1959), *Railroad Transportation and Public Policy*, Washington, DC.

Norton, H.S. (1963), *Modern Transportation Economics*, Columbus, OH.

Overton, R.C. (1965), *Burlington Route. A History of the Burlington Lines*, Lincoln, NB.

Pegrum, D.F. (1968), *Transportation: Economics and Public Policy*, rev. edn, Homewood, IL.

Plattner, S.W. (1983), *Roy Stryker: U.S.A., 1943–1950. The Standard Oil (New Jersey) Photography Project*, Austin, TX.

Rae, J.B. (1965), *The American Automobile*, Chicago.

Rae, J.B. (1971), *The Road and the Car in American Life*, Cambridge, MA.

Rhodes, J. (1988), *Intercity Bus Lines of the Southwest. A Photographic History*, College Station, TX.

Roggero, A. with Beadle, T. (1995), *Greyhound. A Pictorial Tribute to an American Icon*, London.

Rose, J.R. (1953), *American Wartime Transportation*, New York.

Rose, M.H. (1979), *Interstate Express Highway Politics, 1940–1956*, Lawrence, KS.

Sampson, R.J. and Farris, M.T. (1979), *Domestic Transportation. Practice, Theory and Policy*, 4th edn, Boston.

Scharfman, I.L. (1937), *The Interstate Commerce Commission: a Study in Administrative Law and Procedure*, 4 vols, New York.

Schisgall, O. (1985), *The Greyhound Story: from Hibbing to Everywhere*, Chicago.

Schudson, M. (1984), *Advertising, the Uneasy Persuasion: Its Dubious Impact on American Society*, New York.

Seely, B.E. (1987), *Building the American Highway System: Engineers as Policy Makers*, Philadelphia.

Smith, F.A. (1986), *Transportation in America: Historical Compendium, 1939–1985*, Westport, CN.

Sorrell, L.C. and Wheeler, H.A. (1944), *Passenger Transport in the United States, 1920–1950*, Chicago.

Stange, M. (1989), *Symbols of Ideal Life. Social Documentary Photography in America, 1890–1950*, New York.

Stover, J.F. (1961), *American Railroads*, Chicago.

Stryker, R.E. and Wood, N. (1973), *In This Proud Land. America, 1935–1943. As Seen in FSA Photographs*, New York.

Sweeney, D.J., McCarthy, C.J., Kalish, S.J. and Cutler, J.M., Jr (1986), *Transportation Deregulation. What's Deregulated And What Isn't*, Washington, DC.

Szto, S. (1934), *Federal and State Regulation of Motor Carrier Rates and Services*, Philadelphia.

Taff, C.A. (1951), *Commercial Motor Transportation*, Homewood, IL, 1st edn, 1951; 4th edn, 1969; Centerville, MD, 6th edn, 1980.

Thompson, G.L. (1993), *The Passenger Train in the Motor Age. California's Rail and Bus Industries, 1910–1941*, Columbus, OH.

Vietor, R.K. (1994), *Contrived Competition. Regulation and Deregulation in America*, Cambridge, MA.

Wagner, W.H. (1935), *A Legislative History of the Motor Carrier Act, 1935*, Denton, MD.

Wattenburg, B.J. (1976), Intro., *The Statistical History of the United States: From Colonial Times to the Present*, New York.

White, P. (1923), *Motor Transportation of Merchandise and Passengers*, New York.

Wilson, G.L. (1928), *Motor Traffic Management*, New York.

Wilson, J.Q. (ed.) (1985), *The Politics of Regulation*, New York.

Winkler, A.M. (1978), *The Politics of Propaganda. the Office of War Information, 1942–1945*, New Haven, CT.

Winston, C., Corsi, T.M, Grimm, C.M. and Evans, A.C. (1990), *The Economic Effects of Surface Freight Deregulation*, Washington, DC.

Wood, D.F. (1998), *American Buses*, Osceola, WI.

Articles

Anon. (1949), 'By bus', *Photo Memo*, **January**, pp. 12–15.

Anon. (1934), 'Jitney into giant', *Fortune*, **10**(2), pp. 34–43, 110, 113–14, 117.

Anon. (1936), 'Greyhound: From local jitney to big bus system in 22 years', *Newsweek*, 22 August, pp. 29–32.

Anon. (1944), 'Greyhound: Still Growing', *Fortune*, **30**(3), pp. 121–5, 236, 239–40, 242.

Anon. (1946), 'Greyhound Starts a New Lap', *Business Week*, 8 June, pp. 52–4.

Anon. (1949), 'Via bus', *The Lamp*, **31**(3), pp. 19–23.

Anderson, H.V. (1954), 'A history of the bus industry with grass roots in St Louis County', mimeograph, pp. 1–23.

Bail, E. (1976), 'California by motor stage', *California Historical Quarterly*, **55**, pp. 307–25.

Bingham, T.C. (1941), 'The Transportation Act of 1940', *Southern Economic Journal*, **8**, pp. 1–21.

Button, K.J. (1987), The effects of regulatory reform in the US intercity bus industry', *Transport Reviews*, **7**(2), pp. 145–65.

Dieckmann, K. (1989), 'A nation of zombies. Government files contain the extraordinary, unpublished photographs that Esther Bubley took on one long bus trip across wartime America', *Art in America*, **November**, pp. 55–61.

Eastman, J.B. (1937), 'The policy of the Motor Carrier Act', American Transit Association, *Proceedings*, **55**, pp. 288–95.

Ellis, H.A. (1963), 'The growth of Greyhound bus service in the Southeast', *Register* of the Kentucky Historical Society, **61**, pp. 1–21.

Farris, M.T. (1983), 'Evolution of the Transport Regulatory System of the US', *International Journal of Transport Economics*, **10**, pp. 173–93.

Farris, M.T. and Daniel, N.E. (1983), 'Bus Regulatory Reform Act of 1982', *Transportation Journal*, **23**, pp. 4–15.

Flexner, D.L. (1983), 'The effects of deregulation in the motor carrier industry', *The Antitrust Bulletin*, **28**(1), pp. 185–200.

Harbeson, R.W. (1967), 'Railroads and regulation, 1877–1916: conspiracy or public interest', *Journal of Economic History*, **27**, pp. 230–42.

Hitchcock, C.P. (1981), 'Regulatory reform in the intercity bus industry', *Journal of Law Reform*, **15**(1), pp. 1–44.

Huntington, S.P. (1952), 'The marasmus of the ICC: the commission, the railroads and the public interest', *Yale Law Review*, **61**, pp. 467–509.

McCraw, T.K. (1975), 'Regulation in America: a review article', *Business History Review*, **49**, pp. 159–83.

Martin, A. (1974), 'The troubled subject of railroad regulation in the gilded age – a reappraisal', *Journal of American History*, **61**, pp. 339–71.

Nelson, J.C. (1936), 'The Motor Carrier Act of 1935', *Journal of Political Economy*, **44**, pp. 464–504.

Nelson, J.C. (1955), 'Revision of National transport Regulatory Policy', *American Economic Review*, **45**, pp. 910–18.

Nelson, J.C. (1975), 'The changing economic case for surface transport regulation', in Miller, J.C., III (ed.), *Perspectives on Federal Transportation Policy*, Washington, DC, pp. 7–25.

Oster, C.V. and Zorn, C.K. (1986), 'Impacts of regulatory reform on intercity bus service in the United States', *Transportation Journal*, **25**, pp. 33–42.

Peterson, G.S. (1929), 'Motor carrier regulation and its economic bases', *Quarterly Journal of Economics*, **43**, pp. 604–47.

Pinkston, E.A. (1984), 'The rise and fall of bus regulation', *Regulation*, **8**, (September–December), pp. 45–52.

Prizer, J.B. (1953), 'Development of the regulation of transportation during the past seventy-five years', *Interstate Commerce Commission Practitioners' Journal*, **21**, pp. 190–228.

Rae, J.B. (1971), 'The evolution of the motor bus as a transport mode', *High Speed Ground Transportation Journal*, **5**(2), pp. 221–35.

Thompson, Gregory L. (1993), 'Planning Beats the Market: The Case of Pacific Greyhound Lines in the 1930s', *Journal of Planning Education and Research*, **13**, pp. 33–49.

Thompson, Gregory L. (1996), 'The Interwar Response of the Southern Pacific and Atchison, Topeka and Santa Fe Railway to Passenger Road Competition', *Business and Economic History*, **25**(1), pp. 283–92.

Thompson, Gregory L. (1997), 'Railroad Management Influence on the Creation of Two US Bus Systems – With Very Different Results: Pacific Greyhound Lines and Santa Fe Trailways in the 1930s', unpublished paper.

Tower, R.L., Jr (1972), 'The Road to Monopoly. The Development of the Bus Industry in California and Oregon, 1910–1930', Paper in Bancroft Library, University of California, Berkeley, pp. 1–42.

Walker, H. (1950), 'You can't miss America by bus', *The National Geographic Magazine*, **98**(1), pp. 1–16, 33–42.

Walsh, M. (1997), 'Coordination, Cooperation or Competition: the Great Northern Railway and Bus Transportation in the 1920s', in Cameron, R. and Schnore, L.F. (eds), *Cities and Markets. Studies in the Organization of Human Space*, Lanham, MD, pp. 163–89.

Walsh, M., 'In whose interest? Public policy and transport during depression and war' in Garson, R.A. and Kidd, S.S. (eds) (1999), *The Roosevelt Years: New Essays on the United States, 1933–1934*, Edinburgh, pp. 11–29.

Walsh, M., 'Railroad Responses to the Development of the Long-Distance Bus Industry in the United States Prior to Federal Regulation in 1935' in G. Boyes (ed.) (forthcoming), *Cooperation and Competition. The History of the Railways' Relationship with other Transport Modes*, York.

Walsh, M., 'Passenger Connections: Views of the Intercity Bus Terminal in the United States' in Bond, W. and Divall, C. (eds) (forthcoming), *Suburbanising the Masses; Public Transport and Urban Development in Historical Perspective*, Aldershot.

Whiting, J.R. (1951), 'Esther Bubley', *Modern Photography*, **15**, December, pp. 48–53, 118, 120, 122.

Unpublished theses

Berger, M.L. (1972), 'The Social Impact of the Automobile on Rural America, 1893–1929', PhD, Columbia University.

Chandrawatna, P. (1957), 'The Greyhound Corporation', MSc, University of Tennessee.

Cover, V.D. (1936), 'Joseph Bartlett Eastman's Economic and Social Views on Transportation Problems', PhD, University of Illinois.

Ellis, H.A. (1955), 'Southeastern Greyhound Lines. A History of the Management and Financial Policies of a Class I Intercity Motor Bus Company', Doctor of Business Administration, Indiana University.

Fox, F.W. (1973), 'Advertising and the Second World War: A Study in Private Propaganda', PhD, Stanford University.

Jones, D.L. (1976), 'The US Office of War Information and American Public Opinion During World War II', PhD, State University of New York at Binghamton.

Pinkston, E.A. (1975), 'The Intercity Bus Transportation Industry: An Industrial Organization Study', PhD, Yale University.

Index

137, 141, 142, 143, 144, 145, 152n,
222–3, 226
Interstate Transit Lines (Omaha), 99,
104n, 112, 113
Interstate Transportation Company, MN,
109
Iowa, 3, 9, 47, 79, 89–101, 110, 114,
118, 173, 174
Board of Railway Commissioners,
92, 93, 94, 95, 173
'Iowa Bus Queen', 89–101, 112, 174
Investigation of Bus Fares (1946–49), 5,
35–6, 39, 56n, 118, 223
Iron Range district, MN, 19, 76, 78, 82,
84, 85, 90, 107
It Happened One Night, 24, 164

Janesville, WI, 83
Jefferson Airways, Inc., 111
Jefferson Highway Transportation
Company (Jefferson Lines, Inc.), 9,
21, 33, 38, 47, 52, 68, 79, 80, 95,
99–100, 104n, 106–19, 158, 174, 190,
222, 226
'jitney', 4, 17, 18, 29n, 75, 76, 140
judicial decisions (Supreme Court), 24,
140, 142, 150n

Kanona, NY, 199, 214
Kansas City, MO, 9, 52, 83, 98, 99, 111,
112
Kensett, IO, 95
Kingston, NY, 178

labour and labour relations, *see*
industrial relations
La Crosse, WI, 114
and Southern Transportation
Company, 114
Lady Greyhound, 43–4
Lane, Piper and Jaffrey, 82, 83, 84
Lanesboro, MN, 110
Laramie, WY, 2, 221
legislation, *see* regulation
Libsohn, Sol, 194
Lindberg, Fred, 78
Little Falls, MN, 107, 108
Los Angeles, 18, 19, 21, 112
Louisville, KY, 191
Luke, William A, xiii, 124n, 223, 224

Mack (buses), 20
MacMurray, Fred, 51
Madison, WI, 47
magazine, advertising in, 11, 42, 163,
164, 170n, 171n, 181, 193, 225
Mahoning, MN, 19
Maine, 76
Manhattan, New York City, 41, 195,
196, 201
Mankato, MN, 79
Manly, IO, 95
Marble, MN, 76
Mason City, IO, 69, 72, 91, 92, 93, 94, 95,
96, 97, 98, 99, 100, 110, 114, 118, 173
Mason City and Clear Lake Electric
Railway, 93–4, 102n
Massachusetts, 47, 177
McDonalds, 1
Memphis, TN, 191
Mesaba Motor Company, 78, 79, 80
Mesaba Railway Coach Company, 82
Mesaba Transportation Company, 19,
21, 76, 78, 79, 82
Michigan, 82, 83
Milwaukee, WI, 47
Milwaukee and St Louis Railroad, 102n
Milwaukee, St Paul and Pacific
Railroad, (the Milwaukee Road),
102n, 103n
Minneapolis, MN, 38, 75, 77, 79, 81, 82,
83, 84, 106, 107, 108, 109, 110, 114,
118, 173
Minneapolis and St Louis Railroad, 95
Minnesota, 3, 8, 9, 18, 19, 47, 67,
75–85, 90, 91, 95, 107, 108, 109, 110,
113, 114, 118, 119, 153, 173
Bus Association, 112
Warehouse and Railroad
Commission, 81, 82, 108, 109,
110, 112
Missouri, 47, 99, 114, 118
Model T (Ford), 93
Mohawk Stage Lines, 83
Mora, MN, 108
Motor Bus Code (1933), 25, 116, 142,
151n
Motor Bus Society, 222, 224
Motor Carrier Act (1935), 4, 10, 25–6,
116, 137–48
Motor Carrier Bureau, 25, 31n, 145,
146, 147, 152n, 226